Simon Temple-Bennett

STOP FOR BREAKFAST

With Best Wishes
Simon.

HAYLOFT PUBLISHING
CUMBRIA

First published in Great Britain in 2016 by Hayloft Publishing Ltd.,

A CIP catalogue record for this book is available from the British Library

ISBN 978-1-910237-21-2

Designed, printed and bound in the EU

Jacket design: © Henry Jenkins, www.henryjenkins.co.uk
Chapter headers: © Emily Bennett

Hayloft policy is to use papers that are natural, renewable and recyclable products and made from wood grown in sustainable forests. The logging and manufacturing processes are expected to conform to the environmental regulations of the country of origin.

Hayloft Publishing Ltd,
44 Appleby Road, Kendal, LA9 6ES (registered office)
L'Ancien Presbytère, 21460 Corsaint, France (editorial)

t: 07971 352473 ~ e: books@hayloft.eu
www.hayloft.eu

For all those who read and enjoyed *Undressed For Dinner* and who encouraged me to continue the story,

and for the important people in our lives who can be closer than we imagine.

ACKNOWLEDGEMENTS

Anything worthwhile is a team effort and a team is only as good as its members. Our staff regularly refer to themselves as Team Augill but the real team is far bigger than those on the payroll. Every person who has stepped through the front or back door of the castle since 19 September 1997 has played a part in helping us make it what it is today. Like any good story there have been a variety of characters, thankfully the baddies have been far outnumbered by the goodies.

While writing can be a solitary endeavour, publishing a book is also a team effort. Thanks to Andrea, Alison, Allison, Miranda and Mark, my select few advance readers who read and re-read manuscripts and gave me objective and subjective feedback; Wendy as always for her stoical support of yet another writing trip to the sunshine while she stayed behind to mind the fort; Oliver and Emily for providing such priceless pearls of teenage wisdom; all our lovely guests who have given us the strength to carry on and the very few unsavoury guests who often inspired the best anecdotes; Emily for the chapter header drawings; Henry Jenkins for the jacket illustration; Dawn my publisher who was even more excited about this book than the last, Hunter Davies, Eric Robson and Fiona Armstrong who, I think, stuck their necks out to give *Undressed For Dinner* the Lakeland Book of the Year award, giving me the confidence to write this; Nici who has helped enormously with the PR and marketing and Alastair Sawday, one of my heroes, who wrote such sparkling words for the introduction.

FOREWORD

You need to be mad and brave to run a hotel, and to have superhuman patience. The madness is needed to make the early decision to do it; the bravery enables you to keep going, and the patience is a vital survival tool. Without it, you and your family – and perhaps all your guests – would lose the will to live. There is, of course, another vital quality which I have left 'til last, and that is a sense of humour.

Simon, and his whole, heroic family, have all those qualities in bucket loads. On top of that they are expected to cater for, and deal with, the anxieties of others – all focused on a short stay.

When I published my first book about Britain, I was reluctant to include hotels. I was an 'independent', with a deep dislike of the monster hotels that litter our countryside and towns; I need mention no names. They breed like rabbits, grow less and less human; technology welcomes and allocates you and handles your 'needs'. But I learned that small, family-run hotels are among the most imaginative and accessible places. Their owners are often eccentric, delightful, enterprising and very human.

An early favourite was Huntsham Court in Devon, run by Andrea and Mogens Bolwig. The place was a vast Victorian pile, too big to run conventionally, so they let the guests run wild. The house oozed generosity and wit: two baths in a bathroom, two pianos in a bedroom. Vast Victorian 'thunder-boxes' for loos, and communal meals. Time after dinner was often spent around the fire, music on and inhibitions slipping.

Then I found Fingals, also in Devon, and learned another way: an open-hearted, open-house, 'treat us like home, and please only stay if you like this sort of thing' approach. Both beat to the same rhythm as Augill, their owners kindred spirits. Once we had lost our preconceived ideas, we discovered dozens and dozens of terrific little places, some of them challenging traditional notions of 'hotel'.

I turned up at a Welsh hotel, the Cnapan, and the kitchen staff were in with the guests watching a football match. I am no football fan, but it was fun – and no matter that dinner was late. In another place, the owner's vast hound draped itself across my wife's lap while she ate breakfast, all its legs on the ground – a ludicrous but memorable scene. When I stay in a place such as this, such as Augill, I am delighted to find the atmosphere as individual as the owners.

A friend once gave me advice on bringing up children: make memories for them. Wise words, and I'd give the same advice to a hotel owner. Augill Castle needs none of this wisdom; it seems to function with those words engraved into the hearts of the family who live there and all their helpers. Memories almost make themselves at Augill and *Stop for Breakfast* is full of them. Simon will keep you entertained and amused, while you ache with sympathy for Wendy and her annual 'meltdowns'.

We need more Augills, more Bennetts; and they need more of us to dive in at their deep end and share the fun. The rewards are ineffable.

Alastair Sawday

PREFACE

When Wendy and I bought Augill Castle as an empty, near derelict shell in 1997 in a part of the country neither of us knew with the idea of living an idyllic rural life we could have had no idea what it would one day become. Today, the castle is an award winning hotel and wedding venue welcoming guests from every corner of the globe to one of England's most unspoilt corners. Our guests are invited to enjoy a unique, authentic country house experience with the promise that Augill is unlike anywhere they will have ever stayed before.

It isn't for everyone and we don't intend it to be because the guests who get the most out of their time with us are the ones with a genuine interest in other people and there are far too many people in the world who don't give a jot for anyone but themselves. They are not Augill people, although occasionally a couple will make it through the door and do their best to ruin things for everyone else rather than admit gracefully they have made a mistake, and since they can be the source of the best anecdotes they deserve my thanks; we are all, after all, part of the rich tapestry of life.

We don't sell a slick, contrived version of luxury country house living; we seek to share the simple pleasures of country life in a big house. It is a quintessentially English experience – slightly chaotic and sometimes just plain bonkers.

Undressed For Dinner was the first book inspired by our life sharing the castle with other people and its success was testament to the fact that many people could relate to what we do and wanted to be part of the story long after they had stayed. The story is one of hope and disappointment, joy and heartbreak, triumph and disaster; but most of all it is a story with a sense of humour which, now committed to paper, reminds us that life should never be taken too seriously.

It was first published in December 2013 and was judged Lakeland Book of the Year in 2014. A revised edition has been published in 2016 to coincide with *Stop For Breakfast* which picks up where *Undressed For Dinner* finished.

Stop For Breakfast stands on its own as a story about our struggles with events outside our control threatening to tear down everything we built and our struggles raising teenagers, also entirely outside our control, but it is a sequel too, bringing closure to an unfinished story.

In his foreword Alastair Sawday, guru of independent travel and a hero of mine, says to run a hotel you need to be mad or brave but most importantly to have a sense of humour. The sense of humour has never been in doubt – sometimes it has been all there is – but the bravery and the madness have been interchangeable at best and probably, on reflection, totally replaced by naivety.

We are still here, doing what we have always done in a way that sets us apart from the crowd but as our children look out at the world and start to make plans of their own for the future, new horizons are emerging from the haze for us too. We both learnt long ago that making plans is pointless, either there is a path already mapped out for us by another hand or life is such utter chaos that planning is futile, take your pick. The future is made of dreams and we have never been short of those.

Whether what happens next to us, to the castle or both will make another book remains to be seen but one thing is certain: For two decades we have lived an extraordinary life.

To find out more about staying at Augill Castle and becoming part of the story visit:

www.stayinacastle.com

It will add a new terror to the Peace if everybody who has done a year of public life in or about Whitehall is to make a book about it. Not that Mrs C S Peel does not deserve well of her country. She is evidently a capable person and hustled about the country for the Ministry of Food to some purpose before the days of compulsory rationing. Her general idea seems to be that simple folk are tremendously interested in the most trivial and indirect details of important folk. So she will tell you how Sir Henry Rew and Mr Ulick Wintour were fond of tea (Sir Henry likes a bun as well); how Mr Kennedy Jones once lent her his car; how Lord Davenport, asked if biscuits were included in the voluntary cereal ration, said firmly, 'Yes, they are'; how the chauffeur suddenly put on the brake and she bumped into 'poor Mr Faiddes'; how she visited Bath twice and bought a guide book, information from which she retails; how secretaries of Ministers came out to say that Ministers would see her in a few moments; and how, above and beyond all, the Queen, when she inspected Westminster Bridge kitchen, asked of a certain substance, 'What's that?' and Princess Mary at once replied, 'Maize' (just like that)... There are better things than this in the book, but on balance I don't really think it establishes a fair case for existence. The most interesting thing in it is a detailed account of the canteen systems at the Renault and Citroen works near Paris.

Punch, 14 May 1919

Stop For Breakfast is written in the hope of being a read more entertaining and better received.

A Misunderstanding

During which we are invited to Stop for Breakfast

We couldn't be more excited. We have been invited out on a Saturday night. For so long have we turned down weekend invitations that everyone had stopped asking us (so we imagined, although a friend tells us that around here people, quite inexplicably, don't do dinner parties). Anyway, now, after more than a decade of social exile, we have the opportunity to say yes.

Claire and Nigel have recently moved to North Yorkshire from Bristol having bought a large pile a little way up the valley which they plan to use for corporate hospitality and shooting parties. They came to see us for some advice when they first moved in and we all seemed to hit it off. Like us – blow-ins, in-comers or off-comers – they're not slaves to local social conventions and they have invited us for dinner. As we now have help in the kitchen in the evenings we are happy to take them up on the invitation.

Being a rare night out we cajole one of our staff into giving us a lift there and we organise a taxi home. Neither of us enjoys being the only sober one in the room. Nigel, who opens the door when we arrive, is clutching a bottle of champagne. 'Well this is a good start,' Wendy remarks as we step over the threshold.

'I do hope there isn't anybody else here,' I whisper. I hate being hijacked at dinner parties by accepting an invitation on the unspoken understanding that it's just us and then finding that we must be introduced to the host's assumptions of who we will get along with. We are whisked through to the sitting room and as we pass the dining room I am relieved to see just four place settings.

Claire appears from the kitchen in a floaty diaphanous number which leaves very little to the imagination. It reminds me of an article

11

I read on fashion rules. This outfit certainly breaks the cardinal rule of 'cleavage or legs but never both' but hey ho, we're all friends so who's complaining? Forty minutes later, as the third bottle of champagne is being uncorked, there seems to be very little going on in the cavernous kitchen which is odd. We haven't even had nibbles and I'm starting to feel very peckish as well as a tad woozy.

Whether it's all this champagne on an empty stomach, or whether Claire and Nigel were already tanked up before we arrived I can't say, but now Claire is getting uncomfortably close to me on the sofa and opposite Wendy is grappling with a similar personal space issue with Nigel.

'More champagne?' Claire giggles in my ear.

'Errm, do you think we might go through to the dining room? I don't mind telling you I'm starving.' Ordinarily this would clearly be very ill-mannered but this is turning out to be anything other than an ordinary evening.

Claire springs to her feet and disappears into the kitchen. Surely this is a good sign. Nigel is up too, opening another bottle of champagne as Claire comes back in with a bowl of cashews.

'That's bottle number four,' Wendy mouths at me across the room.

'Nuts and bubbles!' Nigel exclaims, 'and then we'll have dinner.'

'Thank God,' I say, quite involuntarily.

'What's that?' Nigel asks, not really looking for an answer which is all to the good as I can do nothing but sit down heavily, my body weighed down by a thickening head, as he refills my glass. By this time I am pressed hard up against one arm of the sofa but Claire is having none of it and shimmies alongside me until her thigh is pressed hard against my undefended flank.

'Help,' I mouth back at Wendy but she is powerless; Nigel is pouring more champagne while trying very hard to focus on Wendy's chest.

As Claire moves in to whisper something in my ear a buzzer goes off in the kitchen. Dinner is ready. I thank God, although I don't think he is listening, for the second time this evening. Wendy and I are first to our feet striding towards the dining room without invitation. Nigel and Claire have no choice but to follow.

The only person keener than Wendy for us to sit together on the same side of the table is me. But Nigel has different ideas and, planting himself squarely next to Wendy slaps his hand firmly on her thigh. I am torn between protest and not wanting to make a fuss, fearful that my judgement of the situation may be addled by too much champagne.

Claire comes in with the first course (which I'm thankful isn't oysters as that'd surely be a step too far) and slides her chair up to mine once she has sat down. But for Wendy, I contemplate dropping my fork, diving under the table to retrieve it and making a break for the door on all fours.

How we manage to get through dinner I do not know – other than with the help of at least three bottles of red wine – but sooner than is decent we are back on the sofas. Nigel says we don't need coffee and breaks out the port and cognac. He pours generous glasses for everyone and then the assault continues. It's well past midnight and I've had enough.

I jump to my feet, 'I'm sorry, call of nature.' Locked in the sanctuary of the loo, I am tempted to bed down for the night but instead I call the castle, 'get the taxi here now.'

'Sorry, who is this?'

'Oh for God's sake, it's Simon, the situation is getting out of hand, get the taxi to come now, I'll explain later.'

Back in the sitting room Wendy has extricated herself from Nigel's advances and is backed up to the fireplace. Both Nigel and Claire are now so pissed that their eyes are rolling independently of each other around the room. This is some relief but is as nothing compared with the relief of the sound of tyres crunching on gravel.

I practically sprint to the front door and can hardly believe that Claire has got there first, barricading our path.

'Sho shoon? Are you shure you don't want choo shpend she night?' she implores, 'We've got a lovely big bed upshtairsh. We were hoping you'd schtop for breakfast.'

'Stop for breakfast? No, I think you have got us wrong. It's been lovely but we really do need to get back. Children. Castle. Sanity. That sort of thing.'

Despite her best efforts Claire is in no fit state to detain us and I fear I push her out of the way a little more forcefully than might usually be decent for a departing dinner guest but by the way her eyes are still revolving I don't think she minds.

In the back of the taxi I turn to Wendy, 'what the hell just happened?'

'I think we've been swung.'

'Is that really what people think of us?' I'm horrified.

'I think when you open your home to all comers, people will think whatever they like my darling. Everything but the truth.'

And she's right. For years the local population have held us at arms length and only now are taking tentative steps towards our door, albeit still armed with their long established preconceptions. Having enjoyed afternoon tea, a group of local ladies start chatting with Wendy. As they leave one turns to her and says, 'you really are very nice people, I shall tell my friends.'

But it all does nothing for my self confidence. Not knowing from one moment to the next what people are going to think, what they might say and whether they are going to like us or what we do is beginning to take its toll. Nigel and Claire's advances have just added to that burden. Socially we are seen as an oddity to be handled with care. It's not true, of course and this does nothing to dispel that myth.

We're just an ordinary couple doing something extraordinary.

Being autumn it's also coming up to the season in which Wendy has her customary melt down. I know it has become a standing joke among our friends – the seasonal nature of what we do leads to an annual cash flow crisis and their reassurances that we're resourceful and creative and will find our way through it are delivered with a little more weariness every year.

But the truth is that every year the numbers get bigger; the responsibility gets bigger. Responsibility for the children, what will their classmates make of our going bust? Responsibility for the staff, it's their mortgages we're helping to pay as well as our own. The responsibility of constantly having to meet the demands of a public wanting ever more for ever less. The responsibility of keeping up appearances because we know that there are many out there just waiting for us to fail, even after nearly two decades. The global economy is in meltdown. It's no exaggeration to say we are in a battle, on many fronts, for our very survival in this corner of rural England.

She: 'And having no parents won't help, I suppose.'
I: 'Jesus, you scared the shit out of me!'

She: 'Sorry lovey.'

I: 'You promised you'd never do this. You know, just turn up.'

She: 'Something told me I needed to. You're not happy and I think you need reassuring.'

I: 'Yes, trouble is, the sort of reassurance I need is more of the living walking through the door and paying sort.'

She: 'I read your book. Well, I didn't read it of course, I watched you write it.'

I: 'Any surprises?'

She: 'Not really. Sadness that we let it all go wrong. But it was hard.'

I: 'It was hard for all of us. It still is.'

She: 'Harder now?'

I: 'Everything changed after you died. I never thought it would, always thought you'd already turned your back on everything so you weren't part of it but of course you were. But then so much else went pear shaped too – the economy, the children's schooling, the banks and their stinking attitude to small people like us. It has just got lonelier and lonelier.'

She: 'But there have been some good times, there's been some fun?'

I: 'Oh, of course there's been some fun. Because, you know, when everything is looking shit, sometimes laughter is all there is left. The saddest thing is that you missed so much of that laughter.

'Let me tell you how it's been since you've been gone but let me also fill you in on what you missed out on before you died. Because, Mum, you know you left us a long time before you left this world.'

She: 'Not in my heart, love.'

I: 'I know that now but we didn't understand that at the time.'

Chapter One

The recession drives us to try to make some cash from our unwanted crap, I get disgracefully drunk and Oliver reminds me how I am not getting any younger

By the time we return home from our holiday in France our heads are spinning. Every foundation stone we have laid over thirteen years seems to be trembling under our feet.

We're still quietly grieving the loss of our last parent, Oliver is about to start at secondary school and we are understandably nervous. How will he cope? Will he make friends? It's fair to say that the social landscape for which the school provides is a tad different from the experience of growing up in a castle. That said, a good deal of the the farmers' children he will be going to school with are a hell of a lot richer than we are but somehow, in this corner of Eden at least, turrets and towers seem to make more of a social statement than hundreds or thousands of acres of green fields and sheep (even if a single breeding tup can change hands for several tens of thousands of pounds). We are also painfully aware of the difference between this and the private education we had originally chosen for him, even if it did go so disastrously wrong.

We have our family home behind the castle but buying it has left us with no spare cash in the business and the attitude towards us from the bank has turned from open arms to a stony faced scowl. Costs are rising and customers, increasingly confusing price with value as they are beguiled by the bargain hunting culture of the internet, are wanting more for less.

We know that we are not alone, it's global, but the idea of chucking it all in and decamping to southern France has never seemed more appealing and swapping one basket load of crap for another might be made sweeter by sunshine, cheap red wine and the opportunity to ripen our own home grown food before the sun dips below the horizon for six months.

'It's our dream, Wendy,' I plead night after night as the summer draws to a close, the nights draw in and Wendy's inevitable melt down over seasonal cash flow looms (a little earlier every year, a fact that hasn't eluded either of us but warrants no conscious acknowledgement).

'This is supposed to be our dream now,' she retorts, 'the trouble with you, Simon, is you're never content with anything. Do you really think you'll be happier anywhere else? There might not be the same problems and worries but there'll still be some. Moving won't heal the damage that bloody school did to Oliver that he is so manfully repairing himself, it won't bring back our parents or magic up an extended family for the kids. We'd all just feel even more isolated than we do here and that acceptance you crave so deeply... in rural France? Forget it!'

'But our problems would be smaller and the sun would be shining on them,' I mutter into my pillow. I'm getting nowhere in this argument so I harrumph down under the duvet and let my dreams take me once again to those wooded valleys of southern France where the lavender, thyme, rosemary and marjoram owns the air and fills it with a heady scent that says, 'this is our place, we belong here' and I dream that I am a herb too and that I no longer have to survive a northern winter wrapped up in layers of fleece. But harrumphing doesn't even cover it – I want to sob, cry. Did we really ever know what we were taking on?

Despite our angst Oliver settles into Grammar School well thanks to the considerable additional effort invested in him by his primary school teachers but it still falls to me to bring his new teachers up to speed about his general mistrust of the school system. Whether or not they see through me and for Oliver's mistrust read mine I can't say but they take on board the warning and we feel confident that he is in a system working with him and his needs rather than against him for a change.

The autumn is filled with mellow days and crisp nights – the perfect antidote to a washout summer and, with blood kissed by the Mediterranean sun and diluted by some very decent red wine still coursing through our veins and a settled weather forecast we decide to throw an impromptu garden party for our closest friends.

We pick the afternoon of a Sunday on the morning of which we have already committed to taking a stall at a local car boot sale. Quite why we are laying out all our unwanted crap for others to pore over is beyond me but Wendy is adamant that we need a clear out and has spent many a rainy day all summer amassing an enviable array of tat to sell which has included a ruthless clear out of the children's unwanted toys. It's not going to turn our finances around but it might raise enough cash to buy some more tat to fill the gaps left by the stuff we sell.

Oliver is now of an age where he is finding increasingly ingenious ways of extracting money out of us and any other gullible individuals. Having already caught him trying to sell items of his wardrobe to his sister, including old pyjama bottoms and smelly worn out trainers, we have told him to find more honest outlets for his entrepreneurial flair. The car boot sale seems an obvious breeding ground for his talent.

And so here we are sitting in the Co-op car park setting up our first car boot sale. I have bank rolled the venture by paying for the pitch, so it will take £6 of sales to break even. The sun is shining and has brought out a decent crowd, so there is every prospect of a profit. Or at least there would be were it not for the somewhat dubious selection of goods the children have brought to market. Added to this, they have been left to formulate their own pricing and their expectations are, to say the least, unrealistic.

At the front of the stall is one of Emily's dolls. It's called something menacing like 'Baby Annie, I can swim, wet myself, vomit and answer back with built in voice recognition unit'. Emily thinks this is worth a tenner but it has had one side of its head shaved, the other side is bright pink spikes and one of its legs has been hacksawed off just below the knee by Oliver. I point out that at the very least this compromises the swimming feature and that perhaps fifty pence would be more appropriate. 'No, we'll start at £10 and see where we go from there,' says Emily.

Oliver is selling a pair of rugby boots for £5 which he thinks a bargain. I point out their limited appeal without studs, but he says they are still good quality and new studs are easily available. The coating of vintage mud presumably adds to their value.

We have a selection of old mugs, some books, a motley selection of soft toys in various shades of grey and some pebbles that, some years ago, Emily collected from the garden and decorated. As original pieces of art, these have been priced at anything between £1.50 and £75 with no correlation between price tag and pebble size. 'Look at the Mona Lisa', Emily reasons, 'it's tiny and worth how much?'

Our pricing is inevitably putting off prospective customers and after half an hour the children are complaining about being bored. They aren't interested in my explanation about how we have priced ourselves out of the market so I take matters in hand, resorting to some old fashioned barrow boy tactics and start calling out: 'Credit crunch busting bargains, everything must go, all offers considered'. Well, of course, the children are horrified and by the time I've got into the swing of things, they're cowering in the front seat of the car. But it's done the trick and within minutes I've raked in 25 pence for a headless Action Man and 75 pence for a dog-eared copy of *A Guide to Steam on the Settle to Carlisle Railway* to a man who is disappointed that I don't also have an edition of *Diesel Multiple Units on Branch Lines of the North West*. I try to interest him in a couple of videos called something like 'Thomas the tank engine and Percy get dirty' and 'Thomas couples up with Annie and Clarabelle' but he tells me it's not the sort of thing he's into.

After a couple of hours we have more than covered our costs and are ready to call it quits but we're penned in by other cars and have to wait to make a break for it. I split the proceeds between the children and send them off to visit the other stalls. Within ten minutes they have both spent every penny and return with more things than we have sold.

Later, as I am setting up for lunch in the garden, there's a commotion from the other side of the garden followed by some frantic shouting.

Friends have come to stay the night and brought their six month old Border Collie. Apparently he's never come across chickens before. Suddenly, frantically from behind the hedge comes a bantam hen followed by an ecstatic collie followed by a red faced brunette. Moments later, the brunette and the bantam are out if sight but the collie comes racing back in the opposite direction in pursuit of another squawking fowl, chased by the brunette with a stick. By the time the dog has been cornered, he's done two full rounds of the garden, taken a mouthful of feathers out of the backside of one hen and chased another two up into the trees. Our friends are mortified but Wendy and I are aching with laughter. 'The hens might have been killed,' our friend exclaims, horrified.

'Oh it would have been well worth it,' we tell her.

Lunch goes well, the sun keeps shining and by tea time I'm ready for a lie down. Having already suffered the effects of too much sun on the back of my head at the car boot sale, in an attempt to stay hydrated I've mistakenly been downing the Prosecco instead of the Pelligrino sparkling water. This on top of not wearing a hat and forgetting the sun cream, means I am wiped out. The only thing for it is to retreat indoors for a cup of tea and a lie down.

I reflect that I am not getting any younger, a fact confirmed a few days later by Oliver at the tender age of twelve. And Emily his ten-year-old sister, concurs.

Not that they've actually said it outright in so many words, but I get the gist. And I know it's true. When you sit in a pub garden and are more interested in the quality of the hanging baskets than how many more pints you can consume, your ideal day out is an afternoon on some friends' narrowboat and your car envy has shifted from a Porsche or a Ferrari to a Landrover Defender you know that a milestone, if not already passed, is certainly looming.

Not solely an age related issue, I have always had difficulty finishing a meal without some of it ending up on my clothes but when I tucked my napkin into my collar in a restaurant a couple of years ago the children and Wendy were horrified. Telling them it always worked for my Granddad did little for my cause. Now I have hit upon an ingenious solution to this problem that obviously isn't going to go away as my aim and steadiness of hand both diminish – I now choose food which is a similar colour to the clothes I am wearing.

But the moment I knew the brow of the hill and I were becoming ever closer came when I bought myself a bottle of caffeine enriched shampoo for my thinning hair. There's no way of hiding such a thing in a family bathroom (it's somewhat impractical to go rummaging around at the back of the airing cupboard every time you want to wash your hair) but I had hoped that the rest of the family would have the decency to diplomatically ignore it. I should be so lucky.

'Ooh look at those luscious locks,' giggles Wendy the day after I start using the shampoo, 'Mind you don't get any on your eyebrows, it already looks as if it's taking effect on your back.' I should have known I'd get no sympathy, especially after last Christmas.

We are gathering to open our Christmas stockings. A few parcels in I come across a CD shaped present. I'm really hoping it might be Susan Boyle's second album or a replacement for my Best of Andrew Lloyd Webber.

But no. It's Now That's What I Call Music 40-something (which, if you don't know, is the annual compilation of the best tracks of the year). The children have both been watching me for a reaction as I open it and say in unison 'it's to bring you up to date Daddy.'

'I see,' I reply, shooting a glance at Wendy as I wonder whose idea this really was. She just smiles sheepishly, undoubtedly feeling a tad guilty as we are all having to listen to her Christmas compilation of Gregorian chants for the umpteenth time since the first of December and before lunch it was The ultimate Yuletide soundtrack prized from the front cover of the festive edition of Good Housekeeping.

Emily seizes the opportunity to replace the musical monks with the new Now CD but only because she wants to play Leona Lewis on repeat. I'm quite happy about this as it is about the only song I recognise.

I don't do myself any favours by then telling the children that I can remember when the very first Now compilation came out. Groans all round, especially from Wendy who has heard that one every year since I've known her and Emily says 'what, forty three years ago? Were there even CD players that long ago?'

'Record players, we didn't have CDs', I begin to explain.

'Oh yes, like that one on the stairs with the big horn and the winding handle, you mean?' Oliver interjects.

Aunty Gloria, our only Christmas guest who I am sure has been here since at least mid-November, causes a timely distraction by nodding off mid-stocking and sending all her presents clattering to the floor.

'Now that's old,' I mutter.

A few days after the car boot sale and garden party, we are taking our MG (which happens to be the same age as me) out for a spin while the weather continues to hold and I am running Oliver into Kirkby Stephen for some sporting event or other. It's a fine day, the roof is down and the engine is purring happily. I start singing Bat out of Hell by Meatloaf as it feels like the right thing to do. After a couple of minutes Oliver asks quizzically but with an accusatory undertone, 'Daddy you haven't been listening to your Now CD lately have you?'

'No, darling, why?'

'Well that's rather an old song you're singing,' he says as he reaches over and pats my thinning scalp.

'Oliver, we're driving a classic car so I'm singing a classic song.'

'Mmm, you're just a classic sort of guy really,' he replies, rummaging around in the glove box for something a little more up to date.

I reflect later that classic is a lot better than old as long as I can continue to inject a bit of cool as well and I think I've pulled that off when I tell everyone that next year, for my birthday, we're all going to a Take That concert.

'Take That?' Emily looks almost horrified when I announce triumphantly that we've got the tickets. 'They're nearly as old as you.'

Well, not quite. And they've still all got a full head of hair.

♛   ♛   ♛   ♛   ♛

As if to compound my feelings of advancing decrepitude Oliver has got himself a girlfriend. This isn't news straight from the horse's mouth, mind you. We have found out via the school grapevine. Apparently he has had her in his sights for quite some time but now he has no choice but to include us in the intrigue of his romance because he needs our help, firstly to take him shopping and secondly for ideas on a date.

The shopping expedition is easily arranged and is to buy a birthday present. I delegate this to Wendy, thinking that I will be better suited to the date advice but when it comes to it I am told flatly that any advice I have to offer will be useless.

'No offence, Dad, but Mum's already told me you didn't have a proper girlfriend until you were eighteen so you're not the best role model.' No offence taken and I resist any temptation to counter with a run down of Wendy's reputation at school.

'Different times, Oliver, different times.'

'Not that different,' he snorts.

Wendy advises that a simple shopping outing to Carlisle together on the train would be a good first date and Oliver agrees. As the date approaches he is obviously becoming very anxious.

'What's the matter?' I ask, 'it's only Carlisle, what can go wrong?' I'm trying to be reassuring but the truth is I know exactly how he must be feeling.

I have been instructed to drop Oliver at the bottom of the station hill. 'Don't take me any further, I can walk up,' are his exact instructions. Mischievously I tell him taking him to the station house door is absolutely no trouble at all.

'Don't. Just don't.'

As he gets out of the car and walks towards the station, even at twelve he's still my little boy. As he tries to swagger nonchalantly up the hill, his coat too big, his shoes looking enormous at the end of his spindly legs, in fact all of him growing so fast and everything out of proportion, as he is swallowed up by the hedgerows, he is still my little boy.

But, in truth, both children are growing up much faster, physically and emotionally than Wendy or I are prepared for. They are a lot less malleable than they used to be. Some friends of ours rejoice in the joy of having young adults in the house and how it has made the trials of raising them all so worthwhile. Frankly they're liars. While it is true that we can all laugh at the same jokes now and there is a new level of intimacy in shared experiences which makes life with both of them often very fulfilling, daily life with adolescents (Emily has been one since she was six), particularly when being balanced with the demands of a business, can be hideous.

We may live an extraordinary life in our castle but as far as the nuts and bolts of everyday family life go, it's pretty ordinary.

Living with a pre-teen daughter and a nearly teenaged son is a daily revelation. And that they are a boy and a girl delivers double the surprises every day.

Having lived in, and shared with guests, almost every part of the castle we now have the luxury of an entirely self contained house. We gathered up all our favourite possessions from the castle to fill our new home as we looked forward to enjoying some privacy; not least so that guests and staff were no longer privy to the often demonic screeching that is the daily ritual of getting up on a school day and which resumes at four o'clock until bedtime (ours often coming before theirs these days).

While it's not quite the same as sleeping in the main castle, we console ourselves that we are, at least, sparing the guests the unpleasantness of actually witnessing any real family life in our family friendly castle. So although a recent Tripadvisor reviewer pointed out that 'we do resent it when we have to suffer poor behaviour from other people's children. Some children appear not to understand "go to bed",' I'm happy to say they were not referring to our children who, in actual fact are invariably delightful in front of anyone who matters apart from their own parents.

A couple of years after we moved in our carefully crafted interior design is already in tatters. Our prize ornaments, so lovingly displayed in the hall and on the piano have given way to such delights as a sweaty pubescent cricket box languishing in the cut glass fruit bowl, and one or two (never a pair) smelly anything-but-white running socks festering at the bottom of the log basket or dangling from the head of a porcelain dog.

It seems both children have grown up completely failing to understand the relationship between rubbish and a bin, presumably preferring to weather the onslaught of parental displeasure at the periodic discovery of snack packets stuffed down the back of the sofa cushions. I once emptied the contents of the bin into Oliver's bed and pulled the duvet up over the rubbish in a vain attempt to make a point. It was a failed gesture as he simply got into bed and kicked all the detritus out with his feet.

The newly laid carpet in Emily's room (oatmeal was never surely a good choice but Wendy says it was an end of roll and cheap) is patterned in multicolours with smears of make up and nail varnish.

'What have you been doing Emily? I'm sure school doesn't allow you to wear nail varnish,' comes the oft repeated wail.

'I'm not wearing any,' she proclaims defiantly, 'it's a Bratz makeover party,' and she holds up two grotesquely painted, tousled and generally defiled plastic dolls. She may not have painted her own nails but her hands and wrists are still sporting as much nail varnish as if she had but there's nothing to be done as the open bottle of nail varnish remover is on it's side in the corner of the room, leaching the last of the original oatmeal colour out of the carpet.

'It was Maisy,' she says, catching the look of parental despair. That one-year-old spaniel has an awful lot to answer for.

Less easy to blame on the dog, and not so easy to hide from us, are the regular iTunes receipts that frequently pop into our email inbox. No matter how many times we change our password, the children figure it out, perhaps not surprising as we only have a repertoire of about four between us as any more would simply be too much for our ageing brains, and so they are able to make random purchases without our consent.

'But it's only 59 pence,' Emily protests when I quiz her about her latest download of 'Talking Finn the Goldfish' for her iPod or her latest acquisition of 200 e-dollars for her own bespoke online runway fashion show.

'Yes, but look, a lot of 59 pences adds up to several pounds.'

'Well it wasn't me,' doesn't wash and then there's a bust up as I tell her it's stealing and she says I just don't understand what it's like to be her. As one of us stomps off down the stairs, Wendy, smugly, will chip in with, 'Some battles just aren't worth fighting.'

'Oh shut up!'

On that note a new row begins after which Emily reappears in floods of tears to tell us she hates this family, wishes she'd never been born and why can't we just stop arguing, it's so unfair, if only she had different parents (oh, and a sister rather than such a hateful brother) her life might just be bearable.

It's clearly very difficult growing up: hormones, emotions and a jumble of immature brain connections but no matter how difficult trying to make sense of it all as a parent may seem, don't make the mistake of buying a book to help you.

We did.

The worthily titled *Teen Owner's Manual* promises operating instructions, troubleshooting tips and advice on adolescent maintenance. It is full of pretty interesting stuff but buried deep within its pages is a paragraph guaranteed to make you feel even more inadequate than your kids already have, especially when it is they that point it out.

'Hey, read this Dad,' says Oliver, smirking.

- If you don't want your son to swear like a sailor, don't use profanity.
- If you don't want your daughter to let her frustration get the better of her, don't give in to your own frustration.
- If you don't want your teen to abuse alcohol, then don't have an after work cocktail every day or get tipsy in front of them.

'Right, Thanks', I say, 'I'm fed up with the both of you, just get me a sodding drink and piss off to bed.'

And so the delicate balance between running a hospitable business and maintaining a functional family life becomes ever more precarious. The son turns into a teenager next August (officially, since unofficially I think there has been a thirteen year old lurking inside his body since he was about eight like an alien life form waiting for its moment to pounce on the unsuspecting care givers that gave it life in the first place). However, without resorting to the pages of the holier-than-thou tome cited above, I have begun to develop a set of rules which I think is working.

So, I'd like to share with you my insights into how to maintain a meaningful father-son relationship when one of you has all the communication skills of a caveman (and which one that is depends entirely on which side of the relationship you are on).

1. Never say 'I know exactly what you're going through because I've been there' because the automatic response to this is, 'nobody knows what I'm going through, nobody understands me, especially not you'.
2. Don't try to be cool by borrowing your son's new white belt with Superman buckle and showing it off in the pub. It's not cool, however well it demonstrates your recent weight loss, and will just make you look like an arse.
3. Don't start deleting the hours of rugby/football/cricket that have been stored on the Sky+ box. Even if there is only 2% space left and the next episode of your can't-miss American trashy serial won't record, just don't.
4. Never enter into a debate about the merits and demerits of censorship and age ratings on DVDs and video games but do always remember that you're right and they're wrong on this one and stand

your ground.

5. Do be prepared for the sudden outpourings of unaffected, genuinely warm affection directed straight at you when you least expect it. Soak it up while it lasts.

6. But don't reciprocate unless you are the only two people on an uninhabited South Pacific island. And there are no ships on the horizon.

7. Never question the identity of the person on the other end of the monosyllabic mobile phone conversation and NEVER, EVER, shout out in the background 'Hello Chelsea/Paris/India/Britney, would you like to come over for tea?'

8. Always knock on a closed door, reasons obvious.

9. Don't stop singing in the shower just because it's 'sooo embarrassing' and remind them you are not too old to audition for Britain's Got Talent (watch their face drain of colour the first time you say, 'If Susan Boyle can do it, why not me?'). If you have a community choir, join it.

10. And finally, for your own sanity and self respect, NEVER, EVER, EVER be drawn into a discussion of the comparative talents and shortcomings of your and anybody else's offspring (and this rule counts from birth). Murderous thoughts are guaranteed to follow.

I have yet to devise any meaningful strategy for managing our father-daughter relationship to my advantage. Some how she always seems to have the upper hand.

CHAPTER TWO

*Reflections on what it is to be middle class and how I wrote
'Undressed For Dinner'*

As winter recedes and spring begins to brighten the horizon our summer adventure becomes a fading memory but my hankering after a change just won't go away. Logic tells me selling the castle now isn't even a possibility. We are in the middle of the worst recession any one can remember, at least since the last recession, and the newspapers are doing everything they can to drive us further into a pit of collective despair. Nobody is buying or selling anything, least of all draughty old castles in the arse end of nowhere.

But, of course, this isn't true. While off-loading the place is not an option, guests are still coming and they are buying into what we do with increasing enthusiasm. New guests are keen to buy a slice of the genuine and authentic, and previous guests are flocking to our door to somewhere comfortable and familiar in an uncertain world.

We are all creatures of habit. Given too much choice on a menu, on the internet, on a street full of restaurants or shops and whether they should be enjoyed in London, Paris or Bordeaux, Milan or Rome, New York or Boston, we often retreat to what we know and what we know we like.

This is never truer than when money is tight and it has proved to be true of castle guests. Throughout the 2000s, as we were growing our business, we were told that repeat custom should be a corner stone of our strategy but it seemed that that repeat custom wasn't happening. Were we doing something wrong? Our business was growing but could it grow faster if more people came back? Why should they? When we looked at our own behaviour it was clear to see why. When everyone has the world brought to them by the internet and endless credit at their disposal then new is more exciting than the old and tested.

When the credit crunch bit all that changed. Having to spend their own hard earned cash instead of easy money thrown at them by the banks, people began a new migration – a flight to safety and many guests we have not see for many years begin to return. What's more, the gap between new guests' first visit and their return shortens. 'When things are tight,' is the oft repeated phrase, 'you look at what you know instead of risking the unknown.'

♛ ♛ ♛ ♛ ♛

We are hosting fewer weddings than we were but still people are getting married and they are enjoying our way of doing things, albeit on a reduced budget.

We have got through another winter, the bank hasn't repossessed the castle, we've managed to pay most of our taxes on time and advance bookings for the summer are looking decent, if not spectacular.

'I reckon,' Wendy reasons, 'that anyone who has still got a job feels a bit safer about keeping it after four years of this shit and with mortgage interest rates at an all time low they have more cash in their pockets.' She's right. The global recession can't go on forever (although it would be a few years yet before the country was truly out of the financial woods).

What we do have is a solid customer base and it is decidedly middle class, in short, we are attracting people like us and at no time of the year are our middle class credentials more apparent than at February half-term.

There's a commotion at the breakfast table. As we begin breakfast service some guests are having an argument. It's the sort of argument parents have in public; full of venom but conducted in stage whispers for fear of being overheard by others who they worry might regard them as inadequate parents (confirming their own insecurities about their abilities) and because they don't want the children to hear them rowing.

Monty and Kate arrive on their way to Scotland. It is the first night of their spring family holiday and is the second longest period of the year they spend in each other's company. They live in Surrey. Monty works in the city doing something nobody other than his immediate colleagues understands but he makes obscene amounts of money doing it. Kate looks after the children.

Secretly the set up works admirably for both of them but they are loath to admit it.

Kate tells everyone she gave up everything for the children, including skiing, and running them around plus keeping the house in order is so stressful. Apparently her former career at the magazine in the West End was a cinch compared with having to ferry the children to and from separate schools, coordinate the schedules of the Latvian cleaner, the Croatian ironing lady, the gardener who is a nightmare and can't be trusted with the roses which she then has to prune herself, 'goodness knows how I find the time!', make sure she's in when Ocado delivers the groceries and get to yoga on time.

Monty leaves the house at six every morning, breathing a subdued sigh of contentment as he closes the front door of his Country Life perfect home and won't need to be back until just before it's time to say goodnight to his marvellously talented but hot-housed and precocious children and his beautifully manicured and preened but neurotic and exhausted wife.

It's suburban bliss of sorts, each going about their daily routine with minimal intrusion from the other. So these family breaks present some considerable challenges to the status quo. Their children, Rosie, seven and Harry, nine, have been awake since five o'clock and Monty knows it is his holiday duty to be up with them, entertaining.

Outside it is raining heavily and Monty and the children have just come in soaked to the skin as Kate walks downstairs. Monty is resentful that he doesn't get a lie-in on holiday as Kate makes it quite clear this is his time to bond with the children (in other words, the kids are his responsibility, not hers). But Kate is quietly seething because she feels guilty (knowing full well that guilt comes from within) and because Monty, frankly, always makes a complete hash of looking after the children. Granted they have fun together but she doubts whether they are properly cared for.

Her suspicions are already reconfirmed and it's only day one of the holiday. They've all had to go upstairs and change so she's already a day's change of clothes down and now she comes into the dining room to find the children helping themselves to Coco Pops instead of Granola.

'No darlings, not that, it's full of sugar and remember your allergies Rosie,' Kate says and the children drop the Coco Pops packets on the table.

'They're on holiday for goodness sake, they've been up since five so could do with a sugar hit and Rosie doesn't have allergies,' Monty counters.

'You know very well what I mean Monty. She's intolerant.'

'Not to chocolate,' Monty replies, feeling his own intolerance to his wife welling up earlier than usual into the holiday.

'Help yourselves to granola darlings,' she says.

'But they don't like granola, they'll just play around with it and leave it.'

Kate shoots Monty a dagger stare. 'I don't know that you have any idea what the children eat for breakfast or even what is good for them. I am with them all week every week and...'

'Oh here we go,' Monty mutters.

Wendy bursts into the dining room from the kitchen. She has met enough Kate and Montys to know when a situation needs diffusing. 'Who's for eggy bread or pancakes?' and to allay Kate's fears she adds, 'Don't worry, they're our own eggs – fresh this morning and totally free range.' Then, directed at the children, 'and perhaps a bit of chocolate spread in the pancakes?'

'Yes please!' the children chime in unison. The deal is done before Kate can speak.

A week later Monty and Kate return for a night. Monty is no longer in charge of the children following an ill-fated sea kayaking expedition off the west coast of Scotland and an unfortunate bout of sickness following a lunch of fish and chips topped off with a Knickerbocker Glory.

In the morning he is up at six for a run while Kate gets the children ready and brings them down to breakfast. Tomorrow, back in Surrey, normal service will be resumed.

We are, of course, selling a dream. It's a slice of a middle class idyll that families are happy to buy into without thinking too deeply about the reality of what life with a young family running a hotel is really like.

I have been writing a blog for a couple of years and decide it is time to turn my musings into a book because, I reason, it's time people knew

31

the truth, that it hasn't all been plain sailing. Quite why I feel compelled to lift the lid on our private life escapes me since I have always been very protective of our family privacy but when I start to canvass opinion among guests, friends and family about the idea I am surprised by their enthusiasm.

In a world where so many of us have everything we need, physical stuff has begun to lose its importance in favour of experience. We know this is one of the cornerstones of what appeals to people about Augill, it is an experience like no other and it is clear that a book about how it all happened is going to add to the experience we are selling.

Wendy wastes no time in harnessing my interest in the project, no doubt seizing upon it as an end to my malcontented unease.

'Take some time, go somewhere and write it,' she commands.

And so it is that a month later I am boarding a TGV in Paris bound for the south of France. I have rung Jacqui and Martin at Les Mimosas, the french B&B I would have as my own, to ask them if they could rent me a room for ten days. As I speed through the French countryside, gradually awakening to spring the further south we go, the words come tumbling out and although I know the story I am writing – I am living it – I have no idea how it is going to read or how, or when, it is going to end.

At Les Mimosas I have a room at the top of the house overlooking the vineyards which stretch all the way from the house to the river. I fling open the shutters, position a little table and a wooden bedroom chair in front of the open window and set my computer down on the gingham table cloth. A baguette and a bottle of good red wine complete the scene and as I stand back and look at my workstation, with its backdrop of vines, rustic plaster and peeling window frame, I can barely imagine I'll ever want to be anywhere else ever again.

For ten days I wake when the morning sun hits my face, eat a breakfast of croissants, bread and honey, walk by and swim (just the once) in the river and then write, first perched on the wide window sill with the spring sunshine on my face and then, when the sun has set behind the trees which line the river, settling down to write at my desk, always with a glass of red wine to help the words flow. Each evening I break for supper, sometimes alone, sometimes with Jacqui and Martin who introduce me to several of their friends in the village and I write long into the night, the flow of words only eventually interrupted by my inability to focus.

It is as if this is a love affair conducted behind Wendy's back but I cannot feel disloyal because this lover is one we both share and when I return home with the first manuscript of *Undressed For Dinner* complete there is no need for any guilty recriminations.

It is a cathartic experience; not quite the closing of a chapter, but rather a laying down of ghosts or an acceptance of the life we have now. On completion I don't know whether the book will ever be published and somehow it doesn't seem to matter, the writing of it being the important thing but nevertheless, I set about the tortuous process of finding an agent and a publisher.

Chapter Three

*I lament the lunacy of health and safety speak, we are sued by one of our own and
Clarissa Blanchard-Cafferty books the unlikeliest of weddings*

We have often remarked that in so many years in business dealing with
the public it is nothing short of miraculous that we haven't been sued.
Health and Safety. The phrase, so often uttered as a disembodied three
word mantra without context or meaning to cover all manner of excuses brings a red mist down on many a hotelier.

'Elf 'n' safety, mate.'

We take our responsibility for the safety and welfare of our guests
and staff very seriously but we also expect each of them to accept responsibility for themselves, something our guests aren't always so keen
to do.

And then, just occasionally, someone thinks they know better than
all of us.

I am working out in the garden and Wendy comes out to tell me
that one of our guests would like to see me. She has a complaint. I am
about to counter with my own complaint that this is not my department
but a single raised eyebrow dissuades me and I down tools to deal with
the situation.

The lady in question is sitting in the hall and jumps up to shake my
hand as soon as I come in. An interesting reaction from somebody with
a complaint, I think.

She begins by saying what a fantastic place the castle is and how we
have got everything spot on so I prepare myself for a very big 'but'
and when it comes it is far from what I expect.

'I am concerned for your safety,' she tells me. 'I have been watching
you in the garden today and I think you are going to do yourself a serious injury.'

I have been hedge trimming with a power hedge cutter and mowing the lawns. 'You haven't been wearing any sort of protection at all and I can't relax while I think you may end up hurting yourself.'

Momentarily lost for words, I want to tell her I think sunglasses and a pair of flip flops are perfectly acceptable workwear when it's this hot and that I have factor fifteen sun cream on my back and shoulders to ensure that I tan safely but feel that she may not appreciate my position.

'I can assure you I am quite safe, perhaps you should just pretend I am not there.'

'But I can't help watching you,' she pleads. Understandable given the Adonis-like upper body I have had on display all morning and I sympathise with her dilemma.

The truth is I have never been keen on all the recommended protective gear that goes with garden power tools and this lady has not been the first to point out that something more that a pair of shorts, a pair of sunglasses and some factor fifteen may be appropriate workwear.

In truth it gives me some peace of mind that Reg, our long-time garden help wears steel capped boots, Kevlar trousers and gloves and a helmet with ear guards – it's not implausible that this is all he ever wears although I'm sure he probably takes at least the boots off for bed – but I have tried all that and once fully togged up nearly succumbed to heat exhaustion just pulling the starter cable on the strimmer. Not to mention that the safety goggles steamed up so that even if I had got going I would have been wielding a spinning steel blade on the end of a long steel pole aimlessly, unable to see a thing.

All that said, it is true that I have had a couple of near misses. Once when strimming the verges of the drive a piece of gravel flew up and hit my sunglasses, cracking the lens. Had I not been wearing the glasses I would likely have been blinded in one eye. Wendy once nearly took off the top of a finger with the hedge trimmer on a rare occasion when she felt she ought to lend a hand outside. She cited inadequate training.

Nobody saw those particular episodes so had no reason to complain but there have been a handful of bizarre health and safety related complaints and incidents over the years.

Owing to some very unpleasant past experiences we don't allow dogs inside the castle (other than, of course, our own). One early summer evening a Land Rover Discovery pulls up outside.

A very doggy sort of lady jumps out and bounds towards the door. As I greet her I am half expecting her to put her arms over my shoulders and start licking me. She has the sort of Barbara Woodhouse demeanour of woollen skirt, padded jacket and hard set hair which speaks volumes of a wholesome life in the country.

'The doggies are in the back of the car. Is it alright to let them out for a run?'

I instinctively know that the doggies are going to be labradors and I advise her they are best kept on a lead as there are hens roaming about the garden.

'Oh, they'll not bother them. They're only trained to bring back dead birds.'

Before I can say another thing she's heading back to the car with a purposefulness of stride that would surely scatter the checkout queue at Waitrose. She has backed the car up to the edge of the forecourt and is now standing on top of the wall, below which is a four foot drop into the flower bed.

The doggies have been in the back of the car for six hours so when she opens the tailgate they're out of there faster than a pheasant. And she is flat on her back, four feet down in the herbaceous border.

What happens next is a sad indictment of the world in which we live. As I go to assist, Wendy comes out to see what all the commotion is about.

'Go and get the camera,' I tell her.

'What for?' she asks incredulously.

'Because we need proof of how close she parked to the wall in case she sues us.'

Happily she never does and, once hauled out of the shrubs which undoubtedly broke her fall, she is calling for the doggies which, of course, have made a beeline for the hen house.

On a different occasion we are accused of having dangerous stairs. A guest who has made liberal use of the bar and drained the sherry decanter in both her own room and her children's finds it difficult to get back upstairs unaided, stumbling several times before eventually making it to the top on all fours.

While she hasn't sustained any obvious injuries, next morning she is ranting about the unsafe nature of the staircase. We can only assume she objected to it's upward trajectory or perhaps, due to the way her head must have been spinning, she mistook it for a spiral staircase.

We are all becoming less tolerant of each other's foibles and the imperfections all around us that actually make life interesting and this in turn seems to be one of the main drivers of the tiresome political correctness to which we are all now subjected. Mind you, none of the sane-minded people I have time for socially give much of a fig for most PC bunkum.

Last spring I went on an electric bike ride with our MP, Rory Stewart. We only cycle about half a mile but are told we cannot go on the highway without a cycle helmet and a high visibility jacket.

'Elf n safety'.

Last year I accompanied Year Six from our primary school on a trip to London. Now, even with thirty kids in tow, a trip to London is an excuse to look one's best. So imagine my horror when, at Penrith Railway Station, the head teacher produces high visibility tabards for us all to wear. 'Elf n safety'.

In neither case is health and safety anything to do with it. It is political correctness and the truth is there is nothing vaguely correct about traipsing around London in luminous yellow – drawing attention to ourselves as a group of vulnerable youngsters – or anything that even slightly improves my safety cycling along a deserted Cumbrian farm lane in March looking brighter than the daffodils.

And I ask you, who looks good in luminous yellow? The damage to my self-esteem is itself a health and safety issue. I don't blame the head teacher or Mr Stewart. The nonsense has become institutionalised.

But this need to dumb down our own common sense and then dress it up as rules for the greater good has got me thinking. I realise that political correctness and the reluctance to call a spade a spade anymore, has altered the very way in which we communicate.

School speak is a particularly good example, although I suspect the same goes for the whole public sector where it seems plain speaking is to be avoided at all costs. I have been a school governor for twelve years, first at our village Church of England primary school, latterly at

Oliver's grammar school and I'm still befuddled. Schools that are now academies must not be referred to as schools anymore. Why? They haven't changed what they do. By the same token, what is a health trust if not a hospital? What is a pupil referral unit or a patient referral unit? For that matter, what is a unit at all?

At school we have teaching assistants, higher level teaching assistants and principal teaching assistants. Apparently they're all members of different job families. There are teachers with TLRs (teaching and learning responsibilities). So is there an option of teaching without responsibility for any learning? What is an Early Years coordinator – a morph of a midwife, health visitor and a primary school teacher perhaps? And a nurse practitioner? What is the different between a manager, a supervisor and a co-ordinator? Is it that job family thing again?

It's all nonsense.

At Augill Castle we are proudly non-PC and most people enjoy us for it. But here are a few suggestions of ways we could modernise our corporate speak without actually changing the way we do anything:

We are often stuck for a concise way to describe what we do at Augill. We are not a full service hotel, but much more than a B and B. We often say we are selling an experience. So, we could be called 'a customer experience fulfilment unit'.

To facilitate this outcome (which can be assessed by the number of measurable deliverables) we must employ people. These are no longer employees, they are now colleagues, grouped into job families. To foster good family morale, job titles should focus on an individual's strengths.

Some are particularly good with children who, of course, are our future customers. We will call these our 'emerging market facilitation agents' or 'future revenue enhancement managers'.

Breakfast is the most important meal of the day so our breakfast chef is now our 'sure start nutritional practitioner'.

We have Reg, a caretaker of sorts but to give him his due he does so much more than his job title suggests so we'll now refer to him as our 'estate and built asset maintenance co-ordinator'.

Our gardener is clearly best described as the 'environmental enhancement manager'. They are both in a job family of their own so should we give them a single carer's allowance?

Housekeeping is one of the most important functions at the castle and our biggest job family. They are now 'accommodation sanitisation specialists' headed up by our very own 'principal slumber and ablution facilities supervisor'.

The men who deliver our gas and oil are 'energy provision operatives' whilst supply of our logs and sawdust heatlogs is outsourced to 'renewable alternative energy consultants'.

I pretty much do whatever is required so I can either be called a 'higher level general assistant' or simply a General Practioner. But then again, that's inaccurate as I am on call 24 hours a day, work before 9am, after 5pm and invariably every weekend. Perhaps I should be included in one of the most important national job families: 'economy backbone maintainers'.

We all share responsibility for the end game, making our guests happy, so our job descriptions should refer to our roles as 'stakeholder satisfaction and gratification maximisers' and our person specifications all highlight the ability to 'smile in the face of absurdity'.

As for Wendy? Despite my repeated attempts at a boardroom coup, she's still simply known as 'The Boss'. Fittingly the most no-nonsense job title for the most un-PC of the lot of us.

It's all part of the game that is caring for the public and we are pretty sure we have covered most bases when it comes to assessing the few actual risks inherent in working, living or staying in an old Victorian building.

So it knocks us completely for six when we do eventually get sued. We are blind-sided not so much by the action but by the fact that the litigation has been instigated by a member of our own staff.

One of the aspects of Augill which has always made the magic has been the way in which we treat our staff as extended family. Of course, we don't live in each other's pockets and everyone has to work hard, but ours has always been a flat structure with open communication. Honesty, integrity and a sense of fairness are at the heart of our relationship with our staff and we always thought that was mutual.

Now our faith in everything we do, everything we have built, is rocked to its very foundations.

The details of what and why are handed straight to our insurers who are quick to investigate and assure us that there is no question of negligence on our part. But the investigator who visits us to explain the process delivers a sting in the tail.

'You have done nothing wrong, you haven't been found negligent or wanting in any way...'

We are both so relieved we almost tune out what he says next and are busying ourselves pouring tea.

'...But,' he pauses just long enough to regain our attention, 'because this member of staff was in your employment and on your premises at the time of the incident you are still technically liable.'

'Liable for what?' I ask incredulously.

'You are liable for the incident.'

'But it wasn't our fault,' Wendy is almost shrieking, 'do you mean they'll get a payout even though we did nothing wrong?'

'I'm not saying it's right, but yes, that's pretty much how it'll go. The insurance company will negotiate but somewhere along the line they'll probably pay out unless there's a clear case to fight in court. I don't think it will come to that. What I need to do is reassure you that you have no more to do with the case, it's between the individual and your insurers now.'

'It's sick, fucking sick,' I spit, but the insurance man is unmoved having no doubt weathered this reaction a hundred times.

The incident leaves us feeling very fragile and more uncertain of ourselves than ever. Our long standing staff do their best to reassure us. They are as incensed as we are, both at the fact that we are being sued by one of our own and the injustice of a system that seems to reward them for doing so.

The staff member does at least have the decency to resign but only several weeks later after claiming that we and the rest of the staff made them feel so uncomfortable that they felt they could not continue. We try to put the incident behind us as we face up to the start of the main summer season but our trust in human nature has been fractured and rather like a crack in glass it can never be truly fixed.

As if expunging one source of unpleasantness from our lives leaves a void which must be filled, a few weeks later we receive a call from Clarissa Blanchard-Cafferty, our high-minded nemesis.

She wishes to engage our services as a wedding venue. That we should be on her radar at all takes us by surprise but that is nothing compared with the details of the event.

Her son has been living in the Scottish Isles eking out a living as an artist and very talented he is, the wide open horizons, windswept landscape and occasional dazzling sunsets clearly stimulate his creative juices. While he may not have chosen to follow his father into a career in banking, since a piece of his work appeared in a gallery in London, his parents have felt able to express their pride for their 'internationally acclaimed artist son' openly.

Ever since leaving university Rupert has shared his artistic life with his best friend Hamish. Clarissa has always said how she admires his loyalty in following his friend to such a remote place, and has seemed quite oblivious of his true motivation. So quite what she and Martin thought when the pair announced their intention to get married can only be guessed at.

Nevertheless, she has taken it upon herself to arrange the wedding and thinks Augill the perfect venue. 'It'll suit them perfectly,' she trills, 'it's so alternative.'

When Clarissa visits to discuss details there is no sign of Martin who, I suspect, is still trying to process how his son has taken a path in life so wildly different from anything he might have imagined.

'We don't want a huge do, there'll be just close friends and family. We don't want to drag Martin's city friends all the way up here,' Clarissa says, knowing there really isn't any need to explain.

'A jolly good houseparty with a wedding thrown in,' Wendy suggests, 'it's what we do best.'

'Exactly, I knew you'd understand. Very discreet.' Clarissa seems a lot brighter than when she arrived and somehow softer, as if we have stumbled upon a vulnerability, a weakness that she'd rather have kept hidden.

'I know how she feels,' Wendy reflects. 'Rupert's choices were never going to sit comfortably with their own outlook on life but I suppose we all have to come to a realisation that our children are our greatest achievement but also expose all of our prejudices, weaknesses and failings.'

She's right. Beyond all the trappings, the status and the accumulation of wealth or debt, as parents we will ultimately be defined by our children over whose destiny we have little control. It's a sobering thought and a great social leveller.

Chapter Four

A guest dies without settling their bill, another wishes to use the castle for alternative purposes and yet other guests are so rich they struggle to see the joy in anything around them

The one thing other than children that exposes our human frailty is death. It is easy to reflect that between us we have seen far more of it than many of our contemporaries. All our parents and grandparents were gone before Wendy turned forty. But while death has touched us personally more than we might believe we deserve, the Grim Reaper has so far refrained from calling at the castle.

There have, of course, been pet mice, a run-over cat, several guinea pigs, the merciful end to our labrador's long and happy life… but guests are slightly less likely to croak at the castle. By the law of averages, in a decade and a half we should have expected to have seen at least one human death but the eventuality has neither been anticipated or discussed.

So, when inevitably we do, indeed, have one fewer guests than expected for breakfast, we find Wendy's comprehensive staff handbook somewhat lacking. There is no section entitled 'Fatality, In House, Dealing With'. For Wendy it's a nightmare. Unplanned anything she finds difficult, but this is just beyond reasonable.

It's a fine afternoon in late May. The season is about to kick off and we're full of optimism for the summer to come. I have dug out a pair of shorts and the first of the half-term families have arrived.

Rick and Stephen have brought Stephen's mother Doreen away for a few days to celebrate her eighty seventh birthday. A frail little lady, about five feet tall and with a classic permanent set blue rinse atop a perfectly pressed tweed twin set, she is every bit the English lady. Doreen is also clearly as devoted to Rick and Stephen as they are to each other. They are booked to stay for three nights.

'My dear,' Doreen enthuses to Wendy, clutching her hand with exactly the right blend of formality and intimacy that nobody born after about 1939 seems to get quite right, 'your castle is magnificent and we will look forward to dining with you.'

Rick and Stephen are equally appreciative. A set designer in the West End, Stephen, a decidedly larger than life character declares the whole castle a theatrical triumph. 'Darlings, if I didn't know better I'd say there's been a Queen at work here,' he says with a wink.

'Oh there has,' replies Wendy, 'Simon's totally in touch with his... erm... theatrical side.'

'Well you've certainly got an eye,' Stephen says as he turns to me and chuckles. Everything Stephen says seems to be accompanied by a laugh, a hearty chuckle or a broad grin. He is devoted to Rick, devoted to his mum and thoroughly in love with life.

'I think we are going to have a lot of fun with those three,' Wendy says, 'they'll definitely be guests to remember,' words that will come back to haunt us.

The evening is one of our most memorable. Stephen has a dozen of us in stitches all night with salacious tales of celebrity carry-ons and theatrical scandal. To add to the entertainment he latches on to an American couple who cannot believe their luck in finding themselves dining with such a character in a castle. It's a dream ticket straight off the set of *Four Weddings and a Funeral* and they completely fail to notice that a good many of the jokes are at their expense.

In short it is an evening for which the castle was built and which makes everything we do utterly worthwhile. All of us fall into bed much happier than when we woke.

The next morning I am on breakfast duty. As I am quietly going about the business of cooking sausages Rick appears at the kitchen door.

'Can you call a doctor?' he is ashen.

'What's wrong?' I ask, knowing full well that if it's anything near as serious as Rick's face suggests, out here in the sticks calling a doctor is useless, and it will be an ambulance, or air ambulance that is required.

'Trouble breathing, lips blue,' he can hardly stutter the details.

'Jesus Christ!' I exclaim without really thinking and, as I dial 999, I tell Rick to get back to the bedroom straight away. What happens next beggars belief. Having requested the ambulance service the operator asks me to describe the symptoms. I do so and she tells me to put the patient in the recovery position and ring back in twenty minutes if there is no improvement.

'I beg your pardon?'

'It's probably just a panic attack.'

'What, with blue lips?'

'We'll get someone there as soon as we can.'

Torn between the sausages and trying to help, it's the sausages which need me less than the unfolding crisis so I bound upstairs and straight into Doreen's bedroom. To my surprise the bed is empty so I must assume she has collapsed in the bathroom. I fling open the bathroom door to be confronted by an 87-year-old lady perched unceremoniously on the lavatory pan.

'Christ, Doreen, you're alive,' I blurt without, obviously, thinking.

'I think so,' she replies, unconsciously checking herself for some sort of pulse and quite unsure whether to reach for the toilet paper or the knickers around her ankles.

Luckily an ambulance crew has picked up the call and, being nearby they divert from another non-emergency call. At that moment they crunch to an emergency stop on the gravel at the front of the castle.

Without another word I leave Doreen to gather herself together and prance theatrically back along the corridor in a vain attempt to make as little noise as possible for the sake of other guests to meet the paramedics and then direct them to Stephen's room.

There's no further need for me as no number of episodes of *Casualty* or *ER* equips me to be of any use now the professionals have arrived and so I return to the sausages.

Ten minutes later there's a juddering sound and the windows begin to rattle. It's the air ambulance landing on the lawn and there are more paramedics running through the castle. By the time Wendy arrives back from the school run chaos has landed.

As she walks into the hall a police officer comes through the front door. 'I understand there's been a death,' he states without any further explanation as Wendy desperately tries to compute this information. When she left for school the castle was quiet and I was cooking sausages. Now there is a helicopter on the lawn, first responders and paramedics seem to outnumber everyone else and a policeman is telling her somebody has died. If ever she needed confirmation of her indispensability, this is it.

'Simon, this policeman says somebody is dead. I've only been gone forty minutes. What did you do?' I suspect she's harbouring uncharitable thoughts about wishing it was me who was dead.

I still can't properly comprehend what's going on. Who is dead? Was the shock of my bursting in on Doreen's early morning toilette too much for a frail old lady?

We all proceed in the policeman's wake, at a dignified pace of course, to Rick and Stephen's bedroom. It is Stephen who has suffered a massive heart attack and it is he who is, indeed, quite obviously, even to the uneducated eye, dead.

Doreen is standing outside the bedroom; Rick hadn't wanted to alarm her earlier. She grabs both my and Wendy's hands. 'My darlings, what an awful thing to have happened to you in your beautiful home,' there are tears in her eyes, 'please believe me when I tell you there couldn't be a more perfect place than this for Stephen to have passed away – he was at his happiest last night.'

We are dumbstruck. We're being thanked for providing the perfect final resting place! How would that go down on Tripadvisor? It's probably best I go to attend to the rest of the guests; Wendy is the best of us to stay to console Doreen and Rick.

Some time later, after all the medics have left and we are waiting for the undertaker to arrive, Wendy reappears in the kitchen. Now it is her face that is ashen.

'What's wrong?' I ask.

'Well you know I like to be helpful…' she begins.

'Yes…'

'I just said, "if there is anything at all I can do please just ask".'

'Oh God…'

Wendy had made her offer thinking it might entail a cup of coffee, a muffin, maybe a sausage sandwich (I have, after all and against all the odds, managed not to burn them).

'Would you mind just popping in to the room and brushing through Stephen's beard before we come in,' Rick had gulped as he handed her a comb.

'What could I say?' she asks.

'Not much I suppose,' I say lamely, 'so what did you do?'

'I didn't have much choice. I sort of did it at arms length with my eyes closed,' she gives an impression, 'but when I opened my eyes they were there and I was hemmed in as they started talking to him.'

She's never even seen a dead body – until now.

When the children return from school later the undertaker's car is just leaving and we recount the day's events. They are, as children must be, suitably underwhelmed by the emotion of it all and much more fascinated by the practicalities.

Emily asks, 'how did they get such a big man into the back of a car? Did they have to break his legs off?'

Oliver is even more practical. 'What about the bill? Did you have to knock off the cost of his breakfast?'

'Bugger,' says Wendy, 'they haven't paid at all.'

'They might have offered to pay for single occupancy,' I quip.

'Oh stop it.'

In the end though, Rick does settle up and the biggest bunch of flowers arrives for Wendy a few days later with a note: 'Thank you for looking after Stephen and us so well, you are the perfect hosts.'

Five years on, Doreen is still going strong having visited us twice and Rick has a new partner. They are regular visitors and maintain that a part of Stephen will forever live at Augill. It seems the incident lives on in the memories of other guests too. A couple who have become regulars tell us that when they awoke that morning, drew back the curtains and saw several police cars, an ambulance and a helicopter on the lawn they thought they'd woken to an episode of *Taggart* or *Silent Witness*.

Just as with the eventual inevitability of a guest death, the longer we do what we do, the more likely the bizarre becomes.

Cliff has sent an email which opens, 'I fully understand if you want to say no...' An inauspicious start I think.

'I am a semi-professional photographer working in the alternative field.' Wendy, who has opened the email, is getting excitable.

'We've got someone looking for a photo shoot,' she exclaims.

'OK, can we get all the facts first,' I am still mindful of our surprise weekend in the company of the naturists.

The email continues, 'I am wondering if you would allow a room or two for hire for two hours at the start of next year? This would be an alternative shoot but would keep nudity to a minimum.' And now the alarm bells are ringing. 'No way, no way.' I am adamant that the conversation is closed.

But Wendy reads on, 'I wouldn't need anything to be moved or a large lighting set-up. I would be as quick as possible and I would promote you to other photographers looking for locations and also for people to come and stay!'

'Yes,' I continue, 'he's looking for an afternoon quickie with the video camera switched on. What sort of photographers would he recommend? Shoots for 'Totty in the Turrets', perhaps, or 'Breasts and Battlements'. No, no no,' and with that I leave the office, sure my position is quite clear.

Next morning I am in the office early and reviewing yesterday's sent emails. The first one is from Wendy and reads, 'Dear Cliff, thank you for your email, we would need to know more about the shoot before we make a decision – i.e. what kind of room you are looking for, what sort of catering arrangements, what publication the shoot is for, would you need any specialist equipment?'

Specialist equipment? For heaven's sake! What is she thinking – that we can make some revenue out of the cellar? Manacles on the walls? Pressing that old torture rack back into service?

Wendy is unabashed. 'He wants to come in January when we could do with the extra cash.'

I'm utterly nonplussed. 'We are a family friendly place. Do you really think…?' Then the email pings. It's Cliff.

'It's not for a publication, it would be for a private shoot. The theme would be fetish, probably latex and bondage outfits.' Just as I am about to gag on my own tongue I am heartened by his further explanation. 'I would keep nudity to a minimum but there would be a few topless shots I imagine.'

'Oh, well that's alright then,' I say sarcastically, still incredulous that anyone else thinks this might be a good idea, 'let's say yes as long as the manacles don't leave any marks on the wall and there is no unpleasant staining on the mattresses.'

But at least Cliff has done his research, 'I want it to be obviously posh, perhaps a lounge or bedroom? I know its a strange request and I totally understand if you're worried about association with the fetish crowd.'

Too bloody right we are, although I can understand the gothic appeal of the castle. And then, as if we might be almost sold on the whole idea, Cliff tries to close the deal, 'I have a website if you would like to take a look, obviously some of the stuff is at the extreme end, but I'm thinking more like, say the Myleen or Casey... the softer stuff.'

'Does he really expect us to look at his...' But before I can continue Wendy has logged on and there is Casey filling the screen cavorting on a bare mattress pushed into the corner of the room with who I can only assume must be Myleen.

'Oh, very posh.'

'OK, OK, I concede, it's not right for us but...' Wendy says as she leaves me to pen a suitably tactful reply about being family orientated and knowing our markets.

'But what?' I ask, keen to know what thoughts are lingering in her head.

'Just but...' she says and walks away.

Just so that I'm absolutely sure of my facts, I quickly press the back button on the browser. There's mention of bondage, a very menacing series of shots of someone looking less than happy in a bath and reference to Casey's expertise with clingfilm although, unfortunately, no pictorial evidence. Still, it might be best if I keep a note of the website address for future reference.

I don't think anyone will find the site in the favourites list if I call it 'Specialist Catering Supplies' and if they do, I'll blame it on Google: 'I was just looking for some clingfilm and rubber gloves. That's search engines for you.'

♜　♜　♜　♜　♜

The summer turns out to be another washout, one of the wettest on record and it's easy to think that if the recession hadn't coincided with a series of such miserable summers we might not all feel so gloomy.

Water is the most destructive of the elements at Augill. Wind can wreak immediate and dramatic havoc but it is the water that constantly and relentlessly erodes all efforts to tame nature. There is a lot of both in our garden: nature to be tamed and water to undo my best attempts.

Our drive is a quarter of a mile downhill of compacted hardcore and the rain, despite all attempts to create alternative channels, will flow nowhere other than down it. On a bad day as much as half a ton of gravel, stone and sand will end up at the bottom of the drive to be manhandled back to the top for the same process to be repeated.

This is one of those days. It is mid-July and we have friends from the south staying for the weekend. It is their first visit to the castle which, in all honestly, I think they didn't believe was real until they got here. That they haven't been until now also throws into question the strength of our friendship as our real friends have stuck with us and invariably been roped in at some point on the journey.

They are fairly gob-smacked by the place and by the enormity of what we have taken on. In fact, it surprises me how we are the only people who appear not to have this reaction to the place. I have stood back from the castle many times since we arrived and tried very hard to feel my gob being smacked, but I just can't get it. Perhaps it's a case of just being too close to the daily reality.

They are also the sort of southerners who harbour a certain ill-concealed but very real disdain for all things northern so it is a triumph to have got them up here at all. But as the weekend progresses and the Cumbrian weather vents its full anger on their invasion from the south, that triumph begins to feel like a hollow victory.

Throughout the night the wind howls and the rain lashes against the leaded windows which make a pretty feeble effort at keeping much of the water out. Our friends emerge next morning un-rested and complaining about the cold, the wet, the noise. I remind them that we haven't asked them to pay anything and show them the country skill of warming their hands on the AGA whilst simultaneously making tea and toast for the rest of us without having to remove any of the steaming footwear from the stove top. They don't utter another word.

The storm has, of course, done its worst on the drive and I feel compelled to make good the damage before any southern smugness can rear its head.

As I am heaving my tenth barrow load of gravel back up the incline our friends sidle up the drive from the castle. 'Can we help?' they ask in that certain way that tells you they have no intention of pitching in. The other tell-tale sign that they are not prepared to chip in being what they're wearing.

'No, no. It's all in hand.' And I press on determined to avoid any discussion about the weather, the inadequate drainage, the merits of tarmac or our sheer selfishness in having moved to such a God forsaken corner of Britain to which they now feel obliged to travel if the friendship is to be maintained. It's a conversation best avoided as I'm inclined, after 24 hours in their company, to tell them we've made new northern friends so no need to bother coming back.

There is more than just bloody-mindedness behind my refusal of help. Apart from clearly being the only man who knows the correct way to fill a pot hole, because potholing is a science, there is a raw pleasure in being out in the elements fighting against nature to single-handedly keep our link with the outside world passable and open; to clear the gutters as they visibly fill with sand and overflow; to spread salt by hand along the drive's entire length to stem the advance of winter ice; to take sole responsibility for checking that the little bridge under the drive is not blocked with debris, holding back the water that could then wash the bridge away.

It's manly, honest work and I wouldn't have anyone else do it. I wouldn't share that feeling of removing aching limbs from sodden clothes and slipping into warm dry things, knowing that it was I alone that kept us and our remaining neighbours (usually conspicuous in their absence when there's work to be done), who share the drive, connected with the rest of the world.

Even Reg, my local retainer, is only allowed to fill potholes in extreme emergency situations: a) if required while I am away skiing; b) if required while I am away on my summer holiday; c) if required due to my unavoidable hospitalisation.

Unfortunately, our friends don't get any of this subtlety and start arming themselves with shovels and a wheelbarrow. This is, of course, a recipe for disaster because a) they're not going to do it right and b) there's no way of telling them, without causing offence, that they haven't done it right.

Luckily Wendy, sensing the situation unfolding and with a complete understanding of the consequences, intervenes, bounding down the drive in the loveable jolly hockey sticks way she has when she's desperate to enthuse.

'Come on everyone, it's the farmers' market in the village and they've got a famous author signing his book there today, let's go and have a gander.' It's enough of a diversion and does the trick.

'Are you going to be alright on your own?' ask the friends. They could as easily say 'leave that and come and have some fun, we'll all pitch in later' but I'm glad they don't.

Later that morning things take a distinctly unpleasant turn. Having toiled for several hours I'm inspecting my efforts from the front door and indulging in a little self congratulation when, from the distance I can hear a low rumbling. As it grows louder I can make out the silhouette of an enormous beast of a truck turning into the top of the drive. By the time I have pulled my boots back on it is tearing its way down the hill, ripping branches and churning up the verges in its wake. 'What the fuck is that?' I ask myself, a little too loudly and two ladies by the hall fire splutter on their Earl Grey.

An often overlooked aspect of hotelkeeping is that if we are responsible for what we feed our guests and for what they drink, we are also responsible for the disposal of their resultant output. This responsibility and, on occasion it's unpleasant consequences, is brought home every time the septic tank is serviced or emptied. If you are unfamiliar with the concept, a septic tank is a big container – it looks not unlike a plastic stomach – buried below ground into which all the household's flushable waste most people don't give a second thought to goes. The liquid gradually soaks in to the ground, leaving a thick sludge which has to be pumped out periodically.

Today is one of those days and the enormous creature lumbering towards me with several limbs of tree already stuck to its sides is the septic tank truck, or sludge separation unit as it is now known since the business of septic tank emptying has gone the way of most simple processes: becoming over complicated by legislation often drawn up by people with no real grasp of what it is they are legislating or why.

The last time we had the septic tank emptied the truck got stuck in the mud and we almost had to back fill the tank in order to lighten the load to get the truck out of the way, so this time I am keen to intercept the mission and keep the vehicle on the hardstanding of the drive. A practical solution but with the downside that the operation carries on in full view of the castle and arriving guests.

When our friends return they are horrified. Septic tanks aren't part of the landscape in West London and while the operation is pretty efficient it comes with a certain aroma.

'Oh you poor things, do you have to do this often? It really is rather grim up north isn't it?' they cackle.

Dave the driver, or sanitisation officer if you prefer, who is from Kent and who I know quite well, reads the situation perfectly. 'Where there's shit there's brass, mate. And the reason there's so much money down south is 'coz that's where we send all this shit for disposal.'

I've no idea whether it's true and don't need to know. It's made my weekend and ruined theirs.

☙ ☙ ☙ ☙ ☙

As the summer drips on the economic mood of the country, and indeed the world, does nothing to brighten things up. Despite this guests continue to come and we are pleasantly surprised by the healthy numbers of visitors from America and Australia. It seems the reach of the internet knows no bounds and, despite the lousy weather, it turns out to be a decent enough, if short, summer season.

So, if business isn't exactly galloping, it's certainly more than just limping for the moment and while we repeatedly go through the process of identifying potential redundancies each January and February, we know we can't do without those same people from May to October and then again at Christmas.

Because our permanent staff are not enough during the summer we find ourselves relying more and more on seasonal staff who are invariably willing, keen and very friendly, if occasionally lacking a little common sense.

Tiffany is joining us for three months during her holiday from university. A straight A* student, with nearly as many A-levels as I have O-levels, she is studying biometric physics or chemistry or something.

'What do you hope to do with your degree?' I ask.

It's usually a reliable ice breaker but she just giggles and says, 'oh you... silly.'

Erm, no.

On her first morning with us I tell the staff not to overstretch her with anything too taxing (showing her where the coat hooks are might even be enough on her first day) and so, as has happened on many previous occasions, with many other new starters, she is put in charge of the toast. We have a rotary toaster which feeds slices of bread between two heated elements at a pre-set speed. What can go wrong? It's bread in... toast out.

It's soon clear that it is possible to be too intelligent to be in charge of toasting bread. Before long she has calculated that better toasting can be achieved with a more optimum speed to heat ratio, pretty much confirming she is studying something involving physics.

Unfortunately, as she begins to fiddle with the controls on the toaster she has failed to take into account possible local difficulties, known scientifically as variables. The dials on the controls are broken and have been put back together in reverse by me in an attempt to avoid paying for new spare parts – even the toast doesn't escape the recession. It's austerity toast of which the Prime Minister would surely be proud.

Soon the kitchen is full of acrid grey toast smoke and what happens next shows Tiffany to be either very resourceful or a few thick white slices short of a loaf.

While anyone else would have simply cranked up the extractor fan, opened the windows and carried on, Tiffany runs to the housekeeper's cupboard, the location of which she has remembered from what we laughably call an induction and by the time I come into the kitchen she is standing in the middle of the room and through the thick smoke it looks as if she is dancing.

'What the hell are you doing?' I ask, removing the still burning toast from the now stalled toaster.

'I'm hoovering away the smoke,' she replies with a grin as she swirls the hoover attachment, on full power, around her head. If there is anyone at home in there I think they must have taken an extended break.

If the general mood of the country is still a depressed one, there is a slice of the population who aren't feeling it and just as our reputation has reached the other side of the world, it has also permeated up the pecking order in this country. On the Glorious Twelfth, the first day of the grouse shooting season, we are preparing to welcome a shooting party. Two couples are arriving by helicopter independently of each other.

'It's the year of the helicopter,' I say, recalling the air ambulance. But Wendy is in a spin all of her own. While I'm just concerned about what happens if both helicopters arrive at the same time, she is fretting about what to feed them, are they going to like the rooms, what they will think of us. I have a more reasoned view. A friend of ours recently enjoyed a private meeting with Prince Charles at Clarence House. He commented on how relatively ordinary the place was – old squishy sofas, lots of clutter. 'Do you think anyone lives in better conditions than what we offer? They'll take us as they find us,' I say but it's clear Wendy thinks that naive.

As tea time approaches I'm in the field to the west of the castle scanning the skies and listening for the distant thrumming of chopper blades. I have mown a big H in the grass to help guide the pilots in although I have absolutely no idea whether this is necessary or if it is the required size. A sound in the distance is growing steadily louder and I'm pretty sure it is a helicopter. A few minutes later it is sounding very loud and the trees to my right are beginning to rustle and sway.

The noise is enough to make the castle windows rattle and scatter the neighbouring sheep and our hens. I'm really starting to feel rather foolish about my amateur attempt at a landing pad as I turn around and see, bearing down on me like a scene from 'MASH' a chinook helicopter, double blades whirring, with a dozen soldiers sitting by the open doors. We are used to seeing military aircraft flying over as Warcop Army Training Camp is just a couple of miles up the road but they are never this low. It can't be more than twenty feet higher than the top of the tower and my heart lurches into my throat as I wonder if my mown H has disrupted a military exercise.

Whether I imagine it or whether it really happens, I can't say, but the helicopter nose momentarily dips in my direction then banks away into the sky and heads west towards Warcop. I have retreated into the hedgerow, pinned against the birch trees, quite stunned and breathless.

No sooner has the chinook disappeared over the horizon than I hear another drone growing louder. Although the approaching cacophany of noise includes the unmistakeable whirring of blades, this is an altogether different sound, high pitched, almost whining. As this helicopter comes into view the trees are less disturbed and I can see why the noise is different. This one, sleek, black and very sexy, has two huge turbo engines on the back.

I am mesmerised as a child by this thing of beauty landing in my field and don't care that it touches down some twenty or thirty feet away from my helpful H.

As the rotors slow, the door slides open and I walk forward, slightly hunched (because that's what they always do on TV) an immaculately turned out lady and man, about my age, step out.

I lurch forward to greet them. 'Very sexy,' is my opening gambit.

'I beg your pardon?' the man enquires.

'Sorry, I mean, the helicopter, very lovely.'

'Oh yes, it's a useful way of getting around,' and he turns to the pilot, 'you might as well fly back and I'll either call you tomorrow or we'll get a lift back.'

'Where have you come from?' small talk is probably all I have in me that will be of any interest.

Imagining the reply to be Nice or Geneva or at least London, I am disappointed by his very matter-of-fact reply, 'Harrogate, ten minutes across the Dales.'

The rest of the group arrive by more conventional means as does the other couple who were planning to arrive by air but have got a lift with friends instead. I'm rather relieved.

Gavin the wealth manager for a large investment bank who has organised the event for his 'premium clients' defines them all in terms of their net worth and, trying to impress us, has a go at adding it all up. Seeing the assembled party as a room of accounts rather than people he delights in telling us we must have a good £500 million sitting down for dinner.

'How pathetic,' Wendy says but it does little to assuage her nerves.

It's a pleasant evening and everyone is very complimentary about everything. But there is something missing. Something we have come to take for granted in our guests just isn't there.

The next morning they breakfast early and are gone. It is the way of shooting parties; in, eat, sleep and out.

'Strange,' I say to Wendy after they have left.

'I feel a complete chump for getting so worked up,' she says, 'just because they're all ridiculously rich doesn't mean they don't enjoy the same things as everyone else.'

'But that's just it,' I reply, suddenly realising what was missing, 'the magic. The Augill Magic, it just passed them by, it wasn't there.'

'What do you mean? We did everything…'

'No, I mean, for most people coming here is a real experience. It is unique and it is special and often staying in a castle is a dream come true. But these people can have anything they want, whenever they want it, so where's the special in anything for them? They enjoyed it but they weren't excited. What do you suppose gets you excited if you can afford absolutely anything you want?'

It's as if their extreme wealth has robbed them of something much more basic, that child-like ability to see the wonder and joy in the everyday. Perhaps surrounding themselves with Gavins rubs off and everything just assumes a monetary value.

It's a sobering thought and we resolve that perhaps we, who are much luckier than most, should remember to see the joy in everyday things because, no matter how much money and stuff any of us have got, we are all at the same mercy: our own frailty and humanity. Surely it's better to go out with less and, like Stephen, go out laughing.

She: 'That was never something you were very good at.'

I: 'No, too introspective. But writing the book helped.'

She: 'Did it help you realise how lucky you are?'

I: 'I don't honestly think luck comes into it. It made me realise how hard we've worked and then how easily it could all crumble to dust. Actually, it was once you'd died that we both saw how lucky we are to have such a strong friendship network – something which is easy to take for granted, a bit like family, until you really need them or they aren't there anymore.'

She: 'Things should have been different between us. I'm sorry for what happened.'

I: 'Look, what happened, happened because of who we both were. Hindsight is a wonderful thing but trying to pretend things could have been different is pointless. Who's to say anything else would have worked out better?

'Why are you here anyway? You said you'd never do this… you know, come back.'

She: 'But I'd like to explain.'

CHAPTER FIVE

Rearing pigs turns out to be even harder work than looking after guests, another summer that hardly happens and I confront something I can no longer ignore

By spring the government's austerity measures are beginning to bite and the national collective tightening of belts is having a marked effect on business. There are fewer guests and they are coming from completely different places – Indian, Chinese and South American visitors are introducing us to new cultures and new sets of expectations whilst our British guests are looking for ever tighter deals. All except the redoubtable Diana Anstruther.

Diana is an actress. She stays with us infrequently but when she does she'll come for two or three weeks at a time. In fact, since every visit seems to be a tad longer than the last, we all fancy that one day she will come and never leave rather like Stephen. Perhaps it is to be the way with theatrical visitors to the castle. Nobody would mind. Everyone adores Diana and would be honoured to think they could play a part in her happy demise. She is unfailingly kind and polite with the staff, showing a genuine interest in every aspect of their lives. She remembers their children, their children's birthdays, their husbands.

Our children worship her. She is everything anyone could wish for from a grandmother without any of the hang-ups. She doesn't judge their upbringing, although she will pull them up on their manners which, of course, she rarely has to as they are impeccably behaved with Diana. She'll watch Oliver play rugby no matter what the weather, she sits for hours painting with Emily and she can sing, oh how she can sing, and together, she and Emily will sing until they are hoarse.

Nobody really knows how old Diana is, I suspect she gave up counting many years ago.

'Age is merely a state of mind,' she will tell you.

Taken in isolation, her skin, or her eyes or her conversation would put her at about fifty. But her body tells a different story – a much longer one. I'd guess at 90 or even 95. She claims she still drives when in London, although her car never appears to move from the same spot outside her house. When she is with us nobody would dream of letting her drive herself anywhere, so keen is everyone to have Diana as company.

She arrives with nothing other than what she is wearing, an extra cardigan, two litres of her 'special gin' and several changes of shoes.

'Darling', she will explain, 'one can always rinse out one's knickers but you can't wash a pair of decent shoes.'

She smokes but only in private. We know she does it and we turn a blind eye. She says she waltzed her way through the Second World War at tea dances at the Ritz, ignoring the blitz. 'The posters said keep calm and carry on so that's exactly what we did. We simply didn't care what was going on because we knew tomorrow we might be dead. Once the whole ballroom shook, chandeliers, the lot. The band didn't miss a note darlings and we didn't miss a step.' Her point is that the law can tell her whatever it wants, but if she wishes to smoke, then smoke she will. Hitler didn't stop her having fun so bureaucrats won't either.

She was classically trained as a ballet dancer and has danced, consorted (slept probably, we'll never know) with some of the great actors and entertainers of the twentieth century. She'll reel off names but only ever the tamest of gossip. 'Discretion, darlings, always show utmost discretion, anything else will always get you into trouble and being discreet gives you a stronger hand to play later when you might need it.'

She understands the value of money but she also understands the value of value so she'll never ask for a discount but will be gracious when it is offered. She, in short is the dreamiest of dream guests and everyone will miss her when she is gone.

'Do you think Diana will live to see my wedding?' Emily asks quite unexpectedly.

'Honestly, darling, no,' I tell her.

'I wondered if she might like to help me design a dress, then she can be there in a sort of way.'

'She'd love that, really she would.'

'So would I.'

For so many reasons Diana is our all-in-one antidote to what unsettles us, to what we are missing.

☙ ☙ ☙ ☙ ☙

Whether because of the cloying air of austerity pervading everything or that I can no longer find any more excuses, I relent and agree to the family's requests to have a go at smallholding.

'Imagine being able to cure our own bacon and make sausages,' Wendy enthuses.

Fencing has never been part of my rural skill set. In fact, I have never done it from scratch, having only repaired existing enclosures in the past but I reckon it can't be that difficult. So I set to it with a sledge hammer, some posts and some wire (no barbed wire as I'm fairly sure if pigs can't fly they can't jump either). The spring weather is warm, the sun is burning my back, a blessed feeling in this part of the world so early in the year and it spurs me on. Once started I refuse to be distracted from the task in hand and three solid days later I have a back sunburnt red raw and two neat paddocks, each with a gate so that my pigs can be rotated between enclosures.

I'm pretty pleased with my efforts but Reg, our man about the castle, who probably thinks he has seen it all in ten years of helping to keep the place standing, just roars with laughter.

'Tha'll ne'er keep a pig in yon place for more than a day,' he tells me, 'they're buggars for escaping an' tha'll have a flattened fence.'

'Smug bastard,' I keep my thought private just in case he turns out to be right.

But Reg doesn't keep pigs, he keeps sheep which, as far as I can see are the stupidest animals alive so I decide he doesn't know what he's talking about and since we're getting two piglets which are little bigger than our cocker spaniel I reckon he is being alarmist. Or maybe he's just jealous that my fence building is better than his.

Two days later Ron and Harry our cross breed Kune Kune - Gloucester Old Spot - Tamworth piglets arrive. OK, so they're not cross breeds, they're mongrel pigs. Unloading them is a cinch and they're soon rooting around their new quarters. Serial guests Liz and Dave Saunders, who have just arrived with their children Becky and

James, are keen to meet the new arrivals. Their assessment of my arrangements is no more optimistic than Reg's.

'I'll bet you they won't still be in there by the end of the weekend,' Liz says, head shaking. What the hell does she know? She lives in suburban bliss in West London so will have had as much to do with pigs as our other southern friends had to do with septic tanks.

The next morning I trot up the bank to feed my two new boys. But they are nowhere to be seen. I search frantically behind the shed that I have erected for shelter and scan the fence line. I can see no obvious way of escape. Just then Reg comes up the bank behind me.

'They're gone,' I tell him, sheepishly, wishing now I had plumped for sheep instead of pigs.

'Nay lad,' he says, smiling broadly and leads me over to the shed, 'look in there, ya'll find them.' And there they are, curled up together sleeping, completely covered in straw. 'Tha's got happy beasts lad.'

It's a sunny spring and as Easter approaches and the weather warms up I am concerned for the pig's welfare. I have read that they can be susceptible to sunburn so I rig up an old garden parasol in front of their shed to give them some extra shade.

'What the hell is that all about?' Wendy chuckles, and Emily adds, 'you sure you don't want to get them a couple of deckchairs while you're at it?'

'Happy pigs make tasty bacon, just remember that,' I remind them.

'Oh you are such a ridiculous man,' Emily says, adding over her shoulder as she turns her back on the whole escapade, 'and that shed isn't going to last five minutes once they get bigger, they'll knock it to pieces.'

I am hurt by my family's lack of confidence in my smallholding efforts, particularly since it is they who wanted these animals rather than me. However, a few weeks later Emily's doom laden prophecy has come true and the pigs have knocked the sides out of the wooden hut. Moreover, they have completely grubbed up the ground in and all around it. What we need is a more robust shelter that can be easily moved from patch to patch.

So I ask one of our neighbouring farmers what he would suggest and as ever, as with so many other situations at the castle, the solution gets temporarily lost in translation.

'Nay lad tha's not got pigs?'

'Well yes I have so what do you suggest for shelter that's cheap and movable?'

'Pigs tha says?'

'Yes, pigs.'

'Swine like?'

'Yes, swine, pigs, you know, oink oink.'

'Aye… what tha needs is a cafoot.'

'I beg your pardon?'

'A cafoot fort swine.'

'A cafoot?'

'Aye a cafoot.'

'And that's what it's called is it?'

'Aye, it is what it is, a cafoot.'

'Well what is it exactly?'

And as if I were a visiting foreign tourist, he says very slowly to aid my comprehension, a c…a…f…o…o…t. Tha can get them from th'Eden Farm.'

So with some apprehension I ring up Eden Farm Supplies.

'I have a couple of pigs and I need some shelter for them that I can easily move. I've been advised that I need…'

Before I can finish I am told, 'Aye, you'll be needing a cafoot.'

'Well I'll have two then please.' And not for the first time do I find myself placing an order for God knows what.

Two days later a delivery truck arrives. 'Two cafoots?'

'Aye,' I reply, somehow sure that delving as far into local dialect as I dare might help with my utter incomprehension of what is going on.

The delivery is swiftly unloaded and on reading the delivery note everything becomes clear. I am the proud owner of two brand new plastic calf huts. Later, as I recount the whole episode to Wendy, she laughs and says, 'well at least you didn't ask for Piggots otherwise you might have been expecting delivery of a famous actor or a small jockey.'

Emily shoots a glance across the living room at us both as we shake with laughter, 'More ridiculousness every day,' she mutters to herself, her head shaking laconically. Little does she know, it's only ridiculousness that's keeping us going.

Naively I assume that having got the pigs and procured them some shelter it is just a matter of feeding them until they are fat enough for slaughter. But I haven't counted on, and nobody has warned me of, the continuing barrage of rural bureaucracy.

It seems we can't live without it. After all, it provides employment for tens of thousands of civil servants. But surely even in their cosseted world, when they're not fretting about their own pensions, some of them must be able to see that the world might just turn a little quicker without quite so much form-filling.

We have kept chickens for several years now without any interference from the authorities but when we decided to add the piglets to our menagerie suddenly animal husbandry took on a whole new dimension. To get a pig licence we had to get an agricultural holding number from the Department of the Environment, Farming and Rural Affairs, affectionately known to all who have dealings with it as DEFRA.

This seemed innocent enough but, two months down the line, having installed the piggies and completed transfer notices for their movement in quadruplicate, we have been told that we have been selected to complete DEFRA's annual survey of agriculture and horticulture.

It's not quite as exciting as the old Reader's Digest 'you've been selected for our biggest ever prize draw' and I must admit that the request landed on deaf ears until today when I receive a gentle reminder with all the DEFRA subtlety of a stampeding bullock.

The survey, I am told, is compulsory under European Union legislation which, of course, means that every French, Italian and Spanish smallholder will have roundly ignored it like me, with only the Dutch and the Germans obediently complying. The Belgians will have been fully employed sending the thing out in the first place, with the Austrians doing whatever the Germans do (because for most Britons there is no difference between the two), and the Greeks refusing to play ball unless they can have a generous cash settlement in return. As for the Irish, Portuguese and all those Eastern European countries, they're all so on the geographical fringes of the club that the tentacles of EU bureaucracy must surely be less invasive.

Keen to be a fine upstanding citizen of Europe, I open the email only to discover that I must log in to start the survey. But I don't have my 'Government Gateway ID or password'. When I telephone the DEFRA helpline I am told that agents are 'experiencing an unprecedented numbers of calls'. Clearly I'm not the only one who has lost their credentials.

I request a call back and, while I'm waiting, take a look at the useful hints on how to accurately complete the questions:

• when calculating the 'Area used by you' (do they mean parking, barbecuing, sunbathing?) figure in the land area section remember to include seasonally rented-in land and exclude any seasonally let-out land;

• your cropping/grassland/bare fallow (does this mean lawn mowing?) should only include land you have 'in hand' and not anything let out to others;

• you can easily check your cropping/grassland running total (the number of lawns I mow in a day, the volume of grass clippings, the size of our compost heap, the number of lettuces in the veggie patch?) against the 'Area used by you' figure you have provided, by checking the land tracker at the top of any of the cropping/grassland sections;

• remember to include yourself in the 'People working on the holding' (OK, will do!) section; and

• sections which are no longer applicable are easily changed through the shaping questions link in the left hand menu and changing the initial question to 'No'.

What the hell is that all about? I am hopeful that applying the last piece of advice to every question might just be the easy opt out.

The phone rings. It's Mandy from DEFRA. 'Is that Mr Bennett?'
'Yes.'
'Can I have your holding number please?'

I oblige and Mandy confirms that I am, indeed, Mr Bennett. 'How can I help, Mr Bennett?'

I explain that I have no idea of my log in details in order to complete the questionnaire and then I ask if it is really necessary for me to complete the survey. 'I'm not really a farmer,' I begin to explain.

'In what way do you mean, not a farmer?' Mandy asks.

'Well, I don't farm. I have two pigs, four chickens and four ducks.'

There's an expectant pause as Mandy waits for me to add something like 'and 250 head of cattle and a flock of a thousand sheep'.

All I can add to break the silence is, 'and one rabbit.'

It's clearly the cue Mandy has been waiting for. 'So would you say farming is your main livelihood Mr Bennett?'

'Mandy,' I'm caught between utter incredulity and unbridled fury at having my time wasted, 'if you can call two pigs, four hens, four ducks and a rabbit a livelihood, it's a sad reflection of the state of British farming.'

The irony is all lost on Mandy for whom I am undoubtedly just one enquiry closer to her retirement and that jealously guarded pension. After a bit of typing and, I'm fairly sure, a little tongue clicking too, I am furnished with my 'Government Gateway' password and ID. With the pigs in mind I muse that this all sounds a bit *Animal Farm* coupled with shades of *1984*. Does having a Government Gateway ID give me access to them, or them access to me?

Mandy offers to help me with any questions I may find difficult to answer but I assure her I should be fine. I have already double counted the stock (2), am fairly sure I have the correct headcount (2) and, after all, how difficult is it going to be to use the 'shaping questions link' I have just discovered lurking in the left hand column to change all my responses to 'No, no longer applicable' and be done with it?

♛   ♛   ♛   ♛   ♛

Whether it's the pressure of keeping everything together, keeping up appearances while the world seems to be crumbling or whether it's delayed grief from Mum's death I can't say but something is very wrong.

I have never been prone to particularly protracted bouts of illness, although I did once pick up a chest infection in the Amazon rainforest (as you do) which lasted three months. Wendy gave me very little sympathy and said it served me right for trying to satisfy my wanderlust in such a hostile environment. 'What would have been wrong with trekking through the hills of Provence?' she'd said.

But this is different. I am listless, tearful, fearful and I'm suffering from some odd physical symptoms. What's frightening is that I can't quite put my finger on any of it, I feel out of control and I am frightened to talk to anyone, even Wendy.

I have withdrawn from attending tourist board meetings, I'm avoiding school governor meetings and taking preposterous steps to avoid contact with guests, even to the extent of hiding in the lavatory when the doorbell rings.

Wendy has her own ongoing battle with depression which should make her an obvious ally but, being a man, rather than discuss things with her in the very likely event that she'll have some valuable insight, I keep it all to myself. But as the summer wears on, usually my favourite time of year, even if it is turning out to be another washout, things don't get any better.

After too many months of pain both bodily and in my head, I decide it is time to speak to the doctor. The decision is made as much because I know Wendy is worried about me and if I don't do something she will. There's little point dithering so I make a same-day appointment, only secured by telling the receptionist that it is an emergency.

'What sort of emergency,' she asks.

'None of your bloody business,' is enough to get me straight on to the doctor's list that morning while she is probably noting on my record 'suspect mental health (anger) issues'. There's no time to change my mind and before I can have any second thoughts I am sitting in front of the doctor.

As I am explaining what's in my head and how I am feeling generally he reaches into the drawer of his desk and pulls out a printed list of questions, explaining they will help to identify my state of mind. That may not be his exact words but it is what I hear and in a momentary state of panic I scan the room for straitjackets or other restraining devices. I'm brought back to the here and now by his first question.

'Have you ever had suicidal thoughts?'

'I beg your pardon?'

'Have you ever thought of killing yourself?' His pen is poised over a tick box.

'Well yes, of course I have, who hasn't?'

I'm not sure it's the answer he is looking for, 'well it's not necessarily a universal thought.'

Oh God, I really am a basket case.

'It can be a sign of stress,' he continues, 'how would you describe your levels of stress?'

'I run my own business, we're in the middle of the deepest recession for a generation, I have two teenaged children and I'm a secondary school governor. What's not to be stressed about?'

'Well have you thought about taking some time off?' he asks.

Now I'm getting agitated, 'what on full pay?' And I think he takes my point. We both take a moment to collect our thoughts and he continues with the remainder of his questions after which he says I am showing signs of mild depression, possibly caused by stress. I'm not feeling particularly enlightened. He tells me that he rarely sees men in my situation, it is nearly always women who seek help for stress related issues, so I am already ahead of the game and suggests a consultation with a counsellor.

'But what about the physical symptoms?' I ask, really more worried about them than what's in my head.

'They can be caused by stress or depression,' he explains.

'Yes, but what if the depression is caused by worry over the physical symptoms?'

He agrees to take some blood samples 'to rule out a range of auto-immune diseases' and I make a mental note to look up what those might be, unsure whether they sound more or less terrifying than the cancer I've already convinced myself I have.

A few needle pricks later I'm out with a leaflet about a counselling service which I can begin over the telephone. 'Sometimes one call is all it takes' the leaflet assures me. I wait a couple of days until I am sure I am alone and not likely to be overheard and am surprised at how helpful it is to be able to talk openly to someone who has nothing to do with my life. The leaflet is as good as its word and one session does my head the world of good. But my body continues to tell a different story.

♛   ♛   ♛   ♛   ♛

By September we are wondering whether we really had a summer at all. Having endured one of the wettest summers on record last year, to have the same again has left us feeling pretty miserable. I am more convinced now that a succession of bad summers is doing nothing for the national psyche and is prolonging the effects of the recession.

In response to my complaints about the weather, Reg, simply says, 'it'll fetch out alreet at th' back end.'

I thought we'd pretty much got over this language barrier. Was I talking about having trouble with my bowel movements? I didn't think so.

'Sorry, Reg, what's coming out of whose back end?'

'Th' weather, lad. It'll turn out alreet in the autumn, th' back end o' the year,' he explains with a grin.

Whether he's been studying the berries on the bushes or the way the birds are flying I don't know but his weather prediction is spot on and for the second half of September and the whole of October the weather is glorious – clear chilly nights, misty mornings and shortening but sparkling days with crystal clear horizons. It's the sort of weather that puts the landscape into pin sharp focus, bringing the fells closer and giving vibrancy to the autumn colours of the trees against the bright blue of the sky.

Today I am eating breakfast on the hoof. But this is not a quickly grabbed sandwich and latte on the High Street, rather a breakfast entirely from the hedgerow. Hazelnuts, blackberries and an apple and I know how lucky I am. Not just because I can do all this without even straying from our own land, not only because, as I crack the hazelnuts in my teeth the late summer sun is beating on my face and is still hot enough to heat my back, but because I can do all of this without any hang-ups. No nut allergy, no worries about diabetes, obesity, heart disease or cancer, no angst about pesticides. If we put aside everything we have done to get here, the sacrifices, the heart ache, the hard work, sore feet, aching backs, financial worries and look at what we have in the here and now, anyone could be forgiven for thinking we lead a charmed life. It's when you feel like this that anything seems possible, a feeling of invincibility imbues your decisions.

It's the sort of weather that spurs us to get on with all manner of jobs, one of which is the next stage of the pig rearing plan. The parasol lasted about two days before the rain started and the calf huts, now predictably renamed Piggots, were a blessing. We might be attached to the pigs but not to the mud and filth that goes with them. There isn't a blade of grass left in either paddock and every one of us has ended up face or arse down in the mud. Pigs, a record breaking wet summer and clay soil are a messy combination and it's time for at least one not so little pig to go to market.

We are feeling very pleased with ourselves at being organised enough to have completed all the paperwork necessary to get the pig to the slaughterhouse which has included details of the type of transport to be used, who is going to be accompanying the pig, what time we will set off and what time we will arrive. Is this to ensure we don't park up outside Starbucks on the way for breakfast? I must give Wendy her due as it is, in fact, she who has done all this, I having been scarred by my experience with Mandy and her DEFRA annual survey earlier in the year.

We have borrowed a neighbour's trailer and all seems set.

Harry is the larger of the two beasts and a fine example of porkdom with every sinew ready to be butchered and it's not a moment too soon either. Enough is enough and I am glad to see the back of him (particularly as it is a very fine long back which should make some excellent bacon).

Harry is less enthusiastic about leaving. In the six months or so that we have had him he has not left his quarter acre paddock. Because the ground is so wet we can't get the trailer up to where he is at the northern end of the estate so we have positioned the trailer at a gate lower down the hillside and are going to entice Harry across a five acre field and into the back of the trailer.

It's a simple enough plan.

Wendy is rattling the food, Emily and Oliver are on either flank and I am ready with metal hurdles to coax him into the trailer. What can go wrong?

With everyone in place, Oliver opens the paddock gate. You have never seen a pig move so fast, let alone two and almost in a blur both Harry and Ron are on the far side (and wrong side) of the field.

Maisy, as any spaniel would, thinks it all an hilarious game and gives chase. Oliver runs as fast as he can to try to round up both the dog and the pigs. Emily, who avoids running at all costs stands, hands on hips and says, 'I could have told you this might happen. This is exactly why I'm a vegetarian.'

'Oh shut up and be useful,' Wendy tells her.

'Well if you're going to be like that I'm going in,' and Emily begins strutting across the field.

Just then there's a loud squeal. Oliver has attempted a heroic rugby tackle on one of the pigs. He is temporarily floored but his strength is too much for Oliver's rugby fly half frame and he is back on his feet, leaving Oliver flapping in the mud.

'Let's just give Harry time to calm down and then he'll come over to where the food is,' Wendy reasons, 'in the meantime we can get Ron back in to the paddock.

Eventually Harry's belly gets the upper hand over his curiosity and he makes for the rattling feed bucket. And so does Ron.

Once by the back ramp of the trailer we manoeuvre hurdles into place behind Harry, the theory being that if we make the space smaller by degrees he will eventually be forced into the trailer. The plan seems to be going well. But pigs are intelligent creatures and Harry knows something is up. All of a sudden he turns full circle and charges for the hurdles, flattening them, Oliver and Emily before making off to the far side of the field once more.

All of this is happening with a castle full of guests – a weekend conference – and in full sight of the road. As I compose myself I look round and am sure I can see gleeful faces watching us from behind various bedroom curtains and two passing cars have stopped.

'How difficult can this be?' I ask nobody in particular.

I suggest a rope around his neck. 'And then what?' Oliver asks sarcastically, 'we ride him bareback all the way to the abattoir?'

Emily sees an even more immediate flaw in that plan, 'he's got no neck,' she sighs. Wendy suggests we lassoo him under his forelegs and pull him into the trailer. 'Ridiculous,' Emily adds, hauling herself onto the fence and resigning from any further involvement in the unfolding farce.

'Let's just all calm down,' Wendy says, her voice shaking, and then the pig will calm down. We all look westward to where the pig is still running about.

As usual, Wendy is right. Eventually the pig gets bored and casually makes his way back to the food. By the time he reaches us I am in the trailer.

'What are you doing in there exactly?' Emily asks, fixing me with a pitiful glare.

'Well perhaps he'll see it's alright in here if I'm in here,' I explain.

'Again, ridiculous,' Emily now clearly questioning her parentage.

'I think perhaps it's not a great idea actually,' Wendy agrees but just then Maisy comes racing at full pelt from the other side of the field, a rabbit just in front of her. The rabbit hurtles between Harry and Ron, sending them in opposite directions. it is enough to startle Harry forward into the trailer. At full speed. Directly between my open, out-stretched legs.

Everything slows down as I see a considerable weight of prime pork careering towards my own meat and two veg.

I scream like a girl. Emily screams even more like a girl. Wendy is frozen and Oliver is just thankful he has more common sense than his father. Luckily Harry's brakes are equally as effective as his acceleration and he stops just short of doing any lasting damage and Oliver is quick witted enough to get the trailer door up and bolted before he realises where he is.

'Helpful,' I mumble from inside the locked trailer.

'Best let him calm down before we open the trailer up again, I'll bring some tea,' Wendy says over her shoulder as she makes her way towards the castle.

It's quite cozy in the trailer with the sweet scent of fresh straw min-gling with pig fart.

'It's just you and me lad,' I say to Harry, tickling him behind the ear. And he gently collapses on to his side, his invitation for a tummy rub, something he has not enjoyed for most of the summer on account of the waist high mud.

'OK just one more time, but I'm not going to miss you, you under-stand? Absolutely not!'

Harry is left to snuggle down in his dry mobile home before being hitched up the next morning for the journey to the abbatoir. If pig keeping is an education, it is nothing compared with what we encounter when we eventually reach the slaughterhouse in County Durham which itself is nothing to what happens on the journey there.

Despite the detailed questions on the various pig licences about the estimated transfer time between the castle and the abbatoir we don't think there can be any harm in stopping off for a quick pot of tea and a sandwich on the way.

Our journey takes us through the centre of the Teesdale market town of Barnard Castle and there's a triple parking bay free right out-side our favourite tea room. We pull up and with no more than a cur-sory glance at the trailer go inside for breakfast. Fittingly, the place does an excellent bacon sandwich.

Being early morning the autumn air is cool and the tea room warm so the windows are steamy so it isn't until we finish our breakfast and step outside that we take in what has happened. Somehow the back of the trailer has unlocked and all we can see is a trail of straw hanging out of the back.

I am frozen to the spot with my bacon sandwich threatening to reappear, 'this cannot be happening, please tell me this is not happening,' I whimper pathetically, wondering whether there is a DEFRA form for such incidents.

There is no sign of a pig careering around the market place and when I peer inside the trailer I am so relieved to see Harry still snuggled up under a blanket of straw I almost want to kiss him, take him home and love him forever more.

Wendy brings me down to earth when I ask her how she thinks the trailer door might have come unfastened, 'Christ, I don't know or care, let's just get this fucking pig slaughtered and be done with it.'

On the way we get hopelessly lost partly because the place is entirely without signage or markings apparently to deter animal rights activists or militant vegetarians and partly because we have both got at least half our attention focussed on the rear view mirror to make sure the pig doesn't get ejected in transit. After several frustrating phone calls we eventually arrive at the facility – a collection of industrial white buildings still with no clues as to where to go. Parked outside is a row of enormous trucks which have already disgorged their loads of pigs, now visible through a window already hung up by their hind quarters on a long conveyor disappearing into the bowels of one of the buildings. It is an eerie place – full of animals but there is not a sound. Even the birds don't seem to be singing here.

A little self-conscious about our little trailer I park up in a corner out of view behind the trucks that are slowly trundling away.

I find a chap in white overalls, white wellies and a white cap. It's not difficult to work out what his job description might be so I reckon it's a safe bet that he'll know where Harry needs to be.

'Excuse me, can you show me where we need to be?' I ask.

'Way aye mun, wass tha got?' he looks surprised and scans a list on a clipboard he is carrying.

'A pig,' I tell him.

'Hay many mun?' he asks scanning the parking area, 'ah thought we'd processed al beast for tha dee.'

'Um, it's just the one pig.'

He flips over a couple of pages, 'Ah, Bennett. One pig.' And just then the final truck drives away and our little trailer is revealed alone in the yard.

'Yes, he's called Harry and he likes having his tummy…' oh shut the fuck up Simon, I admonish myself. I am told to back the trailer up to the loading pen up a 50 metre alley some four metres wide. My reversing skills are questionable at the best of times and with a trailer with a pig inside they are simply non-existent.

'You're joking,' I say, but he's clearly not. Wendy decides she should marshall me down the alley with a series of very unhelpful hand signals. It takes fifteen minutes to get anywhere near the gate to the loading pen and I collide with the wall at least three times.

The man in white just stands there motionless either out of complete incredulity or utter disinterest. I hope it is the latter as, out of sheer frustration, I find myself sticking a middle finger up at Wendy as she tries to help me with a series of random hand signals before winding down the window and shouting at her to fucking have a go instead and as I check the rear view mirror I think he'd better not be shaking his head at me otherwise he'll get some of the same.

When eventually we get the back of the trailer down Harry is cowering right at the back. Hardly surprising.

'Now what?' I ask the slaughterman.

'Now what what?' he replies.

'Well how do we get him out?' I ask, as if I need to.

'Well ya can start by calming down mun. Ya'll have terrified the beast wi' all that screamin'. Did tha bring any pig nuts ta coax him oot?'

I feel very foolish. 'I thought you might have an electric prod or something,' obviously entirely the wrong thing to say as he fixes me with a stern stare telling me animal welfare is their top priority. Well it has been mine until now but I just want the bloody pig out of the trailer. After all, he's going to be dead in under ten minutes. In the end I get into the trailer to try to push Harry out but he's having none of it and rolls over for a tummy tickle instead.

'Oh you bloody shit,' I mutter.

By the time he is eventually trotting down the concrete slope towards a better calling we are both near to tears of exhaustion and frustration. As we drive away we don't give Harry a second look but we can't help noticing the line of pigs through the window on the way out and they look much bigger than ours and there are so many of them I wonder if what we'll get back will even be the same animal.

Forty eight hours later we receive a call from our butcher that Harry has been returned to him and is ready for collection. We have a sausage machine and several large curing buckets ready to go and the kitchen is fully prepped for an all-things-pork day. But I am not prepared for what greets me when I walk into the butcher's shop. There, lying across the slab is Harry. Not cuts of Harry or even two halves of Harry but the whole of him.

'Colin,' I begin tentatively, 'what am I supposed to do with that?'

'He's a fine beast,' Colin replies.

'Oh God,' I whimper, 'who's idea was this?'

Looking at the carcass and then at the car parked outside I can see the only way I will be able to transport Harry back to the castle will be upright in the passenger seat. It's something that won't go unnoticed, is likely to cause an accident and I'm not prepared to try.

'Colin, I can't fit that into the back of the car.'

'Aye, I can see tha dilemma lad.' Every time I get into a scrape and have to involve someone else, no matter what their age in relation to mine, by calling me lad they are signalling their appreciation of my predicament but also reminding me that I am still an alien in their landscape – a rookie northerner.

After a protracted pause Colin, I think slightly reluctantly, agrees to butcher the pig into manageable pieces and a couple of hours later I am at least able to get the pig into the car.

As I hand the meat over to Wendy and Sally, our latest recruit, and a guru of all things self-sufficiency, so this is right up her street, I make a mental note of the lessons to be learnt from the whole experience since Harry's brother Ron has now been joined by Hermione, a pure bred Tamworth who promises to be twice the size and who most definitely will not fit on the front seat when she eventually brings home the bacon.

The telephone rings. It is the doctor. 'I have had the results of your blood tests. When is a good time for you to come in and see me?'

Bad news doesn't have a habit of creeping up on me. I want to ask what the results have revealed but I know he won't want to discuss it over the telephone and I don't want him to.

'Tomorrow, nine o'clock?' I ask.

'Or I can do this afternoon at four?' he suggests, 'sooner rather than later eh?' He's being very matey.

I tell nobody where I am going because I have told nobody about the blood tests. I am sitting in the surgery waiting room, eyes closed when my name is called. When I open my eyes the doctor is at the door. All patients are called through to their appointment in person, it is one of the many niceties of life in a small rural community where the pace of life is not measured in terms of buzzers, bells or intercoms, but now I convince myself that he is affording me a little extra attention.

Following my previous consultation I had looked up the auto-immune diseases he mentioned and I did not like what I read.

'I'm pleased to tell you that the tests didn't find any evidence of any of the things I might have suspected,' it's good news delivered but with the promise of something further, 'but we found something quite unexpected which we weren't really looking for, given your age and relatively good state of general health.'

He goes on to explain the implications of what he's found, the need for a radically modified lifestyle, the long term prognosis and a list of must-dos and definitely can't-dos. All of this washes over me like a tide of words which I hope will recede as quickly as they have come.

He advises me of a series of appointments with specialists that will help to make sense of what I will have to live with for the rest of my life and he reminds me that I am not alone, it is not life threatening, rather life limiting but with the right support I should be able to follow a normal, albeit modified, lifestyle. I thank him for his time and leave.

When I recount things to Wendy she is as floored as I am. 'Are they sure?' she asks.

'I am going for more tests to confirm everything tomorrow, but I think it's pretty clear.'

The next day the diagnosis is confirmed. My hitherto unexplained symptoms are no longer a mystery and I am relieved for that. But from this moment my life, the way I live, the way my family lives, will never be quite the same.

She: 'That must have hit you hard.'
I: 'Well certainly you take your own health for granted.'
She: 'I did, until it was all too late.'
I: 'We all do. I certainly wasn't expecting it but they say there are hereditary factors.'
She: 'Oh?'
I: 'Well it just makes me realise, Dad was 53, you were just 70, your mum was 73, your Dad was only in his fifties. We're not a very long lived family.'
She: 'So...'
I: 'I guess it's live every day but take care to maximise your chances to see the next. It was a big wake-up call but it changed my life because I've seen first hand where not taking care of yourself gets you.'

CHAPTER SIX

A brush with destiny in the nappy aisle at Sainsbury's, a letter from school to strike fear into the most hardened of parent's hearts, revisiting Christmas, and a catastrophe averted at the castle

One of the drawbacks of living in such a rural, sparsely populated place is that Oliver and Emily must rely on us to taxi them to wherever they need to be. While that is something neither of us begrudges them, there are times when they wish they had more independence.

Another facet of this particular aspect of rural life is that when we do take them to a rugby match or a training session or a singing exam they are often too far from home to do a there and back so we have to kill time waiting to bring them back.

In Penrith, our nearest town of note, where Oliver trains with his rugby team every week this usually means a trip to the supermarket – the only place open in a northern market town after five on a Tuesday. Now, even out here in the sticks, supermarkets deliver but Wendy, being the economically minded one of the two of us will not pay a delivery charge for something that can be collected on an existing trip. I, on the other hand, detest having to trawl around Sainsbury's looking for ingredients with which I am not familiar or cart around bulky items that are just a pain in the arse.

All week I repeatedly tell Wendy I am not doing castle shopping in Sainsbury's, she says something along the lines of 'OK, whatever you say,' then presents me with a shopping list on a Tuesday, minutes before Oliver and I are leaving so I have little time to protest. It's one of the many games we play, a bit like the family turning a blind eye to her cheating at cards.

So it is one typical Tuesday and as I'm trundling reluctantly up and down the aisles picking out Harissa, ceps and mascarpone cheese one of the rugby mums spots me.

'Ooh, has Wendy got you doing the family shop? Interesting things in there,' she says tilting her head towards the trolley.

I look into the trolley and survey the ingredients, 'well, Wendy is developing rather exotic tastes these days and, of course, it's not just the four of us I have to shop for anymore,' making, I imagine, a clear reference to the castle element of my purchases.

As I work my way through the list I groan at the mention of sanitary disposal bags and nappy disposal bags. Surely these are easily available online? Assuming these are logically to be found in the sanitary and nappy aisles respectively, I head in that direction. Women always give men standing forlornly in front of the tampons and sanitary towels a certain kind of look. Believe me, I know because I have been there too often. Whether it's pity that we don't know what we're looking for and should, veiled admiration that we are enlightened enough to be there despite our embarrassment or seething jealousy that we are such good partners to our other halves that we really don't mind being asked to be there, I can't say.

Having weathered the strange glances and found the disposal bags, I make my way around to the nappy aisle. Here the looks are likely to be more admiring, if not slightly quizzical about the nature of my relationship with the nappy wearer – dad, uncle or grandparent? Mid forties? It's a tough call.

Just as I am perusing the aisle trying to locate the nappy disposal bags the corner of my eye catches a sudden movement. It's as if someone has turned into the aisle and hastily retreated. I think no more of it.

List completed, I load the dozens of loaves of bread, the dozens of yoghurts, dozens of kitchen rolls, the Harissa, the ceps, the mascarpone cheese, a dozen Somerset goat cheeses that roll all over the place and many other things on to the conveyor belt. 'Would you like some help with your packing sir?' I decline because some is for home, some is for work, it's better done myself.

The trouble is, with the bread and the yoghurts and the kitchen rolls taking up such a lot of room there is soon no room at the other end of the conveyor belt and the checkout boy starts packing anyway. By the time I've finished unloading at one end he has half packed, badly, at the other.

'Oh give me that,' I snap, grab a wholemeal loaf from his grasp and throw it in the trolley, 'there's no point putting them in bags anyway,' from then on there's no more eye contact or, indeed any further form of communication.

Back at the rugby club I catch up with some of the other parents, including the one I'd bumped in to in Sainsbury's.

'Well done you,' she says and everyone else nods and grins.

'I beg your pardon?' a shopping trip is not that much of a cause for congratulation.

'Wendy must be over the moon, isn't she? We wondered why we hadn't seen her for a while.'

'Well, she's at me every week to do it, so I suppose she will be, yes.'

'Oh so were you not as keen? What do Oliver and Emily think? I dare say Emily will be excited about helping out.'

'Ermm… well Emily hates shopping unless it's clothes.'

'Yes, of course, well she's probably hoping it's a girl then, so when's it due? Not long I suppose if you're looking at nappies.'

When I get home and recount this misunderstanding to Wendy she is mortified. 'Do I look like I'm pregnant?' she screeches.

But I'm not really interested, content just to make my point one final time: In future if it can be home delivered it will be home delivered.

'That's ironic,' Emily chips in, 'you wanted both of us to be home delivered but in the end you had to go to the hospital. What a funny old world.'

Paying guests and old buildings don't necessarily make the easiest of bedfellows. There is no doubt a significant proportion of the people who come to stay at the castle don't give a second thought to the logistics of plumbing, heating or electrical current retro-fitted into a Victorian building. For these people, if the heating gurgles, if the hot water isn't instant and if there are insufficient sockets for a family of four to plug in two electrical devices each simultaneously, there is cause for complaint. As for wifi being anything other than perfect in a building with four foot thick walls? Forget that as an excuse and don't even start on the vagaries of broadband signal strength this far from the telephone exchange.

It is these people who trip the electrical circuitry with too many appliances, take up all the wifi by streaming movies and flood bathroom floors by showering without using the shower curtains or filling the bath to within an inch of the rim before both diving in together. So these same people deserve to be the ones who suffer the inevitable consequences.

We are in the middle of a busy breakfast and the dining room is full of gentle chatter. The autumn sun, now lower in the sky, is shining through the leaded windows, creating reflections playing like garden fairies on the wall and everyone is sharing stories of where they have been the day before and their plans for the day to come.

It is the calm of the beach before the tsunami, the tranquility that nature bestows on a place just before an earthquake. Without warning there is an ear splitting screech followed by a crash that really does shake the room. A moment in which everyone is silenced and the entire castle seems to hold its breath is followed by a cloud of dust that rolls into the dining room from the hall.

Tiffany is on duty. She comes running into the kitchen to announce that something has happened in the hall.

'You don't say, Tiffany,' I reply, half expecting her to go straight for the hoover to deal with the dust cloud.

Everyone in the dining room has jumped to their feet but having done so are now unsure what to do. I am just as unsure but am saved by the bell as the dust cloud sets off the fire alarm. Evacuation is the best course of action.

While Tiffany ushers everyone out through the fire exit (having herself been reminded where the fire exit is) I go to the hall to see what has happened.

A four foot square section of original plasterwork has fallen from the ceiling. Victorian plasterwork is much like stone in texture and in weight. Normally held in place by being pushed between the laths above, which can hold an enormous weight when distributed across an area, the plaster can hang for many years. But when the plaster gets wet or when the laths become damp, the integrity of the system fails and failure can be catastrophic.

What has clearly happened is that water from the bathroom above has caused the plaster to become so wet it has pulled itself down under its own weight. Whether the result of a single event or the culmination of years of gradual water damage I can't tell but it's one hell of a mess. It's just lucky there was nobody standing underneath it at the time.

Wendy, who has been enjoying a rare Sunday morning lie-in, walks in on the scene and is not impressed.

'Simon,' she begins, which is rarely a good sign, 'last time I left you in charge of breakfast, I returned to find an air ambulance on the lawn and a corpse in one of the bedrooms. Today I find the castle in ruins.'

I think she's teasing but I can't be sure and even through the dust cloud I can see she certainly isn't smiling. I try to ease the tension, 'I think it looks worse than it is.'

By now she has switched her attention from the plaster coated hall to the two dozen or so guests milling about aimlessly outside asking Tiffany what is going on. 'You think so?' And she sets about taking control. First of all she takes Tiffany in hand by sending her to do something vaguely useful. As if proof were needed the girl has again cemented her dozy credentials by asking if this sort of thing is a usual occurrence.

'What the fuck, Tiffany,' I exclaim and so Wendy diverts her to a different part of the castle out of harm's way.

Being a Sunday we have fewer guests arriving than usual and we manage to clear away most of the debris prior to their arrival. One of the arrivals is our builder who knows instinctively when an immediate call out is required. He takes one look at the scene and pronounces it to be not as bad as it looks. This I am happy to relay to Wendy. Investigation reveals that, while the bath did overflow last night it was a slow leak from a pipe joint that caused the real damage.

'Shit, no insurance then?' I'm imagining a four figure repair bill.

'Ahh, ya'll nay be wantin' ta involve th'insurers. Three hundred poonds and it'll be reet.'

My faith in keeping things local is reaffirmed.

She: 'Your father would have had a fit.'

I: 'So would I ten years ago, but you know things like this just seem to become less of a crisis as you get older.'

She: 'Because you learn to know what you can and can't control?'

I: 'I suppose so. If I'd known that ten years ago I wouldn't have got so screwed up about you leaving and going back down south.'

She: 'You still bitter about that?'

I: 'Not so much now, but it still hurts.'
She: 'because you didn't understand the reasons?'
I: 'Because I didn't want to understand the reasons.'

Christmas in a castle is like Christmas nowhere else, although not always for the right reasons. Expectations of festivities in a Victorian castle are high and we find ourselves under constant pressure to deliver everyone's idea of a perfect Dickensian Christmas. This all starts in about mid-November although I resolutely refuse to put up any decorations before the second week in December and I have been known to hide the key to the Tower, where the decorations are stored, to curb Wendy's enthusiasm for any premature festive frolics. The run up to Christmas with children, however, is pretty much standard no matter what your living arrangements. Take, for instance, the school Christmas play.

Anyone over the age of twelve (and that's being generous) who admits to enjoying a pantomime is, in my opinion, psychologically disturbed.

Wendy says I'd make a fabulous pantomime Dame and I'll confess it must all be more fun to be in than to watch. How could it not be? In fact I was dragged on stage by Widow Twanky a few years ago and I was quite taken by the lights, the smell and the rather fetching frocks. But if there's anything more terrifying than watching a panto, it's the run up to the primary school Christmas production. Oliver's progression to secondary school means that we are no longer subjected to the relentless round of let's-make-sure-everyone-gets-a-part-regardless-of-their-talent school shows of which he was never a star (his talents being reserved for the sports field) but Emily is in her last year at primary school and she does have a talent for singing and performing meaning that she is drafted into everything. Unfortunately, her artistic qualities are not universally shared by her contemporaries.

Dear parents/guardians,
Following the success of last year's production of *Tweeny Sid*, we have decided to be a little more adventurous and stage a production of *The Lion King*.

Children will be auditioning just after the half-term holidays and once they have been assigned a part we will write to you again with suggestions for costumes.

Yours sincerely,

Miss Brightbutton.

Words enough to strike fear in to the hardiest of parents' hearts.

(Wait until she's married with school-age children and see if her Christmas production doesn't morph into a simple heartwarming rendition of carols sung by the children in their own clothes lasting no more than fifteen minutes and rounded off with lashings of mulled wine.)

Tweeny Sid was a sanitised children's version of the classic tale of a murderous Victorian barber in which *Tweeny Sid* was actually a chimney sweep rather than a barber whose black cat stole pies from a struggling pie shop owner... (I can't recall the rest of the story but I felt well rested when I woke to a rousing ovation at the final curtain call). Costumes were a cinch: Something drab and grey topped off with a flat cap and some dirt smudged on the children's faces to make them look Victorian and poor. Admittedly some of the parents, mostly farmers, struggled with the concept of 'poor' so sent their children in dressed as the domestic help.

But *The Lion King*? I ask Emily what part she is hoping for and she tells me she wants to be either of the two lionesses, Nala or Sarabi.

Excellent! I can visualise a lion's outfit and don't imagine it will be that difficult to knock up and being in her final year at primary school she's sure to get one of the major roles.

By the time of the auditions Emily has learnt every word of both parts and practised all the songs. She has a lovely voice and I'm sure she'll walk it. A week later she jumps into the car outside school and thrusts a letter into my chest. 'We've been given our parts.'

Dear parents/guardians,

Following our auditions for *The Lion King*... Emily... has been selected to play the part of... Rafiki, the wise monkey and narrator of the story...

To help you with ideas enclosed are some pictures of costumes from the West End production of *The Lion King*.

We are not expecting costumes to be expensive or elaborate.

Please do let me know if you require any help.

Yours excitedly

Miss Brightbutton.

I catch a glimpse of Emily in the rear view mirror and she's not happy. 'I wanted to be a lion, not a monkey,' she grumbles.

I remain encouraging, 'well in the stage musical Rafiki is played by a woman and she's the most important character as she holds the whole story together.' Emily is unconvinced.

In truth, I am not happy, and Wendy won't be either. How the hell do we produce a decent looking multi-coloured monkey outfit?

'Anyway, it's not a monkey it's some sort of baboon and it's ugly,' Emily wails.

'Very colourful,' Wendy says encouragingly.

'Yes, especially the bright red arse,' I add, not to be helpful but because it is irresistible. Wendy shoots me a look.

Soon after we get home there's a phone call.

'Hi, it's Cressida, Petal's mum. Petal is going to be Zazu the hornbill in the show and we were thinking that because Wendy grew up in Africa you might be able to help us out with a costume.'

What is she thinking? That we have a menagerie of African birds in the garden? The big five roaming the grounds?

'Oh God,' says Wendy, 'she'll not be happy unless Petal is soaring above the rest of the cast on mechanical wings', and she tells Cressida that we are rather too caught up with our own costume dilemma. Cressida isn't happy but she'll have to accept we can't bail her out otherwise word will get out and we'll be responsible for a whole continent of exotic outfits while the truth is we're struggling to find inspiration for our own baboon costume and, anyway, our sewing machine is thick with dust and reeks of neglect.

Over the next few weeks Emily grudgingly admits that Rafiki is quite a decent part although she is less than pleased about the lack of opportunity to show off her singing talent. She suggests to Miss Brightbutton that she could sing some of her lines but Miss B becomes very agitated, explaining that she wants the show to be as true to the original West End production as possible.

Emily's assessment of this is perhaps predictable. 'Ridiculous woman. This is a school play in a village hall. What is she expecting?'

Things greater than will be delivered, we suspect.

We are rather proud of what we come up with costume-wise and as we make our way to the matinee performance of the show we are happy to parade Emily fully made up through the village.

There are two performances of the show which hasn't gone down well with some parents.

Lavinia, mummy of Jonathan and Henry catches us in the street. 'Wend, darling. Don't you think two performances is just too much for the little ones. They're going to be sooo tired.'

'But Lav,' replies Wendy, 'last year you complained that an afternoon performance wasn't good for working parents.' Ironic, since Lavinia's only work experience as secretary of the Parent Teachers Association resulted in her having to take an extended leave of absence after just six weeks due to the stress of it all.

Inside the village hall it's mayhem. Mr Lovegood is trying to keep order but the gazelles are getting over excited, being chased by Lawrence who, being somewhere low down on the autism spectrum has clearly been typecast as Scar, and the lionesses are in a strop having been upstaged by Harry who, as Mufasa, is actually dressed in a real pelt. Apparently his grandfather was a hunter in Kenya.

Meanwhile, Simba is one step away from having to be sedated. Stage fright has got the better of him and he has wet himself. Mrs Cresswell, who should already be warming things up with a medley of show tunes is desperately trying to dry his crotch with a hairdryer without melting the polyester fur.

As everyone takes their seats Miss Brightbutton claps her hands and orders all the rats and spiders to gather at the front of the stage.

'I don't remember rats and spiders in the film,' Oliver whispers to his mum.

'Oh you know they have to create parts for everyone. Remember last year the street urchins outnumbered everyone else by two to one and the year before that Cinderella's kitchen was overrun with ants of all things.'

The show goes with relatively few hitches and I manage to stay awake, not least because I am mesmerised by Petal's costume which must have a thousand feathers. But shedding fast, by the evening performance she's more likely to resemble a bald eagle than an African hornbill.

The highlight of the show is undoubtedly Pumbaa and Timon singing *Hakuna Matata* with broad Cumbrian accents. Oh, and the mulled wine, a first instigated by Wendy on the refreshments committee which makes it all just about worth going through again tonight.

Back at the castle preparations are well under way for our first open Christmas for several years. When we first opened the castle for business, making money at Christmas trumped any spiritual or familial sentiments. In any case, Oliver was only four months old so he didn't care one way or the other. We advertised 'Christmas in a castle' and were inundated with replies. We encouraged each couple to come and see the castle, explaining it is such a unique place they should satisfy themselves in person that we are the right place for their celebrations.

That's how, in 1998 we inadvertently manage to set up interviews for each of our very first crop of Christmas guests.

The first couple through the door are Allison and Andrew. That they have since become part of the family says everything about how they got what we do but they might have just as easily, and understandably, turned on their heels and never set foot near the castle again.

I have become accustomed to doing everything with a baby strapped to my chest, Wendy having made it quite clear that if she is to be burdened with breast feeding, nappy changing and night-time feeds, I have the intervening responsibility. Since this deal was brokered and since Wendy stopped breast feeding a month ago, I do seem to have taken my fair share of night feeds and nappy changing but Wendy is still seldom to be seen carrying the baby.

'I'm not sure this is good for me all the time,' I suggest one day, 'what with my weak back.'

'What weak back' comes the unsympathetic reply.

'The weak back I'll have if I keep having to carry Oliver around, he's getting heavy you know.'

'Ridiculous.'

I know there is no point pursuing the argument as we all remember the drama of the night Oliver was born, the ambulance dash and being stuck in a pub car park with the baby's head crowning, and Wendy has made it quite clear that a lifetime of suffering on my part will never come close to that night.

So, when Allison and Andrew arrive at the front door they are greeted by me, Oliver dribbling at my front, smelling slightly of baby sick and strongly of something altogether more toxic.

'Do come in,' I gesture with the hand that isn't supporting my lower back, 'it's all very relaxed.'

I'm sure they hesitate just for a moment but, at this stage they're prospects for a Christmas room worth a few hundred quid and must be courted.

After tea, coffee and pleasantries they are given a tour of the castle during which Oliver wakes up, burps, farts and then falls back to sleep. It all seems to be going rather well and they are un-phased by Oliver's anti-social behaviour. It turns out they both have young children who will be spending Christmas with their estranged spouses. Wendy and I glance at each other and we each know what the other is thinking, 'lucky bastards.'

Allison and Andrew book, telling us this is their first Christmas together and they think the castle and we are perfect.

'You haven't tasted the food yet,' I quip.

'Oh just one thing, I am a vegetarian, is that going to be a problem?' Allison asks.

My face crumples into a grimace. 'No, no, of course not,' and I'm already wondering what on earth we've taken on. The last time we cooked Christmas dinner for anyone other than ourselves was before we were married. The whole family came. The AGA packed up, the gravy ran out, the potatoes weren't cooked and my grandmother spent a good deal of her time wiping her finger across the furniture inspecting the dust.

'It's going to be such fun,' Wendy chimes.

And so it turns out to be.

As everyone leaves on Boxing Day there are kisses and tears all around. One couple says it is as if the company had been specially chosen and even Glenda, who came with her cat Hortense says it has been simply magical.

'We can do this,' we tell each other when it's over.

We do another three Christmases after that which get progressively bigger until a couple of incidents convince us it is time to set Christmas aside for family. The first is a complaint from an elderly couple who have joined us for Christmas three years in a row. They tell us they find the wait between courses at lunch interminable. That we are trying to cook it, serve it, sit down with them and eat it, entertain everyone and keep our children happy too seems to have passed them by.

The second is that, with several other families joining the mix, Oliver has become overwhelmed by the sheer quantity of presents underneath the tree and, being just three and half, assumes they must all be for him. We find him in a pile of wrapping paper surrounded by presents, which clearly aren't his, in a scrap with another child, Oliver adamant that since he unwrapped the pink doll's pushchair it is his.

Now, nearly a decade and a half later, with Oliver now old enough to read the labels on presents under the tree we figure we're on safer ground but both children are still wailing about the injustice of having to give up their Christmas to guests.

Having not asked the staff to work on Christmas Day for the best part of a decade we're too chicken to ask them now and decide to manfully soldier through on our own. Whether or not the staff think this is a sensible idea we don't know and it falls to two of our longest standing friends to point out that servicing Christmas for a party of thirty odd people consisting of several different family groups each with their own traditions and expectations might be more than even we can manage.

Miranda and Graham ought to know better, having in the past found themselves painting bathrooms, teaching me to wallpaper, rotivating the garden and supporting us sobbing on their shoulders after making similar observations. But they haven't learnt and so they find themselves, together with their two teenage boys, AJ and Sam joining us for Christmas on the understanding that they'll be pitching in. It's a slight sugaring of the pill for Oliver and Emily that the boys will be here to share their pain of another Christmas in public. Oliver has agreed to share his Xbox with AJ and as a result neither of them goes anywhere near the washing up for three days. Emily is more than happy to make room for Sam whom she has adored since they were both babies and both insist they are far too young to be made to work.

Seldom have we been more nervous about anything but happily, by Boxing Day it's clear that, between four of us, we've pulled it off. Whether Miranda and Graham find it an enriching experience is hard to say. They never really do say and we decide better than to ask but I am sure they know how eternally grateful we are.

'We'll do that again,' Wendy says cheerfully as she checks the bank balance a few days later.

'True to your Christian ideals, darling,' I tease, 'but if we do it again we are having some staff.'

'Agreed.'

As 2011 turns to 2012 we'd do well to remember that our constant search for perfection is in vain. If world events have taught us anything this year it is surely that we all inhabit an imperfect world and we should spend a little more time recognising the joy in what is around us rather than searching for something that isn't there.

My new year's resolutions include not expecting miracles from my staff, not to expect miracles from my wife (although that she puts up with me is miraculous in itself) not expecting my children to be perfectly behaved all the time and to stop expecting to see the body of a twenty-year-old each time I look in the mirror. If I can get to grips with those I shall be a more contented person.

At Augill Castle it has been, on the whole, a good year but it has been far from perfect. Business has held up and we have managed to make several improvements to the fabric of the castle and to the services we offer.

There are galley kitchens for guests to use which seem to have gone down well, I redecorate six of our fourteen bedrooms and three bathrooms. We landscape the pond, start a small holding with pigs, ducks, hens and turkeys, start offering afternoon tea, hold open air theatre in the garden (and on both occasions our prayers for perfect weather are answered) have Santa to visit and host Christmas for the first time in ten years.

We lose Harry our very naughty cat who might best be remembered for the time he started to demolish a wedding cake half way through the groom's speech. He is run over by one of our remaining neighbours. And we lose Holly, our fourteen-year-old labrador who was so much a part of the very fabric of Augill. With her natural smile, constantly wagging tail and constant temperament she knew more about customer service than the rest of us ever will.

There are funerals for both. Less theatrical than in the past when mice, rabbits and even moles have been laid to rest in the garden with a full rites service, but no less emotional for that.

There are so many good comments and only a few adverse ones but it is they that make for the best entertainment in the re-telling.

In the spring a couple of guests arrive and leave within an hour. They telephone the next day to ask for their deposit to be returned. When asked why they had left without explanation the reply goes something like this: 'The rooms are shabby and dated, we were expected to eat at the same table as other guests and frankly it wasn't the luxury experience we were looking for. Furthermore, the drive was very well worn and there were children playing on the tennis court.'

Both the rooms to which they were shown have now been redecorated and the drive is under constant repair but as for the children, the restraints in the tower just won't hold and they keep getting out.

Hot on the heels of these disgruntled fellows comes another hard to please couple.

'Frankly we're less than pleased with the room,' I am told on asking how they are settling in. 'There's no hot water.'

'How strange, may I come and check?' I ask without waiting for a reply.

'I hardly think that necessary, we've been running the bath tap and the shower for twenty minutes and there's just freezing cold water.'

I am already holding my hand under a steaming tap when the guest follows me in.

'Well,' he grumbles, 'the hot and cold are on the opposite sides to that in our house.'

'OK, is everything else alright with the room?' There really is nothing else to say.

By the end of May we've enjoyed one of the sunniest and warmest springs on record. But this is lost on a group of four Americans who have booked for two nights but leave after one. 'The castle just is not old enough,' is their main complaint, 'and there's no air conditioning.'

Perhaps a transatlantic language problem? In the US it's called air conditioning, in Cumbria it's called a window.

As summer sets in the weather deteriorates and for a few this is, inevitably, our fault. 'The gardens were flooded, there was absolutely nothing to do and it was freezing cold,' they wail, standing in nothing but T-shirts. We did tell them to come by car but they insisted on the train from London and back in 24 hours. I should have offered to lend them jumpers.

One honeymooning couple declare, on being shown Pendragon, widely held as our most magnificent room, it to be gloomy and oppressive.

'I beg your pardon?' I ask when they tell me they'd rather not stay. 'It's a gloomy place.' the man replies. His wife is nearly in tears and so am I but perhaps for different reasons. Wendy walks in at that moment.

'Darling, here's a new one,' I start, knowing it is deeply unprofessional but really past caring, 'our home is gloomy and oppressive apparently.'

We invite them to find alternative accommodation and they end up booking a room at a very traditional hotel in Bowness-on-Windermere whose speciality is coach parties of old ladies. Enough said.

We prepare for our two forays into open air theatre in July with trepidation. The summer weather has turned monsoonal but days before both *Romeo and Juliet* and *Alice in Wonderland* (complete with a Mad Hatter's children's tea party) the sun comes out and shines through both performances. Each is a quintessentially English picnic-on-the-lawn experience under a crystal blue sky.

However even then someone isn't happy. A local drama teacher apparently found the acting amateurish and the whole thing very unprofessional. Well the food and service isn't unprofessional and she surely is a prime candidate for trying harder in 2012 to see the joy in just being.

By the end of the summer we've had a stream of wonderful people to stay. Some returning after a decade or more, others returning for their second or third stay this year. The only gripe any of them seem to have is with the weather which has treated none of us kindly, unlike the press which give us rave reviews in national newspapers, regional rags and glossy magazines.

We are not even knocked off the crest of our wave when the *Daily Mail* sends an undercover reporter who finds things a little less to his liking, declaring the castle too kitsch, objecting to our family photographs on the grand piano (is it the photos he didn't like or the fact we have room for a grand?) and feeling positively insulted by rickety Victorian windows and breadcrumbs in the butter dish.

Ironically, on the same Saturday *The Daily Telegraph* lists us as one of Europe's best places to spend Christmas and Tom Chesshyre from *The Times* stays in the very same room as the *Daily Mail's* anonymous reporter and says of his stay: 'Staying at Augill Castle is like entering a Gothic fantasy world (with posh toiletries and a very good cooked breakfast). What a lovely, friendly Gothic retreat.'

It's not perfect, this castle. It never will be and neither will we. No apologies for that. The thing is, our guests aren't perfect either so, on the whole, I think we all go together rather well most of the time.

One guest's comment stands out from the rest this year: 'Perfectly imperfect'.

As we welcome in 2012 we try our best to cast aside the gloom in the hope that everyone might just expect a little less from each other.

Chapter Seven

A jacket fit for a sailor, a sailor not fit for sailing, marmalade envy, goats and a life changing diagnosis

As 2012 dawns there is a faint glow of optimism lightening the economic horizon. It's the year of the London Olympics and the Queen's Diamond Jubilee and a collective feeling that this will be Britain's year seems to be loosening people's purse strings.

I buy myself a ridiculous (Emily's now standard assessment of everything I do) and totally impractical red, white and blue jacket made from vintage Union flags which I fancy I am going to have to wear almost every day for a year to justify what I pay for it. By April it has not been out of the wardrobe and every time it glimpses the light of day Wendy is mentally totting up its cost per wear.

This cost per wear thing is something she first formulated to justify her own purchases, arguing that if a dress cost £200, that cost could be divided by the number of wears so that by the time it has been worn ten times it actually only cost £20 per wear, about the same as a cheap dress from Primark which might fall apart after one wear anyway. It's a strange logic but appears to be one to which many of our female friends subscribe. Unfortunately the same formula is often used to beat me up about my sartorial extravagance because I, apparently, have a more extensive wardrobe and am not getting good value for money out of it. The truth is, in my opinion, men don't tot up the value of their clothes in the same way and therefore designers can't get away with charging as much.

Admittedly the Union jacket is currently running at £295 per wear (and that's when I tried it on in the Rugby Store at Twickenham) but you can't put a price on patriotism or eccentricity and since we are spending our family summer holiday at the Olympic Games in London its return on investment will be enhanced.

Personally, rather like London, I am feeling invigorated. Following my diagnosis last year I became a research bore, consuming the contents of internet forums, books, journals, taking on board what was good, learning to discount the cranks and the misleading, sifting through the contradictory and eventually devising a plan to take back the self-control that I felt had been threatened.

The medical establishment's first and almost instantaneous solution was to throw pills and medication at the problem that would have rendered me a prescription junkie for the rest of my life. With Wendy's blessing, because she knew as well as I that this was going to affect her life too, I set about devising a more holistic solution. To my surprise, when I ran this past the doctor he was very supportive.

Now, some three months later, I am, because I feel I am, a different man. My self-inflicted regime began with an extreme diet of just 600 calories a day followed by a completely different lifestyle to the one I had previously taken for granted. I lost three stone in weight and now I look better, feel better and have a self confidence which a year ago I thought I had lost forever.

As a mid-forty year old man I have regained a feeling of youth and invincibility which comes with middle aged weight loss and self empowerment. That my friends have noticed the change and go out of their way to comment on it serves only to enhance my sense of well being.

I am subject to a regime of routine tests which show that my new lifestyle has had a dramatic and positive effect both on my current state of health and the long term prognosis.

However, this renewed self-awareness has, apparently, manifested itself in ways which aren't universally popular. Wendy accuses me of an excess of vanity.

True, running a hotel may be the ultimate vanity exercise but as I bump my body hair trimmer over my abs before applying a fabulous new hair product to my head I wonder if she is being a little harsh. Then again, keeping up appearances is important. Everything we do at the castle is about creating a 'wow factor' so why should what we do with ourselves be any different?

A friend recently bemoaned the fact that nobody dresses for the theatre anymore. Or dinner. Wendy and I recently attended the opera in Covent Garden and dressed properly in white tie and full length evening dress. Our fellow opera-goers who had paid no less for their seats but who had clearly stopped investing in decent clothes some years previously, regarded us with a mix of suspicion and fascination as if we were celebrities they couldn't quite place. I bet, as a result of making an effort, we got far better value out of our ticket price than any of them because we felt fabulous.

I go to business meetings with people who turn up in Trespass fleeces and Craghopper trousers. I know this is the Lake District but if they're planning a hike up Scafell Pike afterwards, what's wrong with a quick change of clothes in the gent's after the meeting? I firmly believe that dressing for business instils a different mindset. What happened to teachers wearing a jacket and tie? How can they berate students for not being smart if they're not themselves? God forbid that MPs start turning up at the House of Commons in tracksuits and trainers or shorts and flip flops, what sort of a state would the country be in then?

That's not to say there is anything wrong with a well tailored pair of jeans and indeed I live much of my life in nothing else. But I have jeans for working in, jeans that go with sports jackets and jeans for the evening. Each pair knows its place.

This has also rubbed off on the children. No longer can we go shopping and pick out their clothes for them. We can't even offer a suggestion (unless we want to employ a bit of reverse psychology and steer them away from something truly unsuitable by raving over it). Clothes are no longer acceptable unless they sport the correct label or have been sported by the right celebrity. The look is everything at the particular expense of practicality – in recent bitterly cold weather Emily has been dressed in spring fashion because spring is what is in the shops and 'this is what everyone is wearing'. In California perhaps but not in Cumbria but with a Union jacket hanging in my wardrobe who am I to talk of practicalities?

As I moisturise and pluck a stray hair from my left eyebrow my thoughts return to the business of hotel keeping. Is it all vanity? I prefer to call it attention to detail and it runs through everything we do.

There is no doubt that we are proud of what we have. Our entire business model revolves around sharing what we have created with others. To ask people to share in your own personal creation, to share your vision of what is tasteful, tasty and attractive is, of course, a form of vanity. To want to make something as beautiful as you can, to want to create in others a sense of belonging in your own home, to have a desire to create friends out of strangers takes a lot of self-belief – even a dose of vanity.

We have been accused of arrogance. I don't think we are arrogant people. In fact we are, on the whole very self-deprecating but yes, to be able to do all of those things, to create what people will pay to experience does take a little bit of arrogance. Perhaps vanity and arrogance are not such unfamiliar bedfellows. After all, do we dress well just for ourselves or do we also do so on the assumption that others will notice and appreciate our efforts?

The ultimate in vanity are awards. As hoteliers we seem not to be content with the compliments of our guests. We seek the approval of our peers. The trophies in the hall are gathering dust so we decide it is time to have another pop at an award. For all sorts of reasons, this feels like the year to have a go.

Knowing something of the politics of industry award schemes there is no point going for the same bed & breakfast award we won in 2009 so we plump for sustainability instead. After all, we have been trying to make the running of the castle as cost effective as possible ever since we arrived and several years before the popular green agenda took hold, when being environmentally friendly still had connotations of Woodstock and free love in the long grass. It proves surprisingly easy to put together a convincing case as most of our green measures come as second nature and we are pleased but not overly surprised to be told we have been shortlisted as finalists.

As the awards evening looms we check out the competition: another bed & breakfast, a visitor centre and a campsite where everything is composted and poo is used to power the lights.

'Not sure I'd want to stay somewhere where the brightness of the lights depends on the amount you shit,' I observe, 'you'd have to fart before you could turn on your kindle.'

'Well at least your tent would be the brightest in the campsite,' Wendy voices the truth again.

It's a pretty academic exchange as camping has never featured on our wish list since the time we joined friends on a campsite in Filey on the North Yorkshire coast. We had brought wine for four to last a long weekend but at the end of the first night we were crawling into the tent, having drunk everything, only to discover it simply wasn't big enough for two. Wendy slept fitfully at best, I dozed outside under the stars. In the morning our friends, whose tent next door was one of those with sleeping rooms off a central communal space, stumbled upon my frozen body and asked why I was outside.

'No room in that little tent,' I replied dozily.

'But it's a tent for two,' they said.

'No it bloody is not,' Wendy retorted from inside.

We approach the awards quietly confident of a trophy to add to our collection. But it isn't to be. The other bed & breakfast wins the award with the evening's compere excitedly announcing that one of the mainstays of their submission is their homemade marmalade.

'Homemade marmalade,' Wendy snorts, 'is hardly going to save the planet,' and for several weeks she is heard repeatedly to mutter about the injustices of homemade marmalade.

Whilst I don't share Wendy's resentment of the marmalade B&B I do harbour a feeling of injustice. After all, how many other businesses of our size run cookery workshops for local primary schools at cost, have raised their own pigs, made sausages and cured bacon? The castle is now almost entirely lit by low energy lighting and we recycle or compost practically everything. But we do all this, not for awards but because it is the right thing to do and our reward is to feel good. If I repeat this often enough I am sure I will begin to believe it.

Having decided not to repeat the pig rearing experiment, although much was learnt from our first foray and dispatching another two pigs was a much less traumatic experience than the first, Wendy decides it would be fun to have some goats.

'What the…' I restrain myself, 'what for?'

'Milk, cheese, they're lovely and the visiting children would love to pet them. I'm sure they'll be less trouble than the pigs and they eat everything.'

When Wendy announces an idea, she expects action. If there is none she will take matters into her own hands. So, when two weeks later, no action has been taken on the procurement of goats, she is on the telephone to our local animal sanctuary organising for the delivery of a pair.

I try to sound a note of reason but Wendy shuts me up, 'they can go in the same paddocks the pigs had, use the same shelters and we'll maybe even be able to make our own cheese. It'll be just as if we'd moved to France all those years ago.'

Christ, I am thinking, what's she on? 'Ah, but you only get milk from goats which are lactating so…'

'Don't worry, I've arranged for a breeding pair.'

'Oh Wendy, for fuck's sake…'

On hearing the news Reg, who by now thinks he has seen and heard it all, is incredulous.

'That'll ne'er keep em in lad.'

'Well you said that about the pigs Reg but they never escaped.'

And because it seems too good an opportunity to resist, I explain, 'They'll be living in the caffots which became the piggots and will now be the gottuts'.

The goats are called Amy and Ben.

'What ridiculous names for goats,' Emily says. We would have expected nothing else.

'Well what would you call them?' I ask.

'Stupid Idea One and even Stupider Idea Two,' Oliver interjects from the next room.

'Wendy, can you see that nobody else is invested in this idea?' I ask my wife.

'But they're lovely and they are no trouble, they're so friendly, come and see,' so we all go and see.

Amy is, indeed a lovely, gentle creature and I can see that visiting children are going to adore her. As for Ben, adorable isn't the first word that comes to mind, he is very stand-offish but perhaps he's just shy. Wendy assures us that they eat grass, kitchen leftovers, anything.

'Including the garden?' I ask.

'They can't jump, Ben's got arthritis…'

'Oh a quality specimen then.' I'm being mischievous.

Wendy ignores me and continues, 'and Amy isn't a jumping sort of goat, they told me that at the animal sanctuary.' She has been well and truly taken in.

'OK, we'll give it one summer but what about the milking?'

'If we're happy, we'll let them mate in the autumn and have a couple of kids and we can milk Amy after that.'

'How much milk do you think you're going to get out of one goat?' Emily snorts but Wendy chooses to ignore her too.

So it is that Wendy's plan involves not two but potentially four goats and she is ignoring all the warning shots her family is trying to fire across the plan.

☙ ☙ ☙ ☙ ☙

In June I am offered a unique opportunity. We have, to date, rarely gone away separately and whenever Wendy has we have joked, with some justification, that the castle is a rudderless ship without her but on this trip the sailing metaphors take on a whole new relevance.

There are two categories of once-in-a-lifetime experiences. There are those that you are never going to get another chance to repeat and then there are those you'd never want to repeat.

I have been invited to join some army friends on an 'adventure training' sailing voyage across the English Channel. I don't know why or how I have been drafted as an honorary member of the armed forces. I am not a good sailor but I accept the challenge in the knowledge that this is definitely going to fall into the former category of once-in-a-lifetime experiences and in the hope that it does not qualify for the latter. The elements will decide.

As the adventure draws closer I am getting more nervous about my ability to cope with whatever the English Channel – apparently widely acknowledged as one of the most challenging stretches of water in the World – is going to throw at us. On hearing the news of my trip, Miranda, who has known me longer than almost anyone exclaims, 'What are you thinking of, you get sea sick on a skateboard.'

She's not far off the mark but Oliver reminds me with typically sanguine teenaged wisdom that 'you might not get another chance like it Dad, you're not getting any younger.'

Thanks son.

Our yatcht is moored at Portland marina on the south coast. It's a six or seven hour drive and I leave none of my shipmates in any doubt about what they have taken on in inviting me along by insisting, like Aunty Gloria who will not be moved once she is settled, that I must sit in the front of the car for the whole journey because of my propensity to travel sickness.

When we arrive at Portland we are greeted by the Regimental Sergeant Major whose opening gambit is 'It's a fucking small boat sir.' I take an instant liking to him. He introduces himself as the RSM but says I can call him Dean as I am a civilian. It never does sound quite right and because it just suits him better, he remains RSM for the duration of the voyage.

As soon as we set foot on the marina pontoon I begin to feel queasy, not helped by our first look at the yatcht. The RSM's initial assessment may have been a little generous. Seven men will spend five nights in a boat no bigger than the one in which the Owl and the Pussycat set sail.

Of course, this being the army I'm not about to say anything and don't have to because the rest of the crew are soon whining like a bunch of pansies about where to put their kit, who's going to sleep where and the dubious stains on one of the pull out hammocks. These are our defenders of the realm. By keeping quiet while they are all dealing, with varying degrees of confusion, with their admin (that's unpacking for non-military personnel) sitting down on the best berth and spreading my stuff out I manage to bag it for myself.

After a lively debate over whether we should go out into town for fish and chips or eat some of the onboard rations that the Training Major (herein known as the TM) has brought, I am over-ruled as the only one plumping for fish and chips and we have to endure mountains of rice topped with tinned chicken in white sauce. It's filling but tasty would be stretching the truth. We all politely decline seconds.

We spend our first night in the marina waiting for the tide which takes us out into open water at 8am the next morning and then the fun begins.

The TM has nominated himself as ship's cook and insists, against everyone's better judgement that we should fill up with fried egg and fried spam sandwiches before setting sail. It's a decision that will come back, literally, to haunt us time and again before the day is over.

Roughly two hours into our twelve hour crossing of one of the most congested and unpredictable tracts of sea in the world (these are facts that were not contained in the pre-board briefing) Captain Preston (Regimental Organisation Support Officer, herein known as ROSO) has offered up our first gift to the sea. Whether or not the fish appreciate the regurgitated fried egg and spam, it's clear that ROSO did not enjoy tasting it all again. He remains motionless for several hours whilst I and our valiant second lieutenant Charlie join the chunder club with further offerings to Neptune.

For a while I feel fit enough to take the wheel which helps enormously as there is no time to dwell on how I am feeling. Unfortunately I have overdosed on my sea sickness medication which has made me feel not quite myself and when I suddenly exclaim that I have sighted land I am told it is just another ship. I am not to be dissuaded as the effect of the pills is strong and I steer a course for salvation. I remain convinced that we are heading for land even though it is moving away from us and there is a plume of smoke coming out of the funnel shaped top. Later I read that one of the side effects of too many pills is hallucinations.

By now the weather is closing in and our skipper, who I think has developed a particularly dry manner from too many years on the water, tells us that the wind and tide are fighting each other, resulting in an ever larger swell, there is no way we can get to France and the tide may even push us past our safe haven at the channel island of Alderney. I dare to ask where we'd end up if we missed Alderney and don't much care for 'the Atlantic' as an answer. It's news that neither I or Charlie can stomach and we're over the side again. By the time I have recovered sufficiently to focus again there is rain lashing our faces, we're bobbing around like a cork, the yacht is practically on its side and I would be near to tears but for the fact that the repeated vomiting has left me practically dessicated.

Unfortunately, during my stint at the wheel we have steered off course in my quest for the mythical island and failed to take heed of a fast approaching super-tanker. By the time the skipper comes on deck (apparently he was checking the tide times but I suspect he was actually swigging rum) the tanker has had to take evasive action by way of a 360 degree turn around us.

This is not good seamanship on our part and puts us in potential peril. I fear whatever badge I might have been in line to receive for taking part in this folly of an expedition will now elude me.

Once danger has been averted and land is eventually sighted by someone less medicated than me I can barely raise a smile. ROSO is still motionless. I've known ROSO for some years and this is the longest I have ever known him be silent so I know things must be serious. They are made no more bearable by the TM's ridiculous efforts to cheer us all up by taking on the mantle of Captain bloody Beaky and offering everyone a cheese and ketchup sandwich whilst singing sea shanties.

Through all of this the RSM has been making no effort whatsoever to familiarise himself with the routines of sailing and has been asleep below deck. I decide that this is the best place to be as we are now being drenched by bucket loads of water at the bottom of every wave. My stomach is completely empty, possibly even inside out by now, so I retreat to the lower quarters.

Once laid down I dare not move and am determined to hold on to whatever I can, no matter what. My resolve is soon put to the test. An hour off Alderney we hit what can only be described as a maelstrom. Two currents, the tide and what feels like seven winds are conspiring to create the perfect storm through which we have to pass to get in to harbour. The contents of the galley are flying through the cabin, everything is falling out of lockers (this is called bad admin) but I am holding on.

All of a sudden the RSM, a big man by his own admission, comes flying horizontally through the air from the front to the back of the cabin accompanied by tea bags and the remnants of the rice from last night. He is closely followed by ROSO who apparently now thinks the whole thing is worthy of a video. Sadly he can't operate the camera because he can't see anything through his salt encrusted glasses. His request for help with the camera proves too much for the RSM who simply says 'excuse me sir' as he lunges for the toilet.

He is a jolly polite sort of chap. Unfortunately he becomes entangled in a bungee cord on a rucksack and can't quite reach the toilet bowl. The other end of the bungee is caught around ROSO's ankles. They are both desperately trying to pull in opposite directions. I can do nothing to help as both my hands have a firm grip on something solid and immovable. ROSO is once again rendered motionless and the glance he throws me is one of sheer panic. He would later tell me that the look I returned him was one of pure terror and I wouldn't disagree.

By the time we reach the relative calm of Alderney harbour (which isn't all that calm) I have packed my bag (or completed my admin) and am making plans to return home by plane, train, mule or foot. The RSM has vowed to join me. I ring home as soon as I am ashore and recount the experience. Wendy reassures me that I'll have found my sea legs now. I remind her that I'm still missing my stomach and when Emily warns me not to get eaten by a shark I tell her that that would have been a blessed relief. So, how it is I set foot back on that yacht the next day I will never be able to fully explain.

Call it peer pressure. A sense of belonging. Needing to feel accepted. The tale of how we got back to England three days later is one for another time. Or perhaps it's enough to say the sea was calm, the sun shone and my eyes stayed shut for a good twelve hours.

>*She: 'Dad would have enjoyed that story. Do you remember how he loved messing about in that dinghy of his?'*
>
>*I: 'Yes, you hated that thing… I always imagined that wherever I went in the world I would be able to count on being accepted for my choices and decisions by someone back home. That home and that someone were always the same thing, you and Dad. Parents. It made being accepted in another place, by other people less crucial. On that yacht I wanted to be accepted as an equal.*
>
>*As children we want the acceptance of our parents and expect it unconditionally, as parents we hope to be accepted by our children but don't expect it.'*
>
>*She: 'I'm sure you mean unconditional love because that's a very different thing from unconditional acceptance.'*
>
>*I: 'I'm not sure I'm talking about either. Maybe it's more about approval. Anyway, when that cycle of mutual whatever it is was broken, I became almost desperate for acceptance in other quarters – as part of a different set of relationships because the primary one that God gave me was gone.*
>
>*'We both felt that with no parents left and so for us it was always about social acceptance – to be accepted by the community we had chosen but which had been given no choice about our arrival.*
>
>*'That put all the onus on us to do the work to earn that acceptance. The difference was that the work you put into familial acceptance is subconscious whereas this acceptance is hard fought for and hard won and we're still far from sure the battle for it is over.'*
>
>*She: 'Careful, you're starting to sound a little needy.'*
>
>*I: 'Is it needy or just insecure?'*

CHAPTER EIGHT

Olympic fever, an ill-fated birthday surprise, father and son bonding, goats on a mission and Wendy gains an unlikely ally in need of support

After the questionable heroics of my cross-Channel adventure come the much more worthy heroics of the London 2012 Olympic and Paralympic Games. We had decided nearly two years ago to forego our annual fix of Mediterranean sun in favour of a fortnight in London. With a handful of tickets in our possession none of us really know what to expect but an extraordinary summer it turns out to be. Against a backdrop of doom-laden news, gloomier forecasts and less than perfect weather the world has turned its sights on London, and England. And the world likes what it sees.

As a family we are lucky enough to be part of it all. For ten days we revel in the carnival atmosphere of the Olympic Games and return to London for the final weekend of the Paralympics.

Highlights include watching Andy Murray, Usain Bolt, Chris Hoy, Victoria Pendleton, Jessica Ennis and Mo Farrer all win gold, being up close when Jess Ennis meets the fans, cheering with the crowd at almost anything inside the Olympic Park, marvelling at the sheer scale of the aquatic centre, the stadium and even the Olympic Park McDonalds! We feel every stroke of the rowing and two of us are inspired to take up the sport.

We roar Oscar Pistorius across the finish line for gold in the 400m at the end of an inspiring last night of athletics and we are there at Buckingham Palace when David Weir wins Team GB's final gold in the marathon, closely followed by Shelley Woods taking silver.

We party in the park to celebrate the close of the Olympic Games and we feel the beat of triumph in our chests in the Olympic Stadium when Coldplay rock us to the close of the Paralympics.

And, for one last hurrah and the ultimate end to London 2012, we cheer as Team GB parade past us in Trafalgar Square, the athletes saluting the crowd as much as we do them, and then we sneak in through non-existent security while everyone is still on a high to join the party in the Mall where Boris Johnson, London's Mayor, outshines the Prime Minister without even trying but where the real stars are the athletes and the volunteers.

Yes, it is an extraordinary summer but mostly not because of any of this. What makes 2012 extraordinary is the humanity and decency with which everyone in London treats each other. The legions of volunteers – the Games Makers as they are called – lead by example. Theirs is a genuine hospitality and proof that it isn't just facilities that make a great experience. Above all, it is people.

That the Games Makers' enthusiastic friendliness is so intoxicating is largely down to how it is received. Games Makers and Games Goers all on a high, accepting, open, forgiving and good natured. We see not one crossed word exchanged. We fall into animated conversation with strangers as if we are friends, show consideration to others as part of something bigger than just a crowd.

In short, an epidemic of friendliness breaks out because we are all part of an extraordinary shared experience. *The Daily Telegraph* later calls it Britain's summer of sporting love, when not only do we fall in love with the games and their heroes, but also each other.

What we learn is that if we all approach each other with an open mind our hearts will follow. A little seed of kindness and consideration grows and like a tree, unless you intentionally uproot it, will continue. All human encounters happen because our individual paths have crossed, however, fleetingly. Sometimes that may be as brief as sharing a doorway as we go our opposite ways. But a simple smile or greeting in a doorway, a ticket queue or waiting for a train can lead to a longer lasting convergence. In fact, it can change life's course.

At the castle our paths converge with others' not by accident but by design. Over fifteen years we have offered our quite individual home, and our own home grown brand of hospitality to anyone who wants to accept it in a spirit of honesty and openness. People are drawn here as we were. Nobody is forced to come.

What London's summer teaches us back at the castle is that to be open, genuine and honest is more important than anything physical we can provide. Those who accept our offer at the castle in the same way are rarely disappointed. Just as the openness of everyone we meet in London diffuses the minor irritations of an overcrowded Tube station or a chaotic queue for food outside the Olympic velodrome, an open hearted guest, accepting of genuine hospitality will forgive a slight delay at breakfast or a piece of peeling wallpaper. That makes up 99% of our guests and we know we are lucky to have met every single one.

For the rest of the year I use this as the basis of an inspirational address I deliver to the staff who have been fabulously loyal throughout what has been a crappy few years. They are all, bar one, utterly understanding of our inability to give them pay rises and they just seem to have a genuine desire to pull together and get the castle through this most difficult of times. I also speak on a similar theme to various business groups and warm to my subject to the point of evangelism.

As we look forward from 2012, if there is to be an Olympic legacy that goes beyond sport it is surely that we can all learn a little bit of humility, to be more tolerant of each other's shortcomings and that random kindness doesn't have to be confined to a summer of sport.

That said, sometimes random acts of kindness can backfire.

Rory is six. It's a sunny late summer Saturday and his parents have brought him and his fourteen year old brother Sam to the castle to celebrate, perhaps under sufferance as it is immediately apparent on arrival that this is not a family given to spontaneous celebration. They have asked us to bake a cake but that's about it.

Later on we sit all the children who are staying down to supper and they tuck into fillet steak and chips. Wendy is at pains to remind all the parents (there are several families staying) that it is fillet steak – that's f-i-l-l-e-t steak, but there's no sign of enthusiasm.

'Jeeze,' she mutters, 'I might as well have given them horse meat.'

'Perhaps that's what they've all got used to recently if their mums have been going to Iceland,' Oliver observes dryly.

We have baked a big chocolate cake which Wendy thinks is best served as dessert for everyone to share. Rory's mum decides she'd like to come into the kitchen to inspect the cake before it is presented.

To be fair she'd told us Rory was sporty and although she hadn't actually asked for a novelty cake it's clear that's exactly what she is expecting, probably covered in astroturf with little marzipan men playing with their balls.

Reading the situation as only Wendy can, she says, 'well it's round like a football,' and refrains from saying that while we do a good line in novelty castle hotels we've never set out our stall as novelty cake decorators, that particular hell having been reserved by our own children and their increasingly sophisticated demands twice a year.

Meanwhile I have taken my own steps to warm up the party by pouring Wendy and I some very stiff pink gins. It does the trick, for us at least. By cake time we are both in a decidedly 'hang it all' frame of mind which is just as well.

I put the six red and white candles on the cake together with a set of golf clubs made of sugar left over from a novelty wedding cake (nobody actually specified a sport) while Wendy nips to the office to remind herself of the birthday boy's name (there have been far too many incidents of her befriending guests on first name terms only to discover, on checking out, that they are somebody completely different). Having downed the gin a little too swiftly she's taking no chances.

On her return the two of us dim the lights and parade the cake in to the Music Room, heartily singing 'Happy Birthday to You'.

At this point it is usual for everyone to join in as the lights are dimmed. Not a peep. Nobody is singing, not even Rory's parents. It's as if they have never heard of such an outlandish custom and not until the last verse does anyone open their mouths. Even then it may just be to ask if there's something wrong with the electrics.

As the candles are blown out we breath a sigh of relief but it is short lived because Rory is quietly but heavily sobbing at the end of the table.

Wendy looks crestfallen as Rory's mum explains that he is an avid Everton football supporter whose colours are blue and white but the candles are red and white, the colours of their arch rivals Liverpool.

Wendy sits down heavily. It's clear she's in need of another pick-me-up because I can see she's thinking that football is as alien to her as Paul Smith and Chanel are to this bunch of un-cultured sports fans. So I bring her another drink. 'Here you go darling, another cranberry juice,' I say with a wink, 'it's packed with antioxidants.'

Inspired by the Olympic Games Oliver asks me which sport he

thinks is going to give him the best chance of winning a gold medal in eight years' time.

Rugby Sevens seems an obvious choice as rugby is his passion but he favours something involving more individual endeavour. 'The trouble with rugby,' he says, 'is that you're too dependent on the rest of the team so even if you play brilliantly, if you don't win you don't get a medal.'

I'm not sure this is quite the attitude I've been trying to instil in him but I do see his point.

'So I thought about rowing,' he continues.

I begin to research rowing clubs near us, naively thinking that, being on the edge of the Lake District they'll be ten-a-penny. Surely every lake of a respectable size is going to have a rowing club? No. Every river seems to have a rowing club on the other side of the Pennines but the nearest I can find to us is at Talkin Tarn, an hour plus drive away on the other side of Carlisle. A tarn is a small lake and this one is perhaps half a mile long. When I enquire I am told that the club is running some learn to row courses for all ages of beginners following a surge of post-Olympics interest.

Since I am going to have to drive Oliver to the club I reckon I might as well enrol myself. This is not music to Oliver's ears, 'What? I'm not rowing with you,' he spits in disgust.

'Don't worry, there are separate boats for juniors and seniors,' and then, just because I can, I continue, 'and then when we both know what we are doing we can make up a father and son pair and enter some regattas.' It's the sort of fantasy most fathers have; being able to participate in sport alongside their sons. Whether it's a bonding thing or just a lame attempt to recapture some lost youth, who knows? Certainly playing alongside Oliver on the rugby field would be preposterous (although a friend of ours whose boys play with Oliver has overcome this obstacle by getting involved as a coach and touch line judge. His boys were at first horrified but, powerless to resist, they are now resigned to it.

The truth is, in rowing, it is possible for us to compete together, mainly because it involves sitting down but this was a consideration far from Oliver's mind when he first suggested taking up rowing.

Oliver takes to the sport with great enthusiasm, he has natural rhythm and that coupled with his all round sporting prowess makes him an instant hit at the club. I am equally keen but my enthusiasm most definitely outweighs any natural ability but I also know it is good exercise as I am bent double by the time I clamber out of the boat after a two hour session.

As the nights start to draw in and autumn takes hold the impracticalities of a two hour round trip for a two hour rowing session become apparent and, having both passed our learn to row courses we concede that it is just too far away in the winter and that we will have to be fair weather summer rowers. The secretary of the club is not surprised, 'You'll be like 80 per cent of the rest of the members so don't worry, there are plenty of regattas just for fun during the summer, perhaps you could row as a father and son pair?'

I look at Oliver, he looks anywhere but back at me. We've got the winter to make a decision on that. He suggests we acquire a rowing machine which I can see gathering dust in the garage. It may be that marathon running is a better bet for us – no costly investment in equipment to put a price on failure.

'It's something the whole family can get involved with,' I enthuse one Sunday morning.

'I'll drive the support vehicle carrying water and sponges,' Wendy offers.

Oliver seems vaguely engaged but Emily makes quite clear the futility of even bothering to canvas her opinion.

'Or cycling,' I add 'it's pretty much sitting down.'

'Ridiculous,' is Emily's considered response.

The goats are a big hit over the summer. They do, indeed eat everything we give them and they are loved and petted by a constant stream of guests. Amy remains the friendlier of the two but as autumn approaches Ben's mood changes. He begins to bare his teeth and make strange grunty, barking noises. Reg tells me it is his response to Amy's readiness to mate. Armed with this knowledge I tell Wendy there are decisions to made, if we don't want baby goats in the spring now is the time to separate them.

She wavers ever so slightly from her initial idea of a small milking herd and it's enough of a chink in her armour for me to exploit.

'They're lovely, but really, are you going to sit on a milking stool at the back end of a goat in February?'

We decide separation is the best plan. Unfortunately, Ben does not agree and he is dragged very reluctantly to an adjoining field. Amy, on the other hand, couldn't seem to care less, perhaps relieved to be free from Ben's constant attentions which latterly have involved the prominent display of a long, thin pink and very unsightly penis. It's a display which hasn't gone unnoticed by some guests' children and another compelling reason for discouraging further goat conjugal relations.

'He's not happy,' I tell Wendy as I leave Ben butting furiously at the wire fence, 'I think we've taken on more than we bargained for.'

A few days later we are driving home from picking up the children from school. There's a commotion ahead and someone is standing in the road signalling for the traffic to slow.

I wind down the window and ask what is going on. 'Two goats are running around on the dual carriageway,' we are told. Cold sweat, heart in mouth, lurch in the stomach doesn't really cover it.

Thankfully Wendy, realising this is ultimately a situation of her making, jumps out of the car to take charge. 'Stay here,' she commands.

'Gladly.'

Emily, plugged into her music and therefore plugged out of life, looks up, removes one earphone and asks what's going on. I explain, pretty sure of her response.

'Ridiculous,' her head shaking in disbelief and she plugs herself back in.

Oliver shows marginally more interest in the unfolding debacle. 'Well this sort of thing doesn't happen every day. Never a dull day at Augill Castle. Maybe you could put that in your marketing Dad.'

Wendy, with the help of a couple of local farmers manages to get Amy and Ben into a neighbouring field. Whether due to the excitement of the escapade or the trauma of the capture, Ben's penis seems to be bigger than ever and very shiny and something tells me this is not good.

Pretty much everyone we ask shares my feelings and so it comes as no surprise that the following February we have two new kids. Billies.

'Not exactly a milking herd then.' I point out.

'Oh but aren't they cute?' Wendy is smitten.

As we continue to ride the crest of the 2012 wave, trouble is brewing closer to home. All is not well in the Blanchard-Cafferty camp.

Following a wildly successful and really very good fun wedding weekend for Rupert and Hamish, Martin apparently descended into something of a black hole. Nobody could really understand it. Clarissa said she thought he was probably just feeling his age, having been surrounded by so many lively young things. Certainly it didn't seem that he had any particular problem with his son's overt affirmation of his sexuality but for several months after the celebration he refused to discuss the weekend, his children or very much else. Clarissa has become increasingly worried and turns to Wendy, of all people, for advice.

'Do you think he's having one of those... you know... mid-life things?'

'What, you mean a crisis?'

'Oh it's such a dreadful word. I prefer to say a mid-life hiatus.'

'Clarissa,' Wendy is taking a direct approach, 'it's still a crisis, even if it's all in his head. We've all been through this sort of thing.'

> *I: 'Everyone needs a sounding board. For us it became each other and we became the stronger for it so that gradually others began to see us a source of strength: "Oh Wendy and Simon are so together; Wendy and Simon can do anything".'*
>
> *She: 'Don't dismiss that. People wouldn't say it if it wasn't true.'*
>
> *I: 'But we always imagined it went with the territory of hotel-keeping. You know, keeping up the facade looking serene while chaos reigns behind the scenes.'*
>
> *She: 'That is what most people's lives are like and I think you know that now.'*
>
> *I: 'I do. But there are still questions that can only be asked of a parent. Not always because they are the only one to have the answer but because they are the only one who would understand the question. We are all products of our past and of our lineage. If there are gaps in our knowledge of who made us what we are, how and why, aren't there gaps in our understanding of ourselves?'*
>
> *She: 'But I don't think you're unique in feeling that. The trouble is many of the questions of which you speak never do get asked by anyone of their parents or grandparents because they often only become apparent when there's nobody left to ask.'*

CHAPTER NINE

Pop tarts, food fads and a wallpaper allergy

Energised by our Olympic experience we feel we can take whatever our guests throw at us. It's that feeling of invincibility again – but sometimes that can be a pretty tough call.

The saying goes that we are what we eat. Now, if food is the key to our identity, I'm a pretty mixed up character. There's very little I won't eat. Our bodies are programmed to crave meat, sugar, fat and salt. They'll put up with fruit and vegetables at a push (which is presumably why they get pushed out so efficiently) but I can't help wondering where some people's food fads come from.

Since we opened the castle we have offered set menus in the evenings with everyone sitting together and eating the same thing. It's like one big happy dinner party and it's supposed to be very jolly. In order to make sure everyone gets something they can eat we ask for food preferences in advance and then plan a meal accordingly.

Simple.

Well, you'd think so. The trouble is we're rather too accommodating and ask such open questions as 'is there anything you can't eat or don't like?' We're no strangers to food allergies, preferences and foibles but even so, some people take things too far.

A few summers ago we employed a chef for the summer. We'd been courting Owen for a couple of years having first found him when he looked after us for a week in a ski chalet. Talented as he was, he was appalled that we should be so accommodating of our customers' whims and suggested we use a different approach along the lines of 'is there anything that might kill you that we should avoid feeding you with?'

A tad over the top but to be fair we have now changed our wording and ask about 'dietary requirements' which sounds a little clinical but change was needed.

No celery, no bananas, no hearts (as if), no brains. No tomatoes and beans together on the same plate, no trout but salmon is OK, no red meat except for lamb, pork, duck and venison. No cheese unless it's cooked, no milk in things but OK on cereal. Things are in danger of getting out of hand and that is without the ethical/religious choices and bona fide medical conditions.

It's Friday and Penny is booking a family room for later in the year. When we ask about her dinner requirements she is quick to tell us that she is Jewish.

'So, no pork or shellfish?' Wendy confirms.

'Well I do like a little bit of bacon as a treat,' she confides, 'and the odd sausage on a Sunday,' but other than that no pork. In other words, as long as it doesn't look like a pig, it's OK and Wendy makes a mental note not to dress the table with a pig's head with an apple stuffed in its mouth.

Paradoxically, when Penny is then asked to pay a deposit she says she can't because it's the Sabbath. 'I'll have to call back tomorrow.' Presumably God doesn't care too much about pork eaters as long as they haven't maxed their Amex card on a Saturday afternoon.

But this is all nothing compared with the guests who give us no warning at all.

Today we have staying a couple who have said nothing during booking about food preferences.

'Oh, just to let you know, I'm pregnant,' I'm told on checking them in.

'Oh, congratulations,' I reply.

She tuts, indignant that I should have the temerity to comment, 'so, is that alright for dinner?'

I'm unsure whether she's asking me if the chairs are going to be big enough, whether she is expecting us to have a birthing pool on standby or whether she's referring to the food. I plump for the latter.

'Well what would you like to avoid?'

'The usual.' Therein lies the problem because everyone's take on pregnancy is different. I give her a quizzical look hoping this will elicit more detail.

'I don't do liver, soft cheese, unpasteurised cheese, eggs or anything cooked in alcohol.'

'OK, no prob…'

'I can't eat undercooked or raw meat, pate…' and then she reels off a list of vegetables which seems odd. It sounds as if the only thing she has been able to eat is a copy of the National Childbirth Trust booklet.

Well, we're having supreme of chicken stuffed with sundried tomato and olive tapenade followed by a trio of lemon desserts.

'Is the chicken organic?'

'No but it is free range.'

'Well I can't eat that, it'll have too many hormones and lemon will be too acidic for me in my condition.'

I can't really see the problem with a few hormones in chicken, maybe the baby will just be born with slightly bigger muscles – saves on baby food but I keep my thoughts to myself. 'Leave it with me,' I say but she is decidedly edgy at the thought of not being in total control.

However, this all pales by comparison with the dietary requirements imposed on children by their parents.

'Tess only eats cheese on toast, American cheese,' I am told one afternoon by a singularly authoritative Californian lady as she pushes past me at the front door (my initial impression is that I wasn't quick enough with the drawbridge).

'Where's your kitchen? I want to see the kitchen and the cheese.' As she is rummaging through the fridge she comes upon some Edam cheese. 'What's this?'

'It's Dutch, it's probably the closest thing we have to American cheese.' This is a punt in the dark as I have very little experience of American cheese beyond Monterey Jack and McDonald's cheeseburgers.

'Ooh I'll try that,' pipes up Tess.

In a sickly sweet voice her mum replies, 'I don't think you're going to like it pumpkin,' confirming exactly who really has the food hang-ups in this family.

Twenty minutes later Mr Food-Fad appears at the kitchen door. He has come to show me how to make the cheese on toast.

It's too much! I brace myself.

'Do you carry on like this everywhere you go?' I ask, 'I can't imagine many hotels allow you to give instructions to the chef.'

He just smiles and says, 'That's what makes this place so special because it's not like most other hotels.'

He's won me over, I can't and don't want to argue with that.

'Well I do know how to grill cheese on toast, trust me.'

He says he does but adds he'll do whatever it takes for a quiet life. The cheese on toast goes down well but Mrs Food-Fad is already stressing about breakfast.

'Tess likes lots of fresh fruit. We're from California you see. You will have fruit for breakfast? Strawberries? Fresh mind, they must be fresh.' As she goes on to demand bottled water as she wouldn't want to risk the the tap water I'm wondering to where she thinks she has come – this is Cumbria not Afghanistan.

Next morning the breakfast table is groaning with fruit. There are blueberries, raspberries, strawberries, mangoes, bananas, kiwi, apples, pears, plums, grapes. All fresh. The food miles could get us all to the moon and back.

It's all ignored. Tess (or rather Tess's mum) has brought her own Pop Tarts.

Mr Food-Fad hands the offending article to one of our girls and says 'would you like me to show you how to cook it?'

I'm glad to say she declines the offer and as she returns with the steaming hot tart he turns to his daughter and asks, 'would you like me to cut the crusts off for you?'

☙ ☙ ☙ ☙ ☙

Somebody who knows me better than is good for them bought me a book last Christmas: *Is It Just Me Or Is Everything Shit?*

Having experienced the Olympic and Paralympic Games first hand we might have been forgiven for thinking that the utter banality and vacuousness of everyday encounters in Britain has been abolished.

Sadly not.

At Augill Castle we have made it our mission to be an antidote to the banal, the pointless and the bland. On the whole, certainly according to the majority of our customers, we succeed, with the facilities we provide, but most importantly in the way we interact with our guests. But just when I manage to deceive myself into thinking that our efforts might not be isolated I venture out of our little bubble into the real world and reality once again presses down on me.

Today is one of those days.

It starts with an appointment with the optician. There's a queue. Eventually I reach the front but before I am even allowed to step up to the counter, banal interaction is instigated.

'Who's next there please?' asks Selina the customer service assistant.

Obviously I am since I'm already here. I'm keeping it brief and businesslike. 'Mr Bennett, I have an appointment at 10.15.'

After a short pause, Selina repeats, 'Mr Bennett, Augill Castle. Ooh, it's not really a castle is it?'

'Yes, it is.' Clearly there is a processing failure here as Selina doesn't react.

'We have an appointment at 10.15 for yourself.' It isn't a question but I know it is meant as one, a) by the upward inflection of the last sylllable b) because why else would she repeat the sentence? And who is yourself? Didn't he once go by the name Cat Stevens?

'I want to say yes, myself has an appointment,' but can't be bothered.

'Please take a seat there for me.'

'I'll take a seat but it'll be for me, not you,' I mutter.

I'm decidedly unfriendly in the optician's little grey examination room. The little grey optician inside doesn't inspire much either, especially after he tells me that my increasing difficulty to read small print close up is an inevitability of the ageing process. Smug little bastard. At least I can see something which is more than he'll be able to once I've poked his eyes out.

'Just pop your chin on this cradle for me.'

What does he mean, pop? And I'm not doing it for him, I'm here for me. Eventually I am released from the little grey cell. 'Janice will accompany you back to the sales floor.' The sales floor – in other words, where the glasses are – is right outside the examination room but am I not to be trusted to find my way there by myself with my geriatric eyesight?

'Would you like to choose some frames there for yourself today?' Janice chirps.

I'll correct your English for yourself here today but I'll come back with my wife to choose some glasses for myself thank you.

'Not today thanks.'

OK, lovely, is there anything else I can help you with there today?'

There? Where? What? 'Oh yes, can I get an oil and filter change for my car and skinny latte and muffin to go please there today from yourself?' I leave Janice looking bemused while Selina continues to happily process the queue.

'How can I help yourself there today?'

In another part of the shop I have some toiletries to buy. I fill my basket and scurry to the counter. There is only one cashier on duty and she is discussing the comparative merits of two types of shampoo in detail with a customer.

'This one will be better for yourself. It's for shine and bounce.'

'Which one?'

'The Pantene.'

'Four pounds ten?'

Lord help us, this is what you get for venturing on to the high street before lunchtime. From the other side of the shop comes a clarion call, 'would anyone there like to pay here at the cosmetics counter.'

I'm here or even there ahead of anyone else. My eyesight might be failing but I've still got a good 30 years on all the other shoppers.

Further down the high street I find myself in a shop browsing through rails of discounted designer label clothes. I am quite happy leafing through the jeans when from over my shoulder comes a familiar phrase, 'Is everything alright for yourself today?'

What is this, a clothes shop or a counselling service? How long have you got? I decide to test the question.

'What exactly do you mean?' I ask as sweetly as my mood will allow. The girl, who isn't unattractive, stares at me. Her mouth pouting like a goldfish is unattractive. 'What does your question actually mean?'

'I just wondered if you needed any help.'

'But that's not what you asked, you asked me if everything is alright. Well, it's not. I am getting old, instead of stocking up on contraceptives for the weekend in the chemist's I'm buying laxatives and my failing eyesight means I can't even read the instructions on the packet. Do you offer a personal shopping service?'

'Umm, no.'

'Do you offer a measuring or tailoring service?'

'No.'

'Do you have further stock in the back room?'

'No, just what's on the rails.'

'Yes, I do need help, but it's not the sort of help yourself can help me with there today. Thank you.'

All by myself I decide on a jumper, take it to the cash desk where there is a queue. When it is my turn to pay I work out that cashier number three is ready to serve me but that doesn't stop a disembodied voice telling me so anyway. 'Cashier number three please.' Another grammatical catastrophe.

'Sorry to keep yourself waiting there today.'

'It could have been worse, myself might have been waiting somewhere else yesterday.'

'I beg your pardon?' It's the most coherent sentence I've heard all morning but I've almost lost the will to live.

'Never mind.'

'Is that everything for yourself today?'

Yes. It most certainly is.

The economic downturn (let's all call it anything other than a depression because that's just too scary) is now in its fourth year. Its effects have been slow to bite and to date business hasn't taken the tumble we'd feared but the number of weddings which are a vital income stream for us have started to fall away dramatically. This hampers our ability to invest and keep the castle in tip-top condition. Trying to get any funds out of the bank or the building society is hopeless so we must just make the best of what we have to hand.

For a couple of years before the economy went pear-shaped we'd had the luxury of being able to employ decorators. While decorating has never been my favourite job I am very good at it, having decorated everything at least once when we first renovated the castle. When we could afford them the decorators' value was always in their speed of delivery rather than the quality of the finish and Wendy always dreaded my litany of complaints about joins in the paper not meeting and unmatched patterns but, as she was fond of pointing out, 'they take about a tenth of the time you do, Simon.'

'Perfection, darling, comes at a price.'

'Oh don't I know it,' and I'm not entirely sure I follow her line of thought.

So, with decorating desperately needed and no spare cash in the bank, I am once more pressed in to action. Apparently it is quite common for people to develop an allergy to something they have been exposed to excessively.

I know of someone who adored strawberries but after years of gorging herself on them every summer (in the not too distant past when strawberries were a delicacy reserved for about six weeks each year) she found herself developing a rash to the extent that eventually she ended up looking like a soft fruit herself and now she can't go near the things. Mother-in-laws are another common example, and while it is often more difficult to limit exposure to them than to soft fruits, the benefits of cutting down are usually profound and long lasting. Happily I have not encountered either of these allergies as I don't much care for strawberries (unless blended and consumed as part of a Daiquiri) and my mother-in-law lives on another continent.

However, I fear that after years of doing it at the castle, I have developed a severe allergic reaction to wallpapering. I'm told that allergies can manifest themselves in many different ways and there are certainly several indicators to suggest this allergy is real. While these symptoms are attributable to me, research has shown that they are common among others of a similar disposition, particularly in conjunction with a rare condition known as crumbling castle (or country house) custodianship syndrome.

The first is behavioural. At every suggestion of a makeover I suffer an outbreak of irrational rage. Thankfully these episodes are short lived but they can be quite violent, damaging and harmful to those nearby. These initial outbreaks are followed by a more prolonged bout of chronic procrastination. Symptoms will vary according to each sufferer's personal circumstances, but for me include unauthorised reorganisation of bookings to occupy rooms due to be decorated, a sudden and inexplicable loss of all decorating equipment and in extreme cases, self harm such as leaping off the top of a ladder and breaking an ankle. Happily this last symptom has only been documented once and whilst the procrastination stage can last up to three months, if caught early and treated with a strong dose of spousal disapproval, usually wears off after about a week. If symptoms persist a holiday is a marvellous cure-all, although sadly not available on prescription.

Once these early symptoms have passed and supposing, as is invariably the case, that the root cause of the problem still persists, there is usually little alternative to working through the condition. This is known as aversion therapy but brings with it an alarming array of side effects. These do not all occur simultaneously (fortunate as death would surely follow), and sometimes one or more of them may not present at all.

First, there is a sort of hallucinogenic state in which I become entranced by the wall to be papered. This can result in periods of total immobility lasting several hours if I am not discovered. The only treatment is a mug of hot tea accompanied by something sweet (custard creams are particularly effective). Note that the consumption of alcohol while actively engaged in any stage of wallpapering is extremely inadvisable as it renders me totally incapacitated and can, in extreme circumstances (particularly at the start of a whole room makeover) either send me right back to a state of irrational rage or intensify the hallucinations convincing me that the job is finished before it has even begun.

If the first dose of tea is not successful further doses may be administered up to a maximum of 48 in any 24 hour period. Usually two or three mugs are sufficient (it remains unclear whether it is the effect of excessive caffeine or repeated urination that has the desired effect of breaking the trance). Medication should rarely be taken on an empty stomach and tea is no exception. The medicinal qualities of custard creams have already been noted, but the added effectiveness of accompanying cake should not be under-estimated.

Once the first drop of wallpaper has been hung, the most severe allergic reactions usually pass, however, in a typical four walled room, (a scenario sadly lacking in most castles) the hallucinogenic trance often reappears at the end of each wall and so it is vital that the course of tea does not cease. Ongoing symptoms which usually do not subside until the wallpapering is complete include breathlessness, excessive sweating, involuntary huffing and puffing, self mutilation (usually with a sharp craft knife) and a gradual loss of the will to live which becomes more pronounced the bigger the job.

These symptoms have no cure but can be significantly alleviated by repeated reassurances from the carer (the tea-bringer) that it is absolutely the best wallpapering they have ever seen. There is no possibility of over-dosing on this particular remedy and it is recommended that this should also form an integral part of the post traumatic recuperation process once the actually allergic reaction has eased. It is universally acknowledged that pointing out any defects such as dodgy pattern matches or overlapping edges can have a very detrimental effect on the speed of recovery.

There are further rare complications, the possibility of which need to be borne in mind. These include temporary paralysis at the top of the ladder, sometimes displaying an array of the above symptoms, internalised rage, very difficult to spot, usually brought on by the discovery of a drop of wallpaper cut too short and often closely followed by self mutilation, irrational screaming at the wall as if it were a living, cognoscente being or berating the wallpaper with warnings that this is its last chance to cooperate, or else. These psychological symptoms can be alarming to anyone who has not encountered them previously and the best advice is not to panic, but to talk through the issue. Further tea usually helps and stabilisation of blood sugar levels with more cake is recommended.

Eventually, of course, the allergic condition passes, once the cause, i.e. the makeover, has been completed. There is often a short but very intense outbreak of uncontrollable euphoria when all the decorating equipment has been safely put away out of sight and this is the one symptom for which tea has no effect whatsoever. The only treatment at this stage is champagne in summer or sloe gin in winter. As both these fruit-based elixirs are clearly bursting with vitamin C, there is currently no medical advice available as to a safe maximum dosage in any 24 hour period and liberal consumption should be encouraged until the equilibrium of body and mind have been fully restored.

Of course, in the most extreme cases there may be no alternative to seeking professional help. This I have had to do on a couple of occasions when I was simply incapacitated by chronic procrastination. However, calling in the professionals should be seen as very much a last resort since once they have completed the job it is common for the allergy sufferer to spin into an uncontrollable rage over how he could have done a better job for a fraction of the cost. In this event, professional help of a different kind may be the option of last resort.

But professionals of either sort are not an option so I do, eventually set to the task and yes, the results are magnificent.

She: '*You have become very sure of yourself.*'

I: '*Oh really? Do you mean that invincibility thing? It's all front.*'

She: '*Your father was the same.*'

I: And you?'

She: '*Oh I was never sure of anything. I died unsure if anyone cared.*'

I: '*That's crap.*'

She: '*But I was taken for granted, although to be fair, many women of my generation were. We were just appendages to our husband's careers.*'

I: '*Yes, well, I think Dad realised that rather too late.*'

She: '*He's been here hasn't he?*'

I: '*He has but he won't be coming back, we made peace with each other and I think...*'

She: '*Don't be so sure of that. If you've made your peace then there's maybe a relationship to be had.*'

I: '*So you've stuff still to say?*'

She: '*I'm listening first, I think there's a lot I missed.*'

I: '*Shall I tell you about some of the shit that really gets me wound up?*'

She: '*I'm a captive audience.*'

CHAPTER TEN

The death of manners, the death of grammar and the death of a neighbour

Whether it's coincidence or just opportunity, the downturn has seen electronic communication transform what we do. There's no doubt that email is quicker and more efficient but there is a basic disconnect between electronic communication and a people focussed industry such as ours and I can't help but mourn the death of manners as a result.

I was brung up proper Guv, honest.

Indeed I was. In a time before mobile phones, personal computers or multi-room TV my formative years were shaped by having to wait my turn to use the telephone (which was in the kitchen so was anything but private, meaning any conversations needing a degree of confidentiality were conducted face to face), accepting without question that my parents had first choice of the three TV channels and engaging in family conversation over dinner every night (and all afternoon on a Sunday as there wasn't anything else to do or anyone to see because my friends were all doing the same with their families).

Of course it wasn't all perfection but it was a different way of life. And while I grudgingly accept that things change and that our reality is now and not then, what I do mourn as a casualty of the communication revolution is the demise of manners. Etiquette which I learnt by osmosis is on it's death bed and not just at the hands of young people – everyone, it seems to me – is becoming a lot less polite and when one tries to do things properly one is lambasted for it.

When Dad died in 1991 the task of relating the news fell to me. I went through his address book and rang those I knew personally and sent a handwritten note on to those I didn't. We still have the dozens of letters that we received acknowledging his passing and eulogising about the part he played in other people's lives. It was an essential part of the mourning process and a decent, respectful way to mark the end of a life. Those letters are a lasting record of my father's worth.

I wasn't taught this at school. We didn't have mourning classes or a dealing with grief curriculum and I didn't know this was the correct etiquette from experience – I hadn't lost a father previously – I just knew it was the right way to do things.

> I: 'When you died in 2009 as I was preparing to embark on the same process I began receiving condolences.
>
> 'By text! 'Sorry 2 hear about ur mum' and 'sad news hope all ok'.
>
> 'What the fuck? In many instances that was all there was. No letters, no cards, no reminiscences, no closure. Just text messages so fleeting they diminished the life the passing of which they were marking.'
>
> She: 'What did you expect, black edged correspondence cards?'
>
> I: 'Well, actually, yes.'

It's nice to receive invitations, because it's nice to have something to prop up on the mantelpiece or the piano, we designed special formal invitation cards for a garden party to celebrate our national award in 2009 (as much as a keepsake as anything because most guests had already been asked to keep the date – yes, by email, of course). But incredibly this little piece of social etiquette has also been greeted with derision in some quarters. It's as if the decline of manners isn't enough and any attempt at formality or correct social etiquette is not only seen as out of place but is actually regarded as the wrong way of doing things in a modern world.

Do Oliver and Emily write thank you letters after Christmas and birthdays? The hell they do, it's a text or a phone call. 'Who writes letters any more,' Emily snorts, 'ridiculous.'

I can't change other people's perceptions but I can stick to my own guns.

Day to day this erosion of social nicety extends into every form of communication. When I call the bank or the phone company, or anywhere for that matter, I am referred to as Simon by complete strangers. Rarely am I asked if I may be addressed as such and my response is dictated by my mood and the reason for my call. If I am complaining then it is Mr Bennett and they shall be Mrs Singh or Mr Patel. But there again I know I am trying in vain to hold back an advancing tide. For our last Christmas gathering we sent out embossed 'At Home' cards. Our friends are not an uneducated bunch but only one person knew the correct way to respond and several people did not reply at all.

So my last stand is email. In the days of letters we would write a reply which would begin something like this:

Dear Mr Jones,
Thank you for your letter of 5 May in which you request a reservation of a room arriving on...etc, etc.

This gives the correspondence context but more importantly it doesn't make the assumption that yours is the only letter to land on Mr Jones' desk or, indeed, the most important one of the day.

Nowadays an email exchange has lost all manners. It intrudes into one's day demanding to be read in a way a letter doesn't – its envelope lending a patience all its own – and if there isn't an instant reply, the sender is often on the telephone demanding to know why. It is the rudest of assumptions that we all have nothing else in our lives but to read your emails Mr Jones.

Furthermore, the laziness and brevity with which communication is now conducted means that its context can be practically indecipherable. I might write an email to a customer like this:

Dear Mr Jones,
Thank you for your reservation of a room on 29 July. We note that you have booked on a bed & breakfast basis. Would you like to book dinner on the night of your stay? etc, etc

It may be days or even weeks later when this reply might come back:
Yes.
Who? What..?
Need I say more? I shall continue to write emails as I was taught to write letters with the courtesy not to assume that I am the most important person in the recipient's day and therefore with the assumption that they do not have copies of all my previous correspondence instantly to hand.

I: 'Perhaps you'll call me pompous for all of this. I prefer to see it as cherishing common courtesy and there is precious little of that left anymore.'

She: 'No, it makes me very proud. It reminds me of your father, he was always very determined to uphold manners. But perhaps you don't want to hear how like

your father you have become.'
I: 'Once, no, but now, I don't mind. We are all our parents and our children too.
It's all part of a continuum which we can't change and it's pointless to try. All we
can do is take the best from the past and pass it on to the future.'

In fact communication is changing across the board and not for the better, especially when acronyms are added to the equation.

My recent dealings with a couple of goats and a pig have brought me into contact with the Department for Animal Health.

DAH just about says it all, particularly with regard to a recent conversation.

The first question I am asked is, 'is this your primary job?'

I know things are tough but, supporting a family with two goats and a pig? 'No dear, I have a supplementary income to make ends meet. Do you need to know about that?'

'Oh that'll be HMRC's department.'

'Will it? I thought HMRC was the department.'

Because my goats, pig and hens make me a farmer I receive an email from WHO (World Health Organisation) warning about the possibility of a new avian flu pandemic. This could be a serious business for my half a dozen hens but the responsibility for ensuring we don't all die of avian flu, or swine flu if the pig gets infected, remains with DEFRA (Department of Extinguishing Festering, Rabid Animals?), with whom I have already had contact.

If we assume we are all going to die, most likely, it seems, from some unplanned casual contact with another species, we'd better just get used to it because the weight of bureaucracy will prevent any timely intervention from the nanny state. But in the meantime, to make life a little less painful, I have a few ideas of my own, most of which, if heeded may make life a little more bearable for all of us, but particularly at the castle:

DOSE (Department for Stupid Elderly) is warning all people over a certain age or below a certain IQ to avoid any buildings with steps for fear of self-harm due to clumsiness. In fact, all people nearing retirement age (a movable feast) are urged not to leave home at all.

SLAP (Society of Lame Apathetic Parenting) is urging parents who can't keep their children under control in public places to apply for a free government backed euthanasia license for their offspring.

RSPCC (Royal Society for the Prevention of Crass Complaints) is offering generous grants to anybody who has lost the ability to see the simple pleasures in life to remain housebound so that the rest of society can get on with creating some wealth with which to fund the pensions and compensation payouts of those who do not heed the warnings of DOSE (see above).

While my newly created organisations are doing their bit, I will be enjoying a new lease of life creating a role for myself at the castle and my new area of responsibility comes with an acronym all its own. I am now responsible for a newly formed FART (Fire Alarm Response Team). It is, of course, an unpaid role but it gives me a nice warm feeling.

I suppose, should I ever be called out of bed to discharge my duties I will have FARTed.

It isn't just everyday communications that are suffering a decline in manners. There are too many people who simply do not understand the importance of social etiquette and one aspect of this is rearing its head more frequently at the castle. It could be explained as a symptom of the downturn but that's being charitable.

Wendy says we should take it as a compliment. I try but invariably end up feeling affronted. 'Sir, my affrontery knows no bounds,' I want to say out loud but only ever mutter under my breath.

I refer to the business of guests bringing their own booze to the castle or, for that matter, any hotel.

Wendy says we should be flattered because it demonstrates that guests feel more as if they are staying in a country house than a hotel which is, admittedly, our central mission, in addition, of course, to turning a profit and keeping our children in shoes.

'Oh yes', I reply to that, 'do come to dinner and bring a bottle. Perhaps some chocolates as well? And where are our flowers?'

I have less of an issue with guests drinking their own tipples in their bedrooms. Maybe because I know there is an element of karma (discomfort and inconvenience), particularly if they haven't the gumption to ask for ice to go with their gin and tonic or a proper glass from which to drink it. The mental image of someone precariously perched on their bed sipping warm G&T out of a bathroom glass last used by someone else's toothbrush is a just and delicious one.

Of course, if asked, ice, lime and the correct glasses would be forthcoming and with guest galley kitchens strategically placed throughout the castle we make chilling a bottle of BYO unreasonably easy. And so it all becomes a bit of sport; spotting the guests with the chinking bags – invariably the ones who refuse help with their luggage.

But shouldn't the self respecting hotelier (or country house host since we are avowedly not a full service hotel) draw the line at guests bringing their own bottles of wine to the dinner table, into the lounge or worse still – and this happened recently – to the bar itself (I mean, you wouldn't take your own beer to a pub would you?)

When it arises the situation is an etiquette minefield.

The Wall Street Journal sums it up well in an article entitled 'Bringing your own wine to a restaurant':

> Take something special. This is key. If you walk in with a widely available Merlot that you could have gotten (sic) at the local wine shop on the way to the restaurant, or something that's likely (sic) on the wine list, you're probably not going to be treated warmly.

That sounds like good advice, but the follow up is better still...

> Offer a glass to the waiter or sommelier or chef. Remember that the reason you have brought this wine is that it's special in some way. It's fun to share special wines, and the waiter, sommelier or chef will appreciate your generosity (and they probably won't take more than a sip anyway).

Well, in our case it may run to a small glass.

Larry and Stephanie have travelled north with their three children, Tamara, seven, Paloma, five and Leonora, three. They live in a fashionable part of north London somewhere between Islington and Hampstead where a half-decent bottle of wine in a restaurant is never going to set you back less than thirty-five quid if you're lucky.

'The drive has been a nightmare,' Stephanie wails even before she has fallen through the front door. But no sooner has she got over the stress of the journey than she is stressing about whether they should have dinner, what they should have, when they should have it. Should the children have baths before supper or after? Will there be hot water this side of six o'clock? Is it going to snow tomorrow? What will we do to keep everyone entertained for three days?

Oh, for Goodness sake! Stephanie is obviously a control freak, further evidenced by the equal spacing in age of her children, their colour coordinated outfits and Larry's air of utter resignation.

'Stop!' I scream in my head, 'you can eat whenever you like, the children can have a bath whenever they like because we do have modern plumbing this far north and there will be plenty to do. And NO, it is not going to snow, it's only October!'

Like many of our visitors from London she has arrived wound up like a tightly coiled spring, but nothing that a good dinner and a few glasses of wine can't remedy. Unfortunately, judging by the chinking of glass inside the bag I am now helping to lug up the stairs, she has BHO – brought her own!

Happy in the knowledge that she might be glugging gin and tonic without ice or lemon out of that bathroom tumbler or, worse, sipping warm Sauvignon Blanc out of a tea cup (albeit an Emma Bridgewater one) I think nothing more of it.

I run into Larry just before dinner. He is striding through the dining room clutching a bottle of red wine with the sort of label whose design clearly cost a lot more to produce than the wine inside the bottle. He clocks me and adjusts his gait to a sort of Monty Python funny walk, his arm straight down his far side holding the bottle, in an ill-concealed fashion, close beside his thigh. Stephanie has presumably commanded him to get the bottle downstairs unnoticed by any means possible. Of course, I am the epitome of discretion.

Later, at the dinner table the same bottle sits between the couple at the end of the table. As I enter with the first of the starters Stephanie turns the bottle so that the label is facing away from me. Well, that must make it OK then although I'm very tempted to ask if they have brought their own dinner for re-heating.

But seriously, what to do? To charge corkage or not? After all, we have a fully stocked bar, a short but comprehensive wine list, all of which costs a considerable amount to set up and maintain. Believe me, it would be far easier to do away with the bar altogether, give everyone a nice cup of cocoa after dinner and have them all in bed by ten but then there would be complaints. We are left struggling to decide the correct etiquette to deal with a guest's complete lack of it.

Unfortunately Stephanie and Larry aren't sharing their wine with anyone. Just as well, it's cheap. *The Wall Street Journal*'s advice covers that too:

Don't do this just to save money. Take your own because it's your birthday and you have a bottle from your birth year, or because you have a bottle that's more interesting than anything the restaurant offers, or because you have a special bottle that you've always wanted to open, or because the bottle is unique in some way.

On another occasion a young couple from Yorkshire visit us as part of their honeymoon. They are loved up, not only with each other, but with life and with the castle.

Gary and Rachel appear at the kitchen door a few hours after arriving. 'We've been given a bottle of champagne as a wedding present', they tell us, slightly sheepishly, 'we were wondering if you'd mind if we chilled it and enjoyed it with you later.' And with that simple gesture the etiquette dilemma is solved.

This minefield isn't a problem confined to us, of course, if *The Wall Street Journal*'s extensive advice is anything to go by:

> Call ahead and ask if you can bring your own bottle, and ask about the corkage fee. From the response, you'll get a sense of how the restaurant really feels about this. Have some of the restaurant's wine first. This shows good faith.

All of this is really just simple common sense and good manners and the maitre d' (that's me!) won't cringe the next time he sees you. There is one final piece of advice from *The Journal* which should resonate with everyone:

> Be discreet. Maybe the restaurant doesn't encourage people to bring their own, but makes exceptions for nice people like you.

Everyone knows bringing their own is stretching the bounds of a hotelier's hospitality but there's a fine line between discretion (a quiet word at the kitchen door) and secrecy judging by the way some guests deal with their empties which we have found stuffed behind wardrobes, hidden under sofas or even sneaked into the bottle bin (that's called TYO: Trash Your Own!). Some guests have even taken their own empties away with them.

So, if you must BYO, offer us a glass and we'll love you forever and if your luck's in we'll be on some desperate diet or other involving no alcohol.

☙ ☙ ☙ ☙ ☙

Just sometimes, while we are being consumed by the little irritations of life, something quite momentus shakes everything down and reveals a whole new world of possibilities.

It's the end of summer, the children are getting ready to go back to school, the castle is full of families enjoying a last gasp of summer holiday before we all share a collective parental gasp of relief as the school term begins.

We have promised our two the now customary family day out in Blackpool but our plans are thwarted with the announcement of the hotel inspector who stayed anonymously last night and now requires a full tour of the castle.

'Well that's OK, Laura can show her around,' I tell Wendy. Just as we are getting ready to leave for the day, Laura comes running up to us, panic etched into every corner of her face, the hotel inspector in tow, consulting a clipboard.

'What's up?' I ask, thinking they must have uncovered something unsavoury in a neglected corner of the housekeepers' cupboard.

'Dead, he's dead,' she gasps. Oh fuck, not again, two guest deaths in as many years might start to tarnish our reputation. But Laura is pointing towards the house of one of our two remaining sets of neighbours and it's the one who lives in the only remaining portion of the castle which we don't own.

To say we had a perfect neighbourly relationship with our neighbour would be a lie. Running a hotel with on-site neighbours to consider has presented some challenges and I'm sure it hasn't been easy for him at times. Tensions have boiled over on occasion and latterly we've both found the best way to rub along is to have as little to do with each other as possible.

His house is part of the stables and overlooks the castle's central courtyard, where we go about our daily business, as well as having an uninterrupted view of the west of the property where we have, as a result, been reluctant to stage parties or events to take advantage of the five acres we own which enjoy the setting sun in consideration of his privacy.

When we first moved to Augill we had bought just the main castle building with all the outbuildings – the Stables cottages, the Orangery, and the Coach House occupied by six sets of neighbours. We have always tempered our commercial activities to take account of their neighbourly sensitivities.

The postman has found him on the ground between his front door and his car and calls 999. As Laura is showing the hotel inspector around, a paramedic comes bounding up to them and tells them what is going on.

'Well this is a first,' the inspector says cheerily, having finished annotating her clipboard. What she is writing can only be summised. 'Good night's sleep but no guarantee of waking in the morning,' perhaps. Just then there's a juddering sound and the windows begin to rattle. It's the air ambulance landing on the lawn.

'Not quite a first,' I reply, wearily, the air ambulance's last sortie to the castle still fresh in our minds. As the prospect of our family day out begins to evaporate I'm unsure whether what seems the inevitable curtailment of our day trip to Blackpool is a blessing or a curse (Wendy has always hated the place, the rest of us love it for what it is – unadulterated, guilt free kitsch).

'We'd better go and investigate,' Wendy says.

'What for, he's dead?' I am no keener on an encounter than she was when our guest died and she was called upon to tidy up the corpse.

'I just want to make sure, I mean, it costs thousands to launch that helicopter, why would they send the air ambulance for a death?' Wendy replies and I can't argue with that.

We tentatively creep round to the site of the incident, Wendy not wanting to see another dead body unless she has to. A first responder, with whom we are acquainted, is crouched on the far side of the car and on seeing us simply shakes his head. It's all the confirmation we need. By this time two police cars have arrived, the air ambulance, clearly not required, has taken off and any chance of the incident being kept from the castle's guests is well and truly scuppered.

Introducing ourselves to the police, we ask if there is anything we need to do. They tell us there is not. It is, after all, a death in a private dwelling not owned by us, even if it is on the same estate and they seem quite indignant that we should have even asked.

Having already been stitched up a few years ago by the local police over a shoddily investigated road traffic accident, for which I was convicted but was clearly not to blame, I have little time for them now and their dismissal of our neighbourly concern is all I need to send me belligerently back on our way to Blackpool. We bid the hotel inspector farewell and she promises that if she has any issues she will be in touch. She's probably just happy to be leaving alive. But on our return, ten hours later, we hear how events took an unexpected and bizarre turn.

No sooner have we left than the police ask if there is anyone on the premises who can identify the body. It falls to Laura, our long suffering PA, to deal with their request.

'Surely Wendy or Simon would have been best doing that?' she asks.

'And who might they be?' the officious little policeman, to whom we introduced ourselves earlier, replies.

Laura, scarred by association by Wendy's brush with death a couple of years earlier, asks a neighbour to do the identification. 'I had little to do with him when he was alive,' she says, 'I definitely don't want to see him dead.'

Then, the police tell her that they are treating the death as suspicious and insist on interviewing all the staff on duty and the guests. By the time we return, Wendy already traumatised from a day of enforced British seaside fun, the entire castle community has been traumatised, involuntarily caught up in a real life Agatha Christie-esque murder mystery. The house has been cordoned off with blue and white crime scene tape and there is a police patrol car stationed outside.

Wendy is incensed. 'This can't be happening! How long is it going to go on for, we have a business to run?' and she goes round to ask what is going on.

'And who exactly are you?' asks the same small policeman.

It's a red rag to a bull, 'I am the owner of the castle, this is my land you are parked on and I'd ask you for a modicum of courtesy,' and then, as if to make a point she spits, 'sir.' The little policemen seems unmoved.

'I presume, having interrogated all of our staff and guests, you'll want to question us.'

'Why?' asks the little policemen, quite inexplicably.

'Because if you're treating it as a suspicious death, surely you'd want to speak to his closest neighbours – we might have vital information,' Wendy says, anger taking over from reason.

'What the hell did you say that for?' I ask her when she recounts the story.

'Because he had little man syndrome and he was rude and pissing me off.'

'Oh, well please don't repeat that when you're in custody.'

The police cordon and the police presence remain for the rest of the weekend until a post mortem reveals there were, in fact, no suspicious circumstances and our neighbour died of a heart attack.

'We could have told them that,' Wendy says dismissively, 'what a waste of everyone's time.'

We are never interrogated so any vital information Wendy thinks she might have been able to impart she is keeping to herself.

She: 'The death of manners, the death of proper English, another death at the castle. My goodness, you'd be forgiven for thinking everything in your life is going to the dogs.'

I: 'No, it's just the death of my youthful optimism in favour of middle aged cynicism.'

She: 'Oh dear me. I remember him. He was a tricky character to get along with although he was always civil to me. Things must have changed when he died.'

I: 'It changed everything. Quite by accident we'd gone from being occupiers of a house as part of a community to being the sole occupiers of an entire castle. It altered the way we run the business, the relationship we have with the whole estate. But it also created a huge dilemma.'

She: 'His was the last part of the original castle building. the final piece of the jigsaw. The key to what you'd always set out to do, to put the castle back together as one property.'

I: 'Exactly. But with the bank's purse strings as tight as ever, what chance did we have?'

She: 'You remember what Wendy always said from the beginning?'

I: 'Oh yes, somehow we will find a way.'

Conflict is not something we encourage or are particularly used to dealing with. Our staff's general longevity might attest to our non-combative style of management. We can be a little more feisty in our own relations with each other and in the privacy of our own four walls the four of us can, on occasion, let rip, especially now we know there is little chance of being overheard. My rage used to be intensified, on the rare occasion a family row did break out at the castle, by Wendy saying 'please stop,' not because it was upsetting her or the children, 'because we've got guests in.'

'Bugger the guests,' usually because the row was something castle related anyway.

There have been a couple of incidents when almighty rows have broken out that have absolutely nothing to do with us – once at a family reunion and once at a wedding. Both events that, in themselves, are second only to Christmas as hot-beds for family disharmony.

At the first we are still living in the main castle, our bedrooms opening off the same corridor as the guest rooms. The family have taken the whole castle for a night to celebrate an 80th birthday.

The family arrives in dribs and drabs on Saturday afternoon, having travelled from all corners of the country and even from overseas. All seem to be in high spirits. There are four generations – the birthday couple, their four children and spouses, their grown up children and spouses with their young offspring, the great grandchildren who are all under ten.

It is obviously the intention of the third generation, the parents of the young children, to get as drunk as possible as quickly as possible. Fine by us, it's all cash in the bank. As their drinking begins there are obviously words exchanged between them and their parents regarding maintaining some sort of responsibility for the younger generation.

'Oh fuck off,' one man says to his uncle. Well perhaps this isn't going to be as fun as we'd hoped.

The children are to have their supper early and then entertain themselves. God forbid that they should sit at the dining table as part of the celebration, that would involve some interaction from their parents whose agenda is quite different. Muriel, whose 80th birthday it is, and her husband Harold, are oblivious to all this bubbling tension, partly due to their extreme age – Harold might be the best part of ten years older than Muriel, but also thanks to their own children's efforts to shield them from what is obviously the clear resentment that their grandchildren feel about having to give up their weekend for such a lame event.

As dinner progresses the volume increases. Our instinct tells us it is the wrong sort of volume, a malevolent maelstrom rather than a benevolent buzz and we do our best to spend as little time in the dining room as possible.

'This is one family,' Wendy says, 'that definitely won't appreciate being policed by us.' Our one concession to the unfolding, or maybe unravelling, family dynamics is to make sure that Muriel and Harold are well looked after. Harold is almost entirely deaf anyway and Muriel is enjoying the close attention of her children to whom she has clearly devoted her life.

At the other end of the table things are getting very heated, enormous quantities of wine are being consumed and it seems impossible that anybody is going to remain oblivious to what is going on for much longer.

'Stop the wine,' Wendy demands, 'they've had enough.'

'Even if I could I can't,' I tell her, already sure that going into a lion's den like that and telling them they've all had enough and 'that's it, it's time for bed', is not the best strategy for keeping all my teeth, 'they're onto their own supplies.'

'Well if there's any trouble, I'm calling the police,' she continues. Fortunately, as with most group drunkenness, not long afterwards they drink themselves into quiet submission, leaving only two, a brother and sister, still intent on keeping up the volume and the arguments. At 2am, with Muriel, Harold, all their children, most of their grandchildren and all the great-grandchildren in bed we retire ourselves.

But sleep doesn't come easily. As we lie in bed the castle seems quiet but there is an uneasiness, impossible to pinpoint. 'I've never felt so uncomfortable in my own home,' Wendy turns to me, 'I feel really edgy.'

'I know what you mean but there's nothing we can do and they'll be gone in the morning.' We snuggle up and try to let sleep take us, pretty sure we're going to need our strength for the aftermath in the morning.

As we both sink into that twilight between waking and sleep there's a sudden commotion on the bedroom corridor. There is shouting, sobbing, pleading and crying. Banging too, doors and something else.

'What the fuck?' I sit bolt upright. 'This has gone too far,' And then from the front of the castle the crunch of tyres on gravel and then again.

'Nobody can be in any fit state to drive,' Wendy is horrified.

'Other than Muriel, she isn't drunk.'

'But she can't see.'

I pull on some night clothes and storm on to the corridor, adrenaline now overtaking my sense of self-preservation. Two or three people are standing in their night clothes outside their bedroom doors with that dazed, gormless look about them that hotel guests have when they have been awakened by a fire alarm in the dead of night.

'What the bloody hell is going on here? I'm fairly sure we didn't cover dealing with this sort of situation anywhere in my hospitality management degree and again Wendy's staff handbook has failed to address such a situation, 'you are guests in our home, paying or otherwise and...' My tirade is cut short by the sight of a perfectly formed fist mark in a plaster wall in front of me. 'What the fucking fuck is that?' I scream, the tirade now a full blown diatribe. I am just about to let rip again when I feel the calming hand of Wendy on my shoulder.

'Come back to bed and let these people sort out their affairs,' she says, and addressing the guests, she adds, 'I don't think there's going to be any more trouble tonight.'

Sometimes it's easy for me to imagine that Wendy was made for just this sort of occasion and certainly that's what the guests are thinking right now.

The next morning I wake feeling a little sheepish, that is until I catch sight of the fist hole once again on my way downstairs. But there is no need for contrition on my part. As soon as I am downstairs I am subjected to a barrage of apologies and even as I go to explain my own reaction I am told there is no need, it was perfectly understandable.

'Michael and Joanna had a major falling out weeks before this weekend,' I am told, 'and somehow they managed to involve all their siblings. Last night it all came to a head.'

'Well, I'm sorry to hear that but I have a fist-shaped hole in a wall upstairs and two very drunk people on the road on my conscience, what can have caused that?'

'A disagreement over their father's decision not to have further treatment for cancer. He's dying you see.'

I've been there, seen how cancer infects the whole family, not just the individual.

> I: *'That got me really angry. Dad died when I was twenty-five. We hadn't had an easy relationship. I had lived in his shadow all my remembered life. He was an accomplished sportsman, I wasn't; he enjoyed school, I didn't; he was witty and charming, I was shy and retiring; he built models and flew aeroplanes, I wrote poetry.*

Although we had the occasional stand-up row mostly our relationship was defined by a quiet lack of mutual understanding given voice predominately through you, 'Why is he always like this?', 'Why doesn't he understand me?' And my favourite, 'You ask him, he'll listen to you' which we all knew to be pure fantasy.'

She: 'He was better at listening than you give him credit for, it was voicing his feelings he didn't do so well but can you blame him for that? He was of a certain generation and a particular class.'

I: 'Well, whatever, I was angry with him for dying. By the time I was twenty-five I had begun to develop into more of the man I imagined he had, unreasonably in my opinion, wanted to see me as a boy.

'I had graduated from university, something he'd failed to achieve, and I was embarking on a promising career. I was about to show him that I wasn't the waste of space I imagined he thought I was.'

She: 'He was immensely proud.'

I: 'And then he died. Cancer. Not the quick kind; the 'I'm sorry it's an aggressive tumour, there's nothing we can do, go home and make the best of the time you have' kind. The slow, lingering 'there may be something else we can try, it's spread but we can offer you another operation' kind; the kind of cancer that permeates every aspect of family life, invites an opinion from everyone, whether they wish to give it or not; the kind that in the end delivers nothing but false hope and withers people before your eyes like vines after the grapes have gone. God knows what it must have been like for you.

'We tried to patch up our differences while he was withering away. He wanted to know all about life in London, my job, my plans for the future, usually over drinks at the village club. But he didn't really listen to what I had to say because he knew he'd never be part of it. And I knew he'd never be part of it, knew he was immune from future disappointment so I told him what he wanted to hear. We became actors in a two-handed play.

'The terminally ill inhabit the world of the undead. They are still there in body but their spirit has already been broken; has already fled so there is no meaningful communication. At the time those evenings seemed ultimately pointless other than to get drunk at the old man's expense but that was the point, to talk about anything but cancer, to pretend that death was not waiting around the corner.'

She: 'I think you know now that time was far from pointless.'

I: 'Oh I do now, but it's taken a long time to get to where I am now.'

She: 'The luxury of youth – time.'

I: 'My point is, in the end, nobody has the right to tell anybody else how to manage their own illness because it is theirs, part of their life to lead as they see fit and particularly when time isn't on their side.'

'I'm sorry but, I've had experience of this…' just as my juices begin to rise again, I feel Wendy's hand on my shoulder, 'time to get the sausages on,' she says.

So while it has been necessary to get involved with family altercations, fights at weddings are much more of a spectator sport, whether because when opening ourselves up to weddings we know that the odd fight goes with the territory or because they are usually so inconsequential as to warrant nothing more than amused detachment.

A wedding between a Mancunian groom and a bride from Liverpool was always going to be a source of potential amusement.

Perhaps not such a rich breeding ground of amusement as one of our earliest weddings which saw the coming together of the bride's Bavarian family who spoke no English and the groom's family from Leeds who definitely spoke nothing other than Yorkshire.

To accommodate a wedding of 40 plus we split our large dining table to make two long banqueting tables but it wasn't our suggestion to have an English table and a German one. Perhaps in Darryl and Jenna's case a Manchester table and a Scouse table would have been a clever idea.

The wedding is very good natured but, as can be expected, drink is in plentiful supply. It's a balmy night so much of the celebration stays outside long into the evening – something that never sits well with us as while we love the fact that people are lucky with the weather, screeching wedding frivolity, particularly when conducted in a scouse accent, barrelling across the fields towards our neighbours' open windows leaves us feeling uneasy.

As is our custom, at about 12.30, when we have made our best efforts to expel all non-residents from the castle, we retire, leaving any stragglers to put themselves to bed. As residents they can, if they wish, stay up all night drinking. Many plan to, none have managed it to our knowledge.

As we are falling into the sort of sleep that comes at the end of an eighteen hour shift, our bedroom door bursts open. Years of experience have taught me to modify my auto response and instead of 'what the fuck?' I call out 'hello, who's there?' This alarms Wendy who wakes thinking she has gone to bed with a stranger.

Shannon is one of the bridesmaids and she is very distressed. Hot on her heels is Trevor who has been trying to calm her down.

'Wendy, get some sleep, the sausages will need you in the morning, right now Shannon needs me to make her some coffee.'

I put on some shoes, I've long since learnt not to go to bed naked when there's a wedding or house party going on, and take them both downstairs.

'So tell me what is going on, which bedroom are you supposed to be in?'

'Well, I'm not with him, he's gay,' Shannon gestures towards Trevor, perhaps a little harshly, given his obvious support.

'Yes, well, I'd guessed that, so where are you supposed to be sleeping?'

'I want to go home,' Shannon wails, 'I can't stay here, I can't face everyone in the morning, not after what I've done,' and she becomes quite hysterical, 'I need a JD and coke.'

'No, what you need is a strong black coffee, especially if you're planning on walking all the way back to Liverpool.'

'Why, how far is it?' She clearly has no idea where she is or what's going on.

I turn to Trevor, 'can you enlighten me here?'

'Well, she's always had a soft spot for Darryl. I told her when Jenna asked her to be bridesmaid it might not be a good idea.'

'OK, but surely she didn't come on to Darryl today of all days?'

'No,' Trevor continues, 'I saw to that, though God knows she tried. The trouble is the other bridesmaid is Darryl's sister and she got wind of what I've been trying to keep a lid on and it all ended up in a bitch fight on the front lawn. Didn't you hear it?'

I might have done and assumed it was copulating cats or hedgehogs but I cringe at what the neighbours will have heard, 'OK, coffee and bed, I suggest she bunks down in your room Trevor, I assume you'll be quite safe. I'm sure in the morning everything will be forgotten.' I'm not, of course, but am past caring.

Chapter Eleven

The race to the bottom, the last piece of the jigsaw and a Christmas to forget

As we soldier on through the recession the children both find their own feet and are growing into fine young people. Emily is now at grammar school, has found her voice and is taking singing lessons. Oliver, after a turbulent first couple of years at secondary school, has taken a long hard look at the contemporaries he has fallen in with and, not liking what he sees, has decided to make a change and buckle down rather than be on permanent report card.

I have always counselled both that school life is a lot easier if the teachers like you and thankfully they have each taken my advice, although Emily can't help questioning my wisdom first.

'Surely all teachers treat all children fairly, I mean it's their job.'

'Well, yes ideally but they're only human like the rest of us. We should treat all our guests the same, shouldn't we, after all they're all paying for the same experience.'

She thinks about this momentarily. 'But you don't because some of them aren't very nice and it's really difficult to be nice to people who aren't nice to you.'

'Exactly.'

We have always had our share of awkward guests, it goes with the job and awkward doesn't necessarily mean unpleasant. It would be easy to imagine that a place which sets itself up to be as relaxed, friendly and open as us would not court unhappiness. But some people are happiest when they are unhappy and being their metaphorical punch bag also goes with the territory.

Unfortunately, the internet has given these people a voice and because it is they, in particular, who generally seem to have an inflated sense of self-importance it is they who will invariably vent their frustrations in public, thinking the rest of the world is bound to be interested in what they have to say. The result, in my very unscientific estimation, is that one out of ten happy guests will post an online review after their stay compared with nine out of ten unhappy guests.

We are in the age of Tripadvisor. We're told it's the age of what idealists might have, at one time, heralded as a new internet driven global democracy but I disagree.

When the global financial crisis began in 2008 we had just sixteen reviews on Tripadvisor and were still scared of it – it promised, or threatened to hand power to the people to make or break a business. We were years away from online booking. Booking.com was still a glint in a web developer's eye and people still understood the distinction of value for money over cheap is best.

We are led to believe the internet has given us all a panoramic view of the world, where everything seems possible and available. The truth is, all too often that it gives us a tunnel vision view, focussing only on what we have already decided to search for, or selecting for us what it thinks we want to search for, telescopically zooming in on far flung options and obscuring those that are right under our nose. And yet almost every week we come across local people from Penrith, Appleby and even Kirkby Stephen, who say 'we never knew you were here'.

The truth is, in the age of the internet it is easier for us to market to the other side of the world than it is on our own doorstep. The thing with the internet is that the closer to home you get, the less effective it can be. Our most effective local marketing campaign, raising local awareness to an all time high was when we stuffed leaflets through letterboxes.

In fact focussing on the local has become more important than ever. It's all too easy to overlook our own local businesses in search of the bargains the internet brings into our homes and I fear we are all in a race to the bottom.

Everywhere we look everything is being flogged off cheap. Booking.com and their ilk have been driving down prices in the travel and leisure industry for some time. Amazon have been screwing everybody and everything for years. And now there are TV campaigns for up to 70% off luxury hotels with Secret Escapes, massive discounts on sofas, beds, computers, TVs – you name it!

A new TV advertisement tells us we could get up to 75% off top high street brands. If the consumer wants everything so cheap that businesses have no choice than to slash their prices, what do we do about the wages of the staff we employ? Want our product for only 25% of its value? Well we'll have to pay our staff only 25% of their value. And guess what? Those staff are the same people who are snapping up the bargains and wondering why they're not getting a pay rise.

It's a spiral that surely is going to keep us all trapped in this bloody recession indefinitely. Will it all end when money is actually worthless, when nobody is prepared to pay for anything because they're not getting paid anything to pay with?

Or perhaps we'll all end up working in sweatshops for tuppence a day servicing the needs of the Russian and Chinese middle classes. Who knows? But mark my words, if this greed for getting everything for the cheapest price doesn't stop, we'll be the masters of our own economic destruction.

What is needed is some balance. For a start, we need to remember that price is not the same as value. Just because something is cheap doesn't mean it's good value. A filthy or tiny or noisy hotel room or a room looking out onto a brick wall can be as cheap as chips but if you don't get a good night's sleep have you had value? Likewise, something that is expensive can still be great value. In a hotel it's usually because the price enables the establishment to go the extra mile with enhanced service and attention to detail that turn a stay into an experience.

Of course, if you're the sort of person fixated only on the price, you are unlikely to even notice the finer touches, you'll still complain about the shortcomings even when you've paid next to nothing and you are every hotelier's worst nightmare – the impossible to please guest and you're probably already well on your way to the bottom clutching your bulging shopping bag of bargains in one hand and your shrinking pay packet in the other, not forgetting to leave a nasty, mean spirited review on Tripadvisor on the way.

The thinking among us can stop to consider how we can make things better for ourselves. There are thankfully still many places out there which are cherished by their customers and which reciprocate.

'Shop Local' is an emerging theme, not just for special occasions, but all year round. Your local high street – the independent bookshop, the butcher, the baker, the greengrocer – is not just for Christmas, neither is your local pub or your favourite country house hotel. They are still there but they need our support to survive this revolution of price over value.

We can start by cutting out the middle men whose cut can be near fatal in itself – the online retailers and the online travel agents who will take a 25% cut for doing nothing, will deliver you no customer service and, while guaranteeing you the cheapest room, certainly won't guarantee you the best.

Buy a book from your local bookshop and benefit from the knowledge of the bookseller as well as being able to revel in the sheer joy of browsing shelves of books you didn't even know existed.

Buy from your butcher, your greengrocer and your baker and start a relationship that will mean you getting exactly what you want because they will know what you like instead of you picking from what the supermarket has already pre-chosen on your behalf.

Book your next holiday with an independent travel agent who can talk to you about the places you're considering because they have been there and you might also be surprised at the better deal they can get you than is available on the internet. We certainly were just last week.

Book a hotel room direct and you'll get personalised service, most likely a better room and a better experience all round. In short you'll get the added value that price alone doesn't deliver.

If we value ourselves and our own worth, we should value the worth of others too. Otherwise we'll all end up poorer for it and there may well be no coming back. It's all a doom laden prophecy but it is borne out of more years than I care to number of having financial doom and gloom shoved down our necks.

We have stayed firm to our pricing, refusing to discount or sign up to online voucher or discount schemes. I might lament the voice Tripadvisor gives to the unenlightened but we have very few bad reviews and those we do have are mostly from crackpots.

Against this backdrop of customers wanting ever more for ever less, Alex Polizzi, the hotel inspector of Channel Five fame and self professed all-things-hotel guru vents her fury in *The Telegraph* at the guests who keep her in the life to which she is accustomed. She seems to have got things wrong which confirms that the way we do things is pretty much on the money.

She begins by trying to justify how hotels have to charge their guests for WiFi access because it is so expensive to install. What nonsense. Firstly, I have not been asked to pay for WiFi in a hotel for at least two years and secondly, we have WiFi throughout the castle and it costs about £40 per month.

Her argument suggests that she has been ripped off but also, by extension, suggests that other elements of a hotel set up which have proved expensive should be charged extra for. In terms of the castle that would probably be everything but the WiFi:

'Welcome to Augill Castle, do come in. The price you have been quoted gets you this far although we must inform you that you have incurred a charge for using the drive because it is costly to maintain. If you'd like to sleep in one of our beds, they are mostly antique so very valuable, the bed linen is Egyptian cotton and costs a lot to launder, so that'll all be extra.

'Do enjoy looking at the sofas in the music room but please be aware that there is a supplement for sitting on them.

'And this is our private cinema. The art deco chairs are from France and the projection system is state of the art...'

Well you get the picture. Ridiculous, as Emily would surely say.

However, as Ms Polizzi goes on, her commentary on modern hotelkeeping turns into more of a tirade and it becomes apparent that she really doesn't like guests at all. She accuses them of being kleptomaniacs and is resigned to losing anything not screwed down to light fingered visitors and says that under no circumstances would she entertain the idea of an honesty bar, likening it to a one way road to financial ruin.

What sort of guests is this lady, a third generation of perhaps the greatest of British hotelkeeping dynasties, attracting?

For our part, trust breeds honesty. It's a formula that's worked (so far) for our children, for each other, for our staff and for our guests. Yes, sometimes things go missing but they are built into the general cost of running a hotel. For every item that disappears forever, three will be returned in the post with an apology – a DVD packed by mistake, a key not returned, a book borrowed from the library.

And, of course, for every stolen item there are many items of left behind property. We have desk drawers full of phone chargers and spectacles which nobody will ever claim. Sometimes clothes end up in the dressing up box. Many larger items are dispatched regularly back to their owners. Just occasionally we receive calls from guests who have lost something, don't know where but refuse to believe that we haven't got it. Quite what I'd do with a pair of second hand hair straighteners is anyone's guess. While we trust our guests, it seems sometimes they don't trust us.

As for the honesty bar, of course we wouldn't let customers loose on one if we were a city centre hotel but our castle dances to a very different tune. This is a country house experience and country houses don't have bar staff. Help yourself and write it down. Trust us not to over charge, we trust you to be honest. There is evidence to suggest that when in doubt most people will over compensate for what they have taken rather that be seen as dishonest. As for the minority who wish to take advantage, well the hit is ours but it is more than offset by not having to pay the wages of an under-employed bar person every night.

Ms Polizzi has made a name for herself telling other hoteliers how they should be running their businesses for better profit. Perhaps she has forgotten that hotelkeeping is about much more than that.

♛ ♛ ♛ ♛ ♛

As 2012 draws to a close and our neighbour's house sits empty we realise we must do whatever we can to raise the money to buy it. Being the last remaining piece of the castle not owned by us it would be easy to assume the seller holds all the cards but I take a different view and reckon a one bedroom cottage surrounded by a hotel is not going to be many people's idea of Nirvana. So we make an offer. Not audacious but fair. To our surprise it is accepted but on the condition that we exchange contracts by Christmas.

'Well that's not going to happen,' Wendy says flatly, 'solicitors start their Christmas wind-down in November.'

We have made the offer with no way of raising the finance so we are playing a dangerous game. I pull together a hasty business plan for 100% funding based on the enhanced value the purchase will bring to the rest of the estate. To my surprise the building society doesn't reject the idea out of hand and with that glimmer of hope we set about a plan to raise funds to pay for arrangement fees, solicitors fees, valuation fees, all of which run to several thousand pounds.

We had promised ourselves, and the children, we would open for Christmas every other year.

But now the children are teenagers and the magic of Christmas is dissolving faster than a Boxing Day morning Alka Seltzer – a concept Oliver will all too soon be familiar with given his recently developed fondness for farmhouse cider – we decide to open for a second consecutive Christmas. Within a month we are fully booked and thirty odd people are coming for three nights. Because it's all last minute we ask the staff to volunteer to work, with some trepidation as they all have families of their own but we are heartened by the willingness of everyone to pitch in.

We have left none of them in any doubt about the precarious nature of the business finances and they know there isn't going to be much work in January but I don't believe either of those is what motivates them to help out at Christmas. They genuinely care for this place and they want to see it succeed. After the castle itself, they are our greatest asset and with goodwill in such abundance it promises to be a marvellous time but by Christmas Eve evening, it's obvious that everyone doesn't share our idea of what makes a perfect Christmas.

Twenty-seven of our thirty guests are revelling in the relaxed, informal, easy going house party style that is now our trademark. But a family of three are stoney faced and glaring at anyone who dares to crack a smile.

Joan, Frank and Tonia are from Liverpool. They have booked Christmas based on the description on our website and have decided to take everything at its word. It is the mildest Christmas anyone can remember so their first complaint is that fires, while lit, are not roaring as described. They take exception to the 'get to know everyone, informal buffet supper' on Christmas Eve being, well, a buffet. The suggested carols around the piano don't happen because nobody expresses a desire to sing. None of my staff is qualified to lead a sing-song, the cat would be a better bet on that front. This isn't good enough and to cap it all nobody goes to midnight mass as the website suggests they might.

'Are you churchgoers?' Wendy enquires.

'Oh no, but it'd be nice to see someone go,' they reply, perhaps in the hope of some form of vicarious redemption.

'I don't think there's going to be any pleasing those people,' Wendy tells me as we climb into bed.

'Well, never mind, I'm sure the magic of Christmas will bring them out of themselves, perhaps they're just shy.'

The next morning they are first up. 'Happy Christmas,' trills Wendy. 'Is it?' they reply. They eat and disappear.

At 1pm everyone gathers for drinks before Christmas lunch. 'Where are the Liverpudlians?' ask some guests who have managed to turn up on time. We had hoped their lack of enthusiasm might have rendered them invisible but apparently everyone has noticed their long faces.

By twenty-to-two there is no sign of them so we all sit down to eat. At 2pm they appear, their faces longer than when they left.

'Hello, sorry to have started without you, we didn't quite know where you'd gone,' I say cheerily. Wendy has bought us all Christmas jumpers and mine has a snowman on the front complete with a two inch protruding orange knitted nose, 'do you like my Christmas jumper?' I ask, lamely trying to break the ice.

'Not much. We went to Kendal but it wasn't how we remember it, all the shops were shut.'

'How ridiculous,' Emily observes later in the day when I recount the story but for now I am momentarily lost for words.

They are served by Oliver who, admittedly has had little customer service training to date but he can turn on the charm when he needs to. We decide it's best to position ourselves as a family next to them at the table but they don't make eye contact or utter a word.

'Most people would consider sitting with the hosts a bonus,' I reflect later.

After lunch we retire to our own sitting room for presents and leave the staff to clear up and guests with tea, cake and newly stoked roaring fires in anticipation of a feast for supper. An hour later John, eighteen and back from his first term at university, finds me. He is shaking.

'Those guests want to see you. They're not happy.' No prizes for guessing who those guests are.

Most guests have retired to their bedrooms for a nap but Joan, Frank and Tonia are in the hall with their coats on and their bags packed.

'We're leaving,' Joan barks, 'you should be ashamed of yourselves, calling this a hotel. The service is appalling, the food is disgusting and the welcome is about as cold as the place.'

Now, like John, who is hiding just out of sight, wide eyed at the lunacy of this exchange on Christmas Day, I'm shaking but determined not to show it, 'well I don't think everyone else…'

She cuts me off, 'Oh everyone else thinks the same, they're just too polite to say anything,' and at that I know, and I think she knows, she has lost the argument.

She throws two twenty pound notes across the hall table at me. 'What's this for?' I ask, 'you've already paid.'

'For our drinks, don't you dare accuse us of not paying our way,' and with that they're gone.

'Well at least they'll have an easy drive home. There won't be any traffic,' John says and there's pretty much nothing else to be said.

It is Emily who has the last word when I explain what has just happened. 'Ridiculous people. I hope their heating has broken down and they have to spend the rest of the day with just a cold ham sandwich between them.' She has all the makings of the perfect hotelier.

Later on the remaining guests ask, again, where the Liverpudlians are. When I tell them the manner of their departure, there's a hearty round of applause and everyone passes the rest of Christmas in a much more relaxed frame of mind.

Needless to say that is not the last we hear of them. Letters follow outlining their original complaints with the introduction of a few more and, with no offer of compensation from us, a terrible Tripadvisor review is their final act of retribution. It remains the jewel in the crown of thorns of our crackpot reviews.

Despite them Christmas is a huge success and, as well as making new friends and great memories, we make enough cash to make a deal on the neighbour's house a possibility. That's as long as we can get the finance.

The building society insists on a new valuation of everything 'which doesn't quite match the figures.' I'm not having any of it and ask for an explanation. What transpires beggars belief. The valuer, well known to both us and the building society, although, of course, totally impartial, has determined that, the last piece of the jigsaw though the property is, it brings no inherent 'marriage value' to the estate by bringing it all back into single ownership.

Wendy is beside herself. 'They've supported us all this way, encouraging us to spend, invest, backing each additional purchase and then at the final hurdle, they do this? We're only asking for £100,000, it's peanuts.'

Reminding her a hundred grand is not peanuts to most people and we're lucky to have all that we have, I know I have made a big mistake.

'I don't know what's happened to you Simon, where's your drive, your get-up-and-go. Have you given up?'

'No, of course not, I'm just saying…'

'You were like this over buying the Coach House for us all to have a proper family home. When you've got a million pound mortgage, Simon, a hundred thousand pounds is peanuts.'

Charles, our solicitor, who has been at our side since the very start, is even more incredulous, 'what utter nonsense.' It's all the encouragement I need to take on the building society.

Ten days later, following a stern but reasoned letter, to my astonishment, I receive a letter telling me the credit committee have reviewed our application and the valuer has 'upwardly adjusted his market estimation in light of additional information'. The deal is on and we eventually complete at the end of February. It's two months later than the neighbour's family had stipulated but, unsurprisingly, they didn't hassle us once we told them we had to raise finance, something I really think they hadn't imagined would be an issue. After all, doesn't everyone with a castle have a few hundred thousand spare lying around?

Having ownership of the castle in its entirety is an odd feeling and one we struggle to come to terms with. Perhaps the castle will never truly feel our own, firstly because we do share it with so many people but mostly because a place like this owns its owners as much as they own it.

That said, having now no other incumbents in the castle we realise just what possibilities are open to us to extend the scope of the business and just how restrictive having to be considerate of our more irascible immediate neighbours has been for so many years.

We hadn't been here long when that irascibility made a house call from just a couple of fields away. It's a Sunday afternoon. Oliver is a baby and we are recovering from hosting a wedding. In these early days we don't take any bookings on a Sunday after a wedding as we simply don't have enough staff to do the function and the subsequent turn-around of bedrooms.

It is a glorious afternoon, Oliver is happily playing on the grass naked with Holly, our loveable labrador. We have cracked open a bottle of wine and are enjoying the sun. It is, after all, our own front garden and nobody is coming to stay.

Three quarters of the way through the wine, we are contemplating opening another bottle when a rattly old Volvo pulls up on the gravel behind us, out of which steps the scruffiest old man I have ever seen not begging on the street. He is fat in that sort of lumpy unwholesome way that comes from inactivity rather than overindulgence, unshaven, his glasses are so filthy it is almost impossible to discern the colour or shape of his eyes and he is wearing a jumper full of holes through which an equally threadbare string vest is visible. I choose not to ex-amine his trousers or shoes.

Without introduction, he bellows, 'I suppose we must all be sub-jected to this every weekend from now on?'

I walk up the steps to face him.

'Sir put on a shirt,' he demands. Rich coming from someone who might just as well not have bothered.

'I will not, sir. What is your point and why are you here?'

'My name is of no importance to you, we shall not be friends. I live two fields in that direction. The music, if that is what you can call such a cacophony, and merriment of last night kept me awake.'

I can't help a little snort of derision, 'the cacophony was jazz and it was all over by 11.30, we made sure of it.'

'I like to be in bed by nine. This is a quiet place but I suppose you'll ruin that now with your London ways. I can't stop you, of course, but I can make my feelings known.'

It's typical of the lack of understanding from many quarters about just how accommodating of our neighbours' peace our business plans have been and we would reflect in later years how different owners might have made their lives quite unbearable.

Wendy is having no more of this. She jumps to her feet, scoops

Oliver up in to her arms and mounts the steps to join me. She is wearing her bikini with a sarong wrapped around her lower half. She is readying herself to put this dullard in his place but before she can open her mouth he puts out his arm to stop her advance. 'Madam, come no nearer, you are indecent,' and then, 'and so, madam, is your child.'

'How dare you. I don't know who you are, I don't care to know but sir, I would ask you to get off my land.' Seeing there is nothing to be gained from further intercourse with these young southern upstarts he retreats huffily to his car. As he drives away she adds, 'and don't come back.'

We later discover the chap is a reclusive academic for whom nobody really has much time or a good word; a shame as he is probably a fascinating character but, as with many like him in the country, exile is inevitably self-imposed. We have little to do with him for several years other than through reports from some guests who followed a footpath that goes past his garden gate, and were invited into the garden to join him for tea (they found him charming, if a little eccentric) until a few years later Oliver and I are out for a walk and quite by chance, we find ourselves on the very same footpath. To our surprise we are invited to stop for tea. Saying no seems not to be an option. I take this as a belated peace offering but as tea is poured and biscuits offered it becomes apparent from his conversation that he has no idea who we are. Understandable, since I have grown stouter and my hair has receded and Oliver is no longer a naked infant, but eventually he asks the killer question, 'where do you live?' I turn to point two fields back towards the castle.

'Ah,' he says, rising to his feet, his face darkening, 'I seem to have made a terrible mistake.' He takes the cups from our hands, proffers a handshake and says, 'Goodbye.'

'How strange,' Oliver says as we head home.

'You met him once before,' I tell him, 'he told you you were indecent.'

Wendy's expulsion of uninvited intruders becomes a recurring theme. It's easy to take for granted what we have at Augill: An imposing Victorian castle sitting at the foot of the brooding Pennine fells surrounded by open farmland unchanged for generations (many of the field gates are the cast iron ones fitted when the castle was at the centre of a working farm estate). It is a magnificent sight. So it should come as no surprise that we get a fair number of sightseers trundling down the drive. What is more of a surprise, even now after fifteen years, is our reaction to them.

The issue is not that they come but the manner of their arrival and then their departure which goes something like this: They turn into our entrance, past the sign which says 'Private, Residents & Guests Only', drive a quarter of a mile down the drive, usually stop at the bottom of the lawn to take a photo, drive up to the front door, stare in through a couple of windows, reverse and drive away. If we are outside or at a window, we wave. They never wave back. In the summer this happens almost daily. A friend suggested that we should turn this to our commercial advantage and sell them tea, sandwiches, scones, a £5 tour of the garden, a £10 tour of the castle. All of that is already available, bar the tours, but only to people who actually get out of their car.

Wendy finds it all so aggravating that she has been known to run out of the front door in the direction of the departing sightseers, waving both arms above her head, shouting 'wait, come back, what did we do to upset you?' adding 'fuckers' for good measure as she sees fit.

The usual response to this is a discernible increase in speed as the visitors assume they have stumbled across an asylum or some sort of rehab centre.

Only on one occasion did the visitor stop and wind down their window. Wendy might have been momentarily non-plussed by this but she didn't show it.

'Yes,' enquires the visitor, 'is something the matter?'

'Well, yes actually. How would you like it if people drove up to your front door, had a nosey through your windows and then drove away, ignoring you as they go?'

'That's not what we did,' the visitor replies.

'Yes it is, I've just seen you, I came out to greet you and you drove away.'

'We thought you were National Trust or something,' says the visitor's wife by way of unsatisfactory explanation.

'So why didn't you get out of the car, did you not like what you saw? this is my family home,' and now she's on a roll.

'Really, dear,' the visitor looks her up and down, 'in your dreams,' and they drive away.

Chapter Twelve

Wedding cakes, a complaint that cheers us up, the delights of the man-turret and getting up close and personal with some sheep

We are creating grand plans for the neighbour's old place, which is to be called The Gatehouse. My business plan to the building society which secured the funds to buy the place talked of an extension to our cookery school but there seems to be little appetite among guests for that sort of thing. To be honest, in common with all my business plans to date, it's absolute cobblers, born of desperation to get something on paper in the timescale his family had originally specified. The impracticalities of that idea prove to be a further barrier as it is a one-up-one-down dwelling so accessibility would be a big issue and since the only way to fund a project like that would be with grants, it is a non-starter, particularly since, for all our many skills, getting our hands on any public funds has always eluded us.

Eventually common sense prevails and we agree that our main money earners are accommodation and weddings and both require more bedrooms so that is what it will be. The only trouble is, we have no cash to make it happen so, for now, The Gatehouse sits empty.

Weddings have been one of our big cash cows but also one of the big casualties of the downturn. So, when we receive a last minute booking for a wedding in February we bend over backwards to accommodate it. It's a pretty low budget affair, in keeping with the times – a sort of austerity wedding – and we have done a great deal on the castle for a weekend. Despite the price tag and my consequential ambivalence we are humbled to be hosting this wedding because, so important to the bride was the venue everything has been homemade, from the dress to the cake, in order to pay for it. Cash is king and, as much for them as us, its divine right of rule is all the stronger for its scarcity.

When it arrives on Friday afternoon, the cake is quite a creation. The bride and her two sisters have made a tier each and their mother has decorated it. Apparently she went to evening classes for just this purpose. I make all the right noises but as the mother of the bride goes to hand me the cake she is taken aback by my refusal.

We're not ones for rules at the castle. It's a pretty laissez-faire sort of place. But there is one rule, or maybe you'd call it a policy, that I have: I no longer touch wedding cakes.

There have been too many instances of being screamed at by demonic mother-in-laws, so protective of their creation that if anyone comes within twenty feet of the thing they risk being cursed to be consumed by the flames of hell and if that isn't scarring enough I have had one too many accidents with wedding cakes too.

The first time I had an altercation with a mother-zilla-of-the-bride was about three years ago.

It's a sunny Saturday morning and the bride's parents have driven up from the Midlands. In the back of their Vauxhall Corsa they have brought the cake.

Given the smallness of the car I suspect they may have set off the previous evening and have been driving at 30 miles an hour for the sake of the cake which has been much anticipated by the rest of the wedding party who arrived the previous evening.

On arrival, I greet the bride's parents at the door and hold it open while they bring in various boxes. One, two, three, four, five… how many tiers can a wedding cake have?

Eight boxes are eventually lined up on the dining room table.

'So this is the famous cake,' I say enthusiastically. 'Can I see?' I ask as I absent-mindedly go to remove one of the cake box lids.

The bride's mother turns on me like a pit bull terrier and with a voice not unlike that unfortunate girl in the film *The Exorcist*, she hisses, 'Leave that alone, get your hands off it…' and then, as if warming to my cinematic metaphors, 'it's my precious, only me can have the precious…'

'Wendy, that woman is mad.'

Wendy explains that the cake with all its intricate decorations has taken six weeks to complete. On seeing the finished article I can see why. It is a fairy castle complete with towers, unicorns, goblins, flowers, enchanted trees and she's even put herself into the tableau because I am sure I can see a Golom-like creature peering out from behind a toadstool.

Still feeling bruised from my earlier encounter I observe, perhaps slightly uncharitably that if the cake has taken that long to create it's going to be pretty well stale by now.

On an equally whimsical note I have grave concerns for the safety of the bride and groom, 'if that's how she reacted to me just touching the box, what on earth,' I ask Wendy, 'is she going to do to them when they take a knife to the thing?'

'We'll probably have to throw a glass of water at her and then she'll dissolve with a little hiss,' she says, 'like the Wicked Witch of the East.'

Another mother of the groom was so protective of her cake that she slept with it the night before the wedding. More often than not brides are just relieved that the cake has got here in one piece and are happy to hand over all further responsibility thereafter. But not this one.

I suspect the bride herself couldn't have cared less what happened to the cake but then she didn't make it. When on Saturday morning, it is finally brought downstairs it is more of a funeral procession than a wedding, with the cake, which is actually encased in a wooden box, brought to it's final resting place.

'Just leave it here, I'll take care of it for you,' chirps Wendy.

'No! Don't touch it please, it's far too expensive.'

'It's just a sodding cake,' Wendy mutters. 'Do they think, after 200-odd weddings we can't be trusted with their cake?'

'Obviously not,' I say. Nor it transpires, can we be trusted with much else when we are presented with instructions on how to pour champagne and how much to put in each glass and then later Wendy is told by the best man that he has several years' experience in cutting cakes so her assistance is not required.

'Darling,' she seethes, 'I've been cutting cakes since you were in short pants.'

It's all pretty extraordinary given there is absolutely nothing re-markable about the cake other than the flowers are exactly the same shade of purple as the mother of the groom's dress and Wendy's rage. Later there is a row as the cake's creator accuses the bride of not making enough of a fuss of the bloody thing and then she scoops it all up and takes it away.

The real clincher comes one late summer weekend after which I am convinced that cakes and me shall never cross paths again.

It has become fashionable to have individual cup cakes on a tiered stand instead of a big cake. Usually these are professionally made confections which in themselves are as artistic as a full-sized cake. On this occasion, however, Auntie Maud has taken it upon herself to make the cakes and presents me with three large plastic boxes full of fairy cakes.

To say they look like the sort of thing you'd expect on the Brownies' cake stand at the church fete is unkind. Brownies, after all, are usually baking for a badge. They may be no masterpiece but Auntie Maud, for whom, it must be said, this may be her cake making swan song, insists I should keep them in a cool place so I promise to put them in the cellar.

Foolishly, I stack all three boxes on top of each other for the journey down the cellar steps. Half way down the top box begins to slide and as I try to rebalance the load I feel the second box begin to go. They land upside down on the stone flags having bounced down a flight of six stone steps.

It is one of those moments of pure horror that seem, cruelly, to last forever. When I eventually regain use of my legs and am crouched over the debris all I can hear is the plaintive sound of my own whimpering.

'Please God, let this not be happening,' and then, ever so quietly because I can hardly admit to what has just occurred in painful slow motion before my eyes, I mutter, 'Wendy, Wendy, I have a bit of a situation down here, I need you.'

When she sees the devastation she silently goes about collecting the cakes, putting them back in the boxes and taking them upstairs to the kitchen. Silently. It's not good. I just follow, silently too.

'Lock the door,' Wendy tells me with an impassive gesture towards the door between the kitchen and the dining room.

'What…' I'm still in shock.

'Just lock the fucking door Simon.' I do as I am told and then we set to work repairing the cakes.

To be honest, Auntie Maud's efforts were never that good in the first place so a new batch of butter icing and a liberal dusting of icing sugar does wonders with only a few cakes having picked up dust and mould from the cellar floor and they are easily washed down.

'There,' says Wendy triumphantly when we have finished the cake makeover, 'nobody will ever know, especially if these six are put at the back.' And then she turns to me. It has taken two hours out of one of Wendy's finely tuned wedding preparation schedules and she is not happy. 'You will never handle another wedding cake.'

'That's fine with me.' So now when a cake comes in the front door, I am usually legging it out the back.

With Easter not so far away it looks as if nothing is going to happen to The Gatehouse this side of the summer. It is costing us an extra thousand pounds a month in rates and mortgage repayments which is simply not sustainable long term but no cash equals no builders so we apply to the bank for a short term loan. We reckon we can do the whole thing for £15,000 so we tell our builder he's got a budget of £10,000 which he thinks is reasonable.

With a revised business plan we approach the bank manager who is open to the idea on the understanding that we combine the new borrowing with our existing unsecured bank loan and secure the whole thing with a second charge on the castle.

'Talk about having us by the bollocks,' Wendy curses, 'and the short and fucking curlies.'

'It's the times we live in,' I add but we know we have no choice if there is to be any chance of getting the place up and running for the summer. Quite how we will service this growing mountain of debt if there isn't a dramatic economic recovery soon is a question best left in a dark, locked cupboard.

As if knowing we need a diversion, Wendy receives a telephone call. She is summoned to London. Alone.

Our dear old friend Diana has contracted pneumonia. She has asked Wendy to visit because she wants to ensure there isn't going to be, in her own words, 'a big hoo-ha when she goes.'

The children are upset not to visit but at the same time say they don't want to remember her the way they remember Nanny.

Diana tells Wendy she isn't in the least bit worried about dying.

'Think of all the fabulous people I'm going to meet all over again.'

She dies three days after Wendy's visit. She doesn't know, but Wendy guesses her last words were probably, 'Darlings, I'm coming.'

Some people leave such a large hole when they've gone that it is almost as if they are still there. So larger than life was Diana that few who knew her seem able to accept she is no longer alive, her presence living in spite of her death.

'Isn't that the way we'd all like to be remembered?' Wendy asks after the funeral.

'No, I want people to miss me, wail to within an inch of their own lives and feel utterly miserable about my departure from their lives for the rest of theirs.'

'God, you're objectionable.'

'It's why you love me.'

Having catered for a wedding on Maundy Thursday we are looking forward to an extended weekend full of guests and, blissfully, (and contrary to what the forecasters said and what is happening in southern England) as Good Friday dawns, the sun rises into a crystal blue sky.

In customary Easter fashion, the phone starts ringing at about 8.30 with people wanting to enquire about availability for…

Easter.

'Do you mean next Easter?'

'No, this weekend.'

'I'm afraid we're full.'

'What, completely full? Not even room for a family of fourteen?'

It's hardly worth going on with any explanation. 'No, but I can take your details for New Year.'

Friday and Saturday pass uneventfully such as any busy high season weekend, but on Sunday morning dawns the realisation that there is the equivalent of another full weekend still to go. Nevertheless, the sun is still shining and we make time for a family breakfast and an exchange of Easter goodies.

Having lobbied to be included on the family Easter Egg list for some seven years, Wendy has bought me the largest egg imaginable. It's rude not to show appreciation and by mid-afternoon on Easter Sunday I've eaten over half of it. It leaves me feeling decidedly bilious and, not knowing what else to do I determine the best remedy to be a generous glass of wine. Unfortunately, prior to scoffing the egg, I have already consumed double the recommended dose of medicinal champagne with breakfast (healthily mixed with orange juice) which has a) added to my current state of nausea and b) rendered further doses counter productive.

It's the icing on the cake, or to be a little more seasonal, the yolk in the omelette of a weekend that already seems to have gone on for a month and I am useless for the rest of the day. Wendy is not best pleased.

Next day, we've organised a lunch for eighteen friends and as many children and an Easter egg hunt for all of them plus a castle full of guests. The sun is still shining and we decide to do the whole thing outside. Wendy has downloaded an elaborate egg-cum-treasure hunt with clues, graphics, the lot. It's supposedly designed for children but I cannot get my head round how the whole thing is supposed to work.

'It's an Easter egg hunt, Simon, get a grip.'

I start to whine about not understanding but Wendy is quick to retort, 'Christ, I'm doing everything else as usual, surely you can manage this. If it's too difficult get one of the children to help you.' Ouch, that stings.

Emily has been outside since nine looking for eggs as usually she manages to pocket a few before anyone else knows what's going on. But this year her search is in vain. She sidles up to me and asks what the arrangements for the egg hunt are so I tell her this year things are a little more elaborate.

'Daddy, you know I have a very bad memory.'

'Do you darling?'

'Yes, so if I help you hide all the Easter eggs, I am sure I shall have completely forgotten where they all are by the time the children get here.'

Her reply to my explanation of Mummy's new egg hunt is predictable. 'Ridiculous. What on earth is wrong with just chucking them all over the garden like we usually do?' Emily and I have much in common.

I try my best to follow Wendy's cryptic instructions but the complexity of setting it all up gets the better of me and eventually Emily and I resort to the old way of doing things with eggs flung randomly from a basket. Despite my obvious intellectual shortcomings, it proves to be the usual success and everyone is happy and when asked why the location of the eggs were so at odds with the clues I am able, rather smugly, to seize the upper hand, 'cryptic clues you see – you either get them or you don't.'

Oliver has started his GCSEs and is manfully buckling down to what needs to be done. Being the boy he is, what needs to be done is the extent of his effort, no more, no less but when we bring this to the attention of his teachers they seem un-phased, 'it is the nature of boys versus girls,' they tell us.

Since his enforced move back to state education from private school he has struggled with being in an academic year lower than his chronological age group. Given the almighty cock-up his private school made of his education, we had no alternative but to keep him back a year and it did enable him to catch up (in the first six weeks of his repeated year six at primary school, thanks to the appropriate support so obviously lacking at his former school, he gained eight months in reading age) but socially we always knew it would be a problem. He has had much time to think for himself about the long term impact that his old school continues to have on his formative years and what impact this may have on his future choices.

'I want you to sue them,' he says without warning, one day in the car.

'Sue who?'

'Sue the school. They've made my life much more difficult than it could have been and I've been socially disadvantaged.'

'Who on earth have you been talking to?' I ask, wondering where this can have come from. But as he explains his thinking I can clearly see that these are his own thoughts, his own reasoning.

When we received the letter from his prep school back in 2009 telling us that Oliver had not done well in his entrance exams and there was only a place in senior school available to him if we were prepared to pay for him to board, his last remaining grandparent, whom he adored, had died the previous week and the last thing he could contemplate was the idea of enforced separation from his remaining family.

Imagine trying to tell a ten-year-old boy as gently as possible that the school he had loved and had been so proud to be part of didn't think he was good enough for them. Of course we didn't put it quite like that but he knew well enough.

He was crushed, a fact that was brought home to us quite unexpectedly, two weeks later when I was hit head on by another car while turning to park alongside the school bus. Oliver, who along with everyone else on the bus had seen the whole thing happen, just said, 'Daddy you took so long to get out of the car I thought you were dead. After everything that's happened I just wanted to be dead too.'

We did take the school to task over its failure to deliver an adequate education and got an apology of sorts and some financial compensation for their shortcomings but Oliver's point now is an interesting one. At what point in a child's future does the failings of a school stop having an impact and how is that impact quantified?

'It's a big thing, suing somebody,' I tell him, recalling our own feelings of being sued by one of our members of staff, 'you might end up having to give evidence in court.'

At the time of its decision the school had gone on to tell us that, on the evidence of his entrance exam results Oliver would have been unable to access the secondary school curriculum. His progress since put paid to that particular lie (although presumably the school would have been able to wave a magic wand had we agreed to the boarding fees).

'But you're doing OK, you'll get decent grades if you keep going the way you are.'

'But it's not just about the exams, I feel different, I don't belong anywhere. It's hard. Please will you think about it?' he pleads.

'Of course, if it's important to you, it probably means you need closure, I understand that.' I tell him I will talk to our solicitor and get his advice.

Our friends are already concerned about us. They have followed our progress over the years and seen our moods ebb and flow with cash flow; shared our elation at the recognition of our hard work that awards bring and consoled us in the face of criticism which, in a place like this, we can't take as anything other than personal. Now we have real angst about Oliver and I can't help feeling it's our decisions that have let him down. With so much else on our minds do we have the capacity for this angst too? Can we afford not to have? A lad who worked for us briefly was fond of telling us how his head was in a spin whenever he got something wrong. It was an oft used phrase and one which we can now relate to. With the spinning speeding up we must just hope there isn't a plughole at its centre.

We are in the fifth year of the economic crisis and beginning to run out of phrases to describe it. While we were relatively unscathed by global events in the first few years, in the last couple of years the bottom has fallen out of our wedding market and for the first time in sixteen years we face not having enough cash to operate from month to month. Things are desperate and even with a summer season looming, we know that a larger than ever chunk of the cash we make while the sun shines will be going to pay off the accumulated debts of the previous winter.

While wanting to leave and chucking it all in has been a familiar mantra of mine every year, this year is the first in which Wendy has openly echoed my feelings. Costs are rising, guests want more and more for less and less. It feels utterly unsustainable.

In the last week of April we receive a letter.

Dear Mr and Mrs Bennett,
We have just returned home from a weekend stay at Augill Castle and feel compelled to write to express our surprise at the gulf between our expectations of our stay and what we actually received...

Wendy, having opened it and begun to read, throws it across the desk. 'I've had enough of it, Simon, enough. Is nothing good enough for anyone anymore?'

I pick it up to continue and then, with a wry smile, begin to read aloud:

Unlike other so called country house hotels in which we have previously stayed, there was an overwhelming sense of ease and contentment which made us feel far more welcome than we are accustomed to from the moment we arrived. In fact we felt this wasn't a hotel at all, but rather just a real country house offering an authentic experience. On arrival we were offered tea and cake by Wendy which we felt was a totally unnecessary gesture, clearly contrived to put us at our ease.

Having overcome our initial incredulity at this spontaneous hospitality, imagine our horror at discovering the further audacity of the owners by presuming to provide softer pillows and bigger bath towels than we are used to in our own home. The toiletries, bathrobes, decanter of sherry and homemade biscuits in our bedroom were far more than we expected and surely should have been more clearly explained in the hotel's website. The latter simply doesn't do the place justice. In fact nothing has been stinted on from the curtains to the rich wall coverings to the well appointed bathrooms, leaving us feeling totally dissatisfied with our own domestic living arrangements.

Imagine our further disbelief on discovering that our small children had been catered for with a fully equipped baby box of things we might have forgotten plus books and soft toys to make them feel at home – surely a cynical attempt to curry favour with your younger guests knowing the influence they have on their parents. The nappy disposal unit in the bathroom was, we feel, a step too far across the boundary of reasonable expectation.

There was nothing to be done but to leave the castle and gather our thoughts in the grounds. But even this seemingly simple task could not be completed without the relentless helpfulness of the staff in pointing out the facilities and the enforced companionship of Maisie the ridiculously adorable cocker spaniel. The tennis court was newly painted (if a little mossy), the climbing frame and swings all in good working order and the treehouse had been newly renovated. In short, there was a conspicuous lack of neglect everywhere.

Once back at the castle we were shown the library and given a full run down of how the honesty bar works by Simon, Wendy's affable, charming and implausibly handsome husband. The door leading to the newly installed cinema was pointed out with an invitation to use it as we wished. How ridiculous that we were expected only to ask for a film of our choice to be screened in the private cinema with no fuss or additional charge.

Later in the day we found it even more unbelievable that we were able to relax in the drawing room while our children played with all of the toys without being looked down on or scorned at for making a mess or a noise. One simply doesn't expect this sort of attitude in modern hotels and we felt almost cheated by not having to trudge to the nearest indoor play centre and suffer ghastly food and drink just to entertain our children on a wet day. Surely this small inconvenience would have mitigated the guilt we felt at having to consume the absurdly delicious afternoon tea we had ordered later that afternoon.

After just one afternoon we were left feeling that things could surely not get any better. How wrong we were. Had we not known better we would have sworn that our fellow guests were handpicked for us, so easy and convivial was the company. We found ourselves in a state of utter discombobulation over the ease with which we made new friends in such glorious surroundings. The free flowing conversation was accompanied by a meal which we can only describe as food for the soul. Where were the tiny portions of overly messed with food designed to leave us still hungry? Where was the simpering service? Why was the log burner stoked to make us feel so cozy, forcing upon us the agonising decision of whether to stay put or move at the end of the evening? To then round off the whole meal with a gargantuan cheeseboard seemed very extravagant and obviously designed to make us sleep too well.

And as if the food wasn't enough, we were invited to help ourselves to the bar or enjoy coffee and tea with hand made chocolates in front of another roaring fire. Quite absurd.

The beds were unreasonably comfortable, the duvets, filled with goose and duck down, unexpectedly warm and inviting and everywhere was so quiet, meaning that we overslept and woke in a panic expecting to hear staff housekeeping noisily outside our door. But there wasn't a sound. We were then further knocked off guard when we came downstairs expecting to scrounge a late cup of coffee only to find that a fully laid breakfast table was still waiting for us. We found it extremely disconcerting that breakfast should continue until everyone has had it. Why on earth is the kitchen not run for the convenience of the staff as in most hotels? The children were given a basket of fresh laid multicoloured eggs from the castle's hens to choose from. Clearly as fresh as can be, we noticed an absence of supermarket date stamps on any of them.

This totally unnecessary level of hospitality, good food and comfort continued for the rest of the weekend resulting in the ultimate disappointment of the whole trip: Having to leave.

You have taken severe liberties in anticipating all the needs of your guests before they have even realised them for themselves and you have created an atmosphere of friendliness which allows families to enjoy quality time together, thus audaciously re-writing the definition of family friendliness. Be warned, this will not please many who are looking for an upmarket creche in which to abandon their little ones for the weekend.

Added together we have had an experience which has left us deeply rejuvenated. But what has left us unsettled is that we now feel sure we will never be able to find a comparable experience anywhere else in England. You have significantly limited our choices for future family short breaks so we have no choice but to return year after year.

We hope you will take all our points on board and ensure that you change absolutely nothing at Augill Castle (other than moving it a tad closer to the Mediterranean – or at least Berkshire) otherwise we will be forced to return and revert to type and take all our meals perched on the end of our bed in our room, for fear of spontaneous social interaction, speak to nobody and continually hush our children, all for fear of upsetting the delicate balance of the household, as is the norm in most English country house hotels, family friendly or not.

Yours disconcertedly

Mona Forfun

Later that afternoon Anna, our friend from the home counties, rings, 'any interesting post this morning?'

'Oh you bugger,' Wendy laughs.

'Just thought you needed cheering up,' and with that Wendy sobs, laughs and cries some more for nearly an hour. That spinning just won't stop.

The following day another letter arrives and this time it's no laughing matter. The bank has got it's wires crossed and there is going to be a delay in approving our funding application for the renovation of The Gatehouse. Our relationship manager has left and our file has been passed to the lending department in Birmingham where the pen-pushers know nothing of the back story.

'That's it then,' Wendy says, 'we won't be getting any revenue from The Gatehouse this year which means by this time next year we're going to be around £15,000 out of pocket. Marvellous, just fucking marvellous.'

But perhaps there is a glimmer of hope. Old guests are continuing to return in greater numbers. Even more significantly, friends of previous guests have been booking on the strength of a trusted personal recommendation (one in the eye for Tripadvisor, whose recommendations nobody trusts) and guests have been returning with other friends or family in tow.

It is a reassuring trend in very uncertain times and something that has helped to keep us sane. Hopefully such loyalty will not dissolve as soon as the good times return but we're quietly confident it won't. It is one of many indicators that we are in a new sort of world now. Our psyche has changed to value value (at least our model guests know the difference between value and price) so with value for money firmly on everyone's agenda and a new risk averseness taking over the national mood we have an opportunity to be a lot of people's 'go-to' place.

For the first time in six years it's a sign of an end in sight. The spinning has yet to slow but we feel a seed of optimism growing, perhaps because it's only when you reach rock bottom and start to rise up again that you can realise the worst may be over.

♕ ♕ ♕ ♕ ♕

During the bleakest moments of the past few years, which have invariably been mid-winter, I have often been found holed up in what many men will relate to as my man-cave.

Every household has a version. A drawer, a cupboard, a shed. That place where anything that may conceivably be useful at some indeterminate date in the future is stored.

Invariably this storage – more accurately termed hoarding – is the preserve of the man of the house and the space, exclusively his, is his cave into which his female strays at her peril. It may be man's last bastion of unilateral authority.

The concept is no different in a castle although the practicalities vary, mostly in terms of space and volume. No run of the mill drawer or shed here, rather a series of unconnected outbuildings which makes searching for the ideal piece of crap for the job, put aside five years ago, that much more of a challenge. And for extra special castle man-stuff there is the ultimate space: the turret.

The turret is the castle's man-stuff HQ, containing both the most recently acquired stuff as well as diehard pieces which have attained a state of inanimate immortality as the indispensables; those bits of stuff which survive every purge, every re-organisation. They are man-stuff royalty, lording it over all the other useful things with an air of self assured superiority.

Stuff is a strange word but it sums up all these disparate belongings, each destined to be useful one day, somehow better than any other.

To service the need for every man to furnish his cave with man-stuff, there are, of course hardware shops and DIY superstores. The best of these are intentionally designed to satisfy modern man's instinct as hunter gatherer. As we are no longer responsible for feeding our tribe we turn to filling our shelter with the stuff that will keep it watertight, warm, comfortable and, most crucially, enhance its market value.

Stuff to achieve this we buy at every available opportunity – just in case. Hence my turret is filled not just with old, salvaged stuff, but with carrier bags of unrelated stuff foraged on numerous sorties to the hardware emporium. Invariably a visit to buy a battery or drill bit will end up with purchases of several tens of pounds. Included might be such impulses as odd shaped light bulbs in case we should ever acquire an odd shaped lamp, curtain hooks in case the curtains should spontaneously fall down, a new shade of furniture wax for when we buy some new furniture (which would never be chosen to match the wax we already have in the turret). Always included will be a new brand of strongest ever mammoth man glue and the world's toughest brand of double sided tape bearing an irresistible image of a giant beast being suspended from a crane attached only by a length of Elephant Tape. Glue and tape are a castle bodger's best friends.

And it is always essential, when buying a drill bit, to buy additional sizes a couple of millimetres either side too. Don't ask why, it just is because when it comes to drill bits, size is everything.

My turret is a preserve of manliness made even more so by the fact that it is topped with battlements. If you've ever suffered shed envy, this is in a league of its own.

Wendy is only allowed in on a biannual basis when the level of disorganisation becomes so critical that all useful output has stopped. At that point a female mind is required to restore order and logic (although too much logic is as damaging to the balance of the cave as none and when she is invited in she knows better than to even think about discarding, labeling or categorising).

A certain level of chaos ensures I can maintain sole control of my empire and my position as lone saviour of any emergency situation. It's a matter of the self preservation of one's indispensability. Organisation leads to transparency of the system and that would never do.

At present we are mid-way between such events and the turret and all associated outbuildings are female no-go areas. If there is maintenance, emergency repair, fixing of any kind or just plain bodging to be done (and there is always plenty), it's my job.

Light bulbs? My job.

Replacement batteries? See me.

New loo seat? I've got a choice of three.

Furniture wax, danish oil, woodworm treatment? Got it all.

Useful lengths of wire, all grades of sandpaper, WD40, screws, nails, staples, glue, roofing tape, washers, jubilee clips, spare TV remote controls, little rubber feet for the bottom of appliances, mouse traps, marker pens, nuts, bolts... they're all in the turret.

But what makes every man's cave truly idiosyncratic is not the useful stuff, it's the useless stuff which is kept just in case. This is the stuff that becomes the bone of contention during the biannual clear out and the exchanges follow the same pattern.

'What are you keeping this for?' Wendy will ask waving an out of date instruction manual for a long expired strimmer or coffee machine.

'You never know,' I will reply, studiously avoiding eye contact.

'And this?' She has no idea when or how the need of a dried up marker pen, a salvaged hinge from a loo seat or half the innards from a yale door lock is going to present itself.

'Why are you asking? Don't question, just put it where I say,' and invariably that's as far as she pushes me.

Granted there are times when I am caught out for a lack of logical thinking. It is just easier to toss the old batteries and blown lightbulbs into the box as you extract new ones from the packet. Eventually there will be no new batteries and plenty of old ones. Finding a working lightbulb becomes a guessing game (gone the days of checking if it's good by rattling it). Rest assured that lurking somewhere in one of those unpacked carrier bags of assorted hardware acquisitions will be a packet of AAA batteries and a bulb of some description.

But there is a challenge to all this. Having just completed a professional flower design course, Wendy wants a place to store all of her floral paraphernalia, tools, equipment and supplies and she has suggested a shared space. All will be boxed, labelled, arranged alphabetically and colour coded.

It won't work. I don't do sharing.

Luckily we have spare turrets! Shelved and organised, I'll be as welcome in hers as she is in mine but it doesn't matter as it doesn't sound like it'll be my sort of place.

As the days lengthen I emerge from my man-turret.

For several years I have been badgering a near neighbour to allow me to have a go at sheep shearing. We are surrounded by the creatures but I know very little about their life cycle or what happens to them during the course of their, admittedly, miserable existence.

From afar sheep husbandry looks like an awful lot of effort for very little reward but if it's hard work, it's honest work too; just the thing to revive my flagging self-esteem and what better way to assert my youthful credentials than to get involved with such an intensely physical business?

That our neighbour has subtly but repeatedly ignored my requests might suggest he doesn't think I'm up to the task but this year he has relented.

Oliver is incredulous, 'you'll not last five minutes, it's brutal work especially at your age.'

This, of course, galvanises my resolve, not only to have a go but to make sure I do the best job I can. Recalling my last novice venture into country pursuits when I nearly took the head off my host's wife with a shotgun and my bright yellow Gore-Tex was quite at odds with the muted green and brown tweed in which my fellow guns were attired, I decide I must be kitted out in the right gear with the right equipment.

I find a website which promises to cater to all my needs, describing shearing trousers as 'very popular, hard wearing, comfortable, at a very reasonable price.' Shearing singlets are 'ideal for cold winter days outside, suitable for farmers, farriers, stonemasons, as well as shearers'. But I am eventually sold on the starter kit: 'Ideal for those going on a shearing course or starting shearing. A singlet, a pair of shearing trousers, a shearing belt, a pair of moccasins and an assortment of accessories.' And at the bottom of the page in large, bold script, 'Includes a free screwdriver!'

A few days later my kit arrives. The singlet extends half way down my thighs which is perhaps why it is so suitable for cold winter days outside – affording a nice warm arse even if your arms are freeze dried

169

from the shoulders down – the trousers are really just jeans devoid of tailoring with extra deep pockets – perhaps to accommodate the free screwdriver – and there are an assortment of tools with no immediately discernible purpose.

There is also a shearer's belt made from a combination of leather and surgical elastic. The family are, of course, agog to see me in my new get-up and I oblige, far from confident that their reaction will be anything other than derision.

Oliver is the first to comment. 'What the hell? You look more like you're going to shag the sheep than shear them.'

Wendy doesn't help by adding that she thinks I bear an uncanny resemblance to one of the Village People. Both the children look at her quizzically. 'Believe me,' she explains 'if only you knew.'

I have to admit that the assortment of accessories, which I have attached to my surgical elastic and leather belt, make me look like a travelling sales rep for a sex toy manufacturer and I still have no idea why I should be getting so excited about the free screwdriver. But it is the moccasins which really take the biscuit.

Emily has, as usual, the last word. 'Why are you wearing slippers? It looks like you've scalped the sheep and then slipped your feet straight into their skins.'

'Look, all this gear came from a specialist website,' I explain, rather lamely.

'Specialising in what exactly?' Emily asks suspiciously, 'you look, well frankly just ridiculous,' and to add to her insult, before I have a chance to object, she whips out her 'phone and I'm all over Snapchat.

A week later, our neighbour rings to finalise arrangements for my shearing initiation.

'Just thought I'd make sure you're still keen,' he begins, 'and a quick word about what to wear...'

I cut him short, 'no need, I have all the gear I need,' I tell him confidently.

'OK then, ya'll be reet.'

'Aye,' I'm getting into it already.

I pull up to the farm the next day filled with trepidation. Not because of what I am about to do – it's an adventure and I'm a novice so there's no pressure to perform – but because I am worried I've got the gear all wrong – a polyester singlet and very unflattering trousers teamed with the moccasins and the strangely erotic belt is all very at odds with my usual wardrobe.

As I step inside the barn where hundreds of woolly sheep are being herded in one end and pink naked sheep in equal quantity are being evacuated from the other I immediately understand the need for a singlet – or even less – it is hot, steamy and there is an all-pervading pungent sweet aroma – not unpleasant. My loose fitting, sturdy trousers are also clearly de rigueur as this is physical work requiring a high degree of flexibility.

But what of my dodgy belt and my moccasins? I need not have worried. I am kitted out almost identically to my fellow shearers. The belt helps with back support and there is some sort of harness which seems to engage with the belt to help further support the shearers, although I never quite get the hang of it. As for the moccasins, they are to help my feet feel the movement of the sheep as they are clamped between my thighs and absorb the quantity of oil and muck that comes off every animal.

After eight hours (apparently a short day), in which a top shearer might fleece upwards of 300 sheep, I manage five. The first two struggle so much I am left on my back as they leg it. The next is left with what could charitably be called a Mohican cut and the next two I manage to fleece look like Chernobyl sheep, all covered in patches with a few lesions for good measure. I spend a good deal of the day herding the beasts and a not inconsiderable amount of that time on my back, knees or face down in sheep shit. But it is exhilarating.

'Tha did well lad,' I am told as the sun sets behind us in a blaze of orange. I don't know about that but that I am invited back to the farm for tea is all the confirmation I need that I didn't actually disgrace myself.

Over tea I learn that many larger sheep farmers rely on travelling shearers from as far afield as Australia and New Zealand who make a living out of it by following the seasons around the world. There just aren't the young people locally willing to learn. Besides, there's no money in it. These sheep, upland varieties which spend much of the year on the moors, produce a coarse wool which might fetch £1 a fleece. It doesn't cover the cost of removing it.

'We do it for th'welfare of sheep, as long wool attracts maggots and the like,' I am told.

Perhaps I am being fanciful, but I can't help but imagine that it also develops a bond between sheep and shepherd. The way the sheep lie motionless between the sturdy and experienced thighs of their master echoes of an unspoken trust between man and beast.

As I leave I am struck by the overwhelming sense of admiration and envy I have for these people, the rituals of their lives rooted in the landscape, hefted to the animals they care for. But I leave with an unanswered question which niggles me and will not go away – what was the purpose of the free screwdriver?

'How was it?' Oliver asks on my return.

'Bloody hard but I reckon it's something every man should try at least once and you know… you're nearly the same waist size as me now.'

CHAPTER THIRTEEN

A tale of castration, plans for a party, sensible footwear and
mystery spotting the mystery shopper

We will have been at the castle sixteen years in September but this June marks our fifteenth anniversary of opening to guests so we decide, with the mood subtly changing but in spite of being unable to afford it, to throw a party. That friendly mantra is something Wendy has taken to her heart, 'if you're going to go down, darling, you might as well go down in Gucci.' But we have survived a lot more than just the economy and it has been our friends and what small family we have that have seen us through. They deserve a party just as much as we do.

The party isn't extravagant other than to take over the whole castle for a weekend. To offset the lost revenue we ask everyone if they will mind paying something to stay and, of course, nobody does. After all, if we lived in a normal house and decided to throw a weekend party for forty on the Saturday night and a hundred for a garden party on the Sunday, we wouldn't be covering everyone's accommodation costs. We settle on 1998 prices and everyone is more than happy with that.

We choose the weekend of the Appleby Horse Fair. The horse fair is the largest gathering of gypsies in Europe and takes place at the beginning of June each year.

It is undeniably a spectacle but the travellers are not welcomed by the local population with open arms and warm hearts. Eden is the most sparsely populated district in England and life is quiet here. The town of Appleby has a population of some two thousand, Kirkby Stephen around fifteen hundred and these are the district's second and third largest settlements. When the travellers come to town there can be as many as ten thousand and the same number of visitors and tourists again on top of that.

There is, of course, money to be made, but it is the clash of cultures and the strain on the local infrastructure that causes the tension. That and the overbearing policing of recent years which has done nothing but turn a simmering pot into a boiling cauldron.

Being out of the way, it is traditionally a quiet one for us and those guests we do have are often associated with the gyspy gathering and eat breakfast early, arrive back late and spend nothing on food and drink so we're happy to fill the weekend with our friends and family instead.

It is turning into a glorious spring; dry, sunny, warm and we tentatively look forward to a sparkling weekend of outdoor celebration. We plan to have afternoon tea and then drinks and canapés outside on Saturday followed by dinner and a casino and the following day a garden party with a hog roast, ice cream van and ceilidh on the lawn complete with outdoor strings of lights, hay bales to sit on and rugs and cushions on the grass.

'What is your wet weather contingency plan?' asks Faye who has lived here all her life and seen enough weddings at the castle rained indoors despite the bride's best intentions.

'There isn't one,' I'm placing all my faith in the power of positive thought.

'You know, we could have had a goat roast,' I tell Wendy, 'or even a nice vat of goat curry.'

The goats, now a family of six since we failed for a second year to prevent Amy and Ben copulating, have, predictably, become my sole responsibility. They have grown to a size where all of them are capable of jumping barbed wire topped fences and it is only going to be a matter of time before my prized herbaceous borders and even those of surrounding neighbours are ravaged. Attempts to find them new homes have been in vain. Unsurprisingly, the animal sanctuary from which the original two came does not want anything to do with them, I have tried a soft sell on several friends without success and although the idea of roast goat or a spicy curry is appealing, I have yet to find anywhere or anyone with the facility to slaughter them.

I made enquiries of the industrial sized abattoir to which we took our pigs, knowing they had separate days for cows, sheep and swine. It was a conversation I should have known not to start.

'Hello, we brought some of our pigs to you a year or so ago and I was just wondering…'

'Aye, pigs are on Tuesdays and Thursdays.'

'Yes, well, no actually, I haven't got pigs any more, I was wondering about goats.'

'Tha want's to get some goats?'

'No, I want to get rid of some goats.'

'We don't buy beasts, this is an abattoir, not an auction mart.'

'No, I want to slaughter them so we can eat them.'

'Eat them? Goats? I've never heard of anyone eating goats, not in these parts anyway.'

'So you don't do goat days?'

'Harry, there's a chap on't 'phone wants to know if we do goat days.'

'What like a festival of goats or summut?' Harry calls back.

'No I mean do you have days when you can slaughter goats, maybe alongside some sheep.'

'Bloody hell, there's no call for goats in these parts. I think you'll need to go to Bradford or somewhere like that,' and he hangs up.

When I recount the story to Wendy she asks what's in Bradford. 'I've no idea, maybe it's the goat slaughtering capital of Britain.'

Emily reminds us that she always thought the idea of keeping goats a ridiculous one and that we now have only ourselves to blame for the current predicament. Oliver says if I'd only follow up on my long over-due promise to apply for a firearms licence we can get a rifle, shoot them and bury them in a pit.

'That's rather extreme,' Wendy says.

'Well they're your bloody goats, so you come up with a plan.'

While a plan for long term disposal of the goats continues to elude us, a more immediate plan to prevent the problem getting any larger is in hand. Our first two kids were billies and rendering them sterile was a simple process of tying a tight rubber band around their testicles when they were little (although I swear there's been a hatred in their eyes that's never left). The second two kids were nannies, not so easily sterilised and the danger now is that in the autumn Ben will try to mate with them as well. Now, in a sparsely populated rural community such as this, that sort of carry on is not unheard of but the quality of the resultant offspring can be less than predictable and whilst in humans that usually manifests itself in some sort of intellectual deficiency, in

175

goats, goodness only knows what might result.

I call the vet and explain the predicament and she agrees to a house call to deal with the situation. 'Are you able to assist?' she asks.

'Um, yes, I suppose so, what's involved?'

'You'll just need to hold him down, I'll give him a sedative and then I'll castrate him. It's a simple procedure.'

I have no idea what castration actually involves and imaging it to be similar to a vasectomy where the tubes are cut I am horrified to be party to a full-on surgical operation out in the middle of a field. Simple for her maybe, but not for me and definitely not for the poor goat – he'll hate me forever now. I take up my post, holding Ben still by the hind legs with a full view of proceedings. The vet slices open the poor creature's scrotum and out pop his assets, snip, snip and they're both rolling away down the slope – the testicles, not the vet and the goat.

'I'm scarred, Wendy, scarred,' I wail theatrically later as I'm recounting the experience.

'Hmm, not as much as the poor goat,' she really has missed the irony of how this is all her problem, not mine.

I honestly don't think I'm cut out for country pursuits. In fact, it took fifteen years for me to eventually succumb to the eminent practicality of that stalwart of the country wardrobe: The Wellington boot.

Having spent far too many days doing ridiculously muddy jobs in even more ridiculously unsuitable shoes, the welly now has me under its spell. Becoming a pig farmer was, of course, the final nail in the coffin of any stylish sort of clothing.

That I have resisted them for this long is something of a miracle. Being a regular follower of *The Archers*, I guess I have always identified with the likes of Brian Aldridge or Nigel Pargeter (God rest his soul, I too got into some trouble on the roof but did live to tell the tale) and the thought of wellies as a permanent part of my daytime apparel has filled me with the horror that I am slipping into the realms of Grundydom. If this all means nothing to you BBC Radio Four, each evening at 7pm will soon put you in the picture.

The truth is that out here in the real countryside the welly is everything and everywhere but they are no fashion item. While this humblest of items has been popularised elsewhere with the addition of spots, every colour of the rainbow, Burberry linings or digital images of your children, spouse, dog, cat or favourite pig surrounding your legs, these fashion statement wellies are obviously designed not to get muddy. Here, where the country is dirty, wet, messy and smelly there are black wellies for really serious jobs and, maybe, green ones for jobs not involving a spade, quantities of shit or machinery and for social occasions – yes, up here people do wear wellies to parties.

Earlier this year we trawled up to Carlisle for one of Oliver's club rugby matches. It had been very wet. Our team coach had come admirably prepared in full club tracksuit and green (suitable rugby coaching colour) wellies which, while perhaps not affording him the best traction on the pitch while refereeing the game, certainly kept his ankles dry. I, on the other hand, was wearing a pair of Oliver Sweeneys, the male version of Jimmy Choos and they were very quickly indistinguishable from the mire despite my best efforts, mincing around like a fairy, to avoid the squasiest parts of the pitch and the puddles. Oliver is now much less keen than he used to be to have support on the touchline, 'Surely you've got other things to do on a Sunday morning – it's your busiest day of the week.'

'Darling, we're never too busy to support our favourite son.'

'Well couldn't you come… you know, a little… well, less well dressed?'

A few years later this simmering embarrassment is crystallised when, at the rugby club's annual awards bash I pick up the poshest supporter award.

Now long standing friends of mine will testify that when it comes to any sort of clothing, but especially footwear, quality and style have won over common sense every time. But episodes such as this and many others have eaten into my consciousness and a frightening practicality has crept in.

There are good reasons why it has taken me so long to go public in knee high rubber. At the Lowther Horse Trials a few years ago, the weather was so bad that the mud was half way up the calves; a sticky smelly mix of mud, horse muck, sheep shit and pig urine – the year round smell of the Cumbrian countryside, so charming for visitors – mixed with the heady festival going mash of spilled beer, sloshed champagne, melted ice cream and the contents of innumerable wild boar wraps and Cumberland sausage baguettes. So bad was it that the usually three day event was cancelled after day two and the ensuing financial conseqences meant it was several years before the long established event was resurrected.

I decided to take the children despite the weather as we are all going stir crazy stuck inside watching the rain outside. It's August, we ought to be enjoying the summer spending days on the beach, by the river or at the lakeside but instead of us seeking out the water, it is finding us.

We arrive just before lunch and I insist that the children wear their Wellington boots. I am togged up in a pair of Timberland boots which I feel is a sensible yet stylish nod to the climatic conditions. I have, of course, completely failed to consider that my fashionably long jeans which extend well below the bottom of my boot heel with the intentional result of wearing them into a frayed and ragged hem are totally incompatible with the weather.

Having parted with the princely sum of nearly £100 for the three of us to get in to the showground we make for the food. Being a curmudgeonly sort I have an intense dislike of running into people I know a) unexpectedly, because I never know what to say, b) out of context, because I never know what to say as I can't remember who they are or c) just because I never know what to say as there is a very good reason why I only ever encounter these people unexpectedly.

Today, this full horror is realised. No sooner have we scoffed our oven baked pizzas from the 'food from Cumbria and absolutely nowhere else because we are completely self sufficient' food court made with organic flour from Melmerby, topped with Furness sun-ripened tomatoes (I don't think so), Cumberland mozzarella, Westmorland salami, Ulverston pineapple, Windermere anchovies and wild garlic from the slopes of Blencathra, than we run into a vague business colleague. Oh God, despite my best efforts to duck behind the mobile lavvies he has spotted me and there is no avoiding him. I can't divert off the metal walkway due to a lack of sensible footwear and there is definitely nowhere to run.

He manages to reinforce all my prejudices about why it is a good idea to avoid casual social contact by insulting me whilst attempting to be funny and boring me to tears with some dreadful name dropping of people of whom I have never heard (other than the Duke of Edinburgh – a Lowther Show regular).

Just as I am finding the will to make an excuse to move on before losing completely the will to live, he introduces me to his wife and mother. I am momentarily at a loss as I hadn't noticed he was with anyone. Then, from behind his six foot frame, from either side, appear two Gollum-like creatures, one dentally challenged, the other just challenged, both grinning but saying nothing. It's just too much. I turn, barking at the children that the sheep show – the sheeptacular – is about to start. Emily turns round, startled. Her wellies, of course, don't move at the same speed as the rest of her and as she rotates to look at me, slowly, oh so slowly, she loses balance, falls sideways and then, trying to correct herself, falls headlong, face first into the mud. The wellies stay stoically upright, discarding their occupant.

It is, of course, the perfect opportunity to extract myself from Gandalf and his two Hobbits and also to allow myself a certain smugness that a more sensible form of footwear with laces and a little foot hugging form and style would have served my daughter much better in such a compromising social situation.

As one hotel reviewer once said of Augill: 'Kick off your wellies by the front door without causing a scandal' (a quote since brazenly purloined by one of our competitors). At our front door now you will find more pairs of wellies than anything else but by the back door I remain determined my shoe rack will retain more style than practicality and Wendy still has a whole cupboard full of shoes in boxes just in case, one day, we return to civilisation.

By the end of May my faith in my no-contingency party plan is increasing, bolstered by my conviction that if this party goes according to plan, everything is going to be alright. It's a reassuring, if irrational, notion. With just a week to go the sun has been shining non stop for a month and even if it rains now the ground will stay firm enough not to present too many problems. The band, on the other hand, have contingency firmly in their heads and rightly so, given that they will have several thousand pounds of amplification equipment sitting out on the lawn. I am able to reassure them that they will have the benefit of a gazebo to protect them from vertical rain.

'Yeah, but rain is rarely vertical up here is it? What about if the rain is horizontal?'

'It won't be,' I must sound convinced as nobody else is.

With just a few days to go until the party I ask Wendy what needs doing. I have organised everything required outside, she has been in charge of everything inside. So far, neither of us has called on the other for assistance.

Working with one's spouse is a tricky business. It took us ten years to work out that we didn't both need to be in the same place doing the same thing at the same time. In truth, it might have been our long suffering staff who pointed out that having both of us in the same room trying to do the same thing was not good for anyone.

We are both very controlling sorts making giving up control of any part of our lives to the other very difficult. This, of course, rarely ends in the job being done better or quicker, only in us disagreeing on the end result and determining that each of us knows best how things could have been handled better. That we are both competitive too doesn't help; it's good in business but makes maintaining domestic harmony that much more challenging.

But now we must grow up and act as responsible, selfless adults. At forty-something we've both realised that we don't need to ask anyone for permission to run our own lives anymore. Also, the business at the castle has outgrown our efforts or desire to remain with all the reins in our own hands and the children are at risk of bolting out of the stable if we don't show them, or at least give them the impression that we show them, the same consideration as the business.

So tonight, I have made a decisive move and suggested that for the rest of the weekend we should split our time so that one of us is doing family things while the other does business things.

Wendy agrees and all is arranged.

As it happens, Oliver has been invited to a sleepover at a friend's house. This is a rare thing as he is something of a nomad. There are plans to camp out overnight in the woods at the bottom of the friend's garden but even though the weather has been glorious, nights are still chilly and so this seems, at best, optimistic. I can see half a dozen frozen, oven ready teenaged boys knocking at the door at midnight pleading for hot chocolate and, although they'll never ask for it, a reassuring cuddle from a familiar pair of arms.

180

Since it's not my door they'll be knocking at, it doesn't warrant a second thought and I turn my full attention to Emily as I have negotiated that Wendy should oversee dinner tonight whilst I spend quality time with our daughter who should enjoy having a parent all to herself without having to vie for attention with her older brother.

So the evening is set. But first I must convince her of how much she really enjoys rugby and is looking forward to this evening's premiership final tussle on the television. The prospect of watching 30 grunting muscle-bound men rolling around on the grass clearly doesn't have the same effect on her as it does on her mother and she fixes me with a look far beyond her years.

'Dad, don't be so redi...' but I cut her off.

'I know what you're going to say, and don't. I've heard it too often so keep it to yourself.'

This is, of course, the sort of conversation opener with a pubescent girl that can only go one way. Emily fixes me with a penetrating, cat's eyes stare. She is weighing up her options. Oh how I love this girl, if she keeps this up she'll be nobody's walk-over.

Yes, she has seen an opportunity to bargain, but more importantly, I think she has gazed into my very soul and sees what is afoot. She clearly does think my plans for the evening are ridiculous and has seen that Mummy would be very interested in Daddy's ulterior motive for having suggested that she should be doing all the hard work while he watches rugby using quality time with their daughter as a feeble veil across the whole deceit.

I watch the rugby with a clear conscience having negotiated with Emily to watch a hideous American teen movie in return for her silence and total cooperation. She ups the stakes by agreeing on the condition that Doritos, dips and Haribo sweets are in constant and ample supply. I agree and my conscience is further cleared by the undeniable fact that Wendy and I are not competing any more, but complementing each other and that it will be me that gets up early in the morning to do breakfast while she stays in bed.

This is something that puzzles most people who know me well. 'But you're so grumpy in the mornings', they all tell me. Well, yes, this is true, but I am also pretty grumpy in the evenings. In fact, I am a grumpy old man. Just not famous enough to be doing it on TV yet.

The truth is that I am better let loose on guests before midday because they are, in the main, with the exception of North Americans who seem to be either disarmingly or disagreeably chirpy at all times of the day and night, more likely to be grumpy themselves, hung-over or just uncommunicative. In other words, I am less likely to do any lasting damage at that time of day, and if I do, Wendy still has a fighting chance of recovering the situation later on.

It's not just the guests that benefit from this division of labour. The staff do too. My priorities are different so that the first thing I do when I get into work is make everyone tea and coffee, then attend to the guests, sausages, whatever else comes as a secondary priority. When Wendy is in charge it's a case of make your own tea or serve breakfast with a tongue and throat as dry as a desert or, indeed, the garden in which I plan to host our Mediterranean style garden party.

She's focussed, I'm not. Wendy's strength is to be able to concentrate all her energy on one task at a time while still being able to keep a controlling interest in half a dozen others. I can keep an interest in half a dozen tasks at a time but will be in control of nothing. That, I like to think, is how we complement each other perfectly but perhaps Wendy has a different take on things. Probably, it's best not to ask.

☸ ☸ ☸ ☸ ☸

We have entered another round of awards this year, going for Small Hotel of the Year as a change from B&B of the Year which we feel we have outgrown. It's a big deal because we don't really feel worthy of being included in the hotel category. But then we no longer fit into the B&B category either – apparently the tourist board, which runs these things, received several complaints from other B&Bs when we won the national competition as B&B of the Year back in 2009.

'If we're inspiring hate mail,' Wendy said at the time, 'we must be doing something right – hospitality is a jealous business.'

The application was submitted a couple of months ago and, as part of the judging process we must be 'mystery shopped', involving an anonymous overnight stay by an inspector (or inspectors) followed by a report which will inform the judging panel. This is nerve wracking enough but the real horror is that, after it's all over, we get a copy of the report whether we want it or not!

So, for the last month we have been on our best behaviour. Wendy has told me there is to be no ranting in the kitchen and that I am not to vocalise my inner most thoughts about any guests unless I am in bed and it's after midnight. She can be such a killjoy when there's a trophy within her grasp.

Now, in these post apocalyptic days of austerity that we are all enduring (in it together and all that as the stock market reaches new heady heights) awards and their associated mystery shops aren't funded by the tourist board any longer. So we have to pay a not inconsiderable sum to be 'shopped'.

Having signed a contract agreeing to be mystery shopped should we become finalists and agreeing to the fee, we receive instructions that we should not try to guess who the mystery shopper might be and to undertake to ensure that all of our staff make no attempt to try to second guess their identity. We should make no special effort to impress anyone we suspect of being a mystery shopper and we should make no attempt to try to tease their secret identity out of them.

Oh come on. Really?

As soon as we hear we have been nominated as finalists I gather the staff together for a pep talk and tell them that from now until the end of the month every new booking must be treated as a mystery shopper. Particular attention must be paid to detail and they should all be eagle eyed for any suspicious behaviour.

'Like what?' they ask, 'skulking in the bushes or something?'

'No, don't be absurd, things like tugging on the curtains or lifting the seat cushions off the sofa.'

Then Wendy puts the fear of God into everyone by telling them she has been tipped off that this year's mystery shoppers will be visiting with white gloves and wet wipes to check for dust in obscure places.

'So carry on and act as normal,' I reassure everyone, 'don't try to second guess who they might be.'

'Talk about mixed messages,' I hear one of the team mutter over cigarettes and coffee, 'we've got to look out for suspicious behaviour - well that pretty much cuts nobody out; be on our best behaviour but act normally.'

A couple of Sundays later Maria and Terry pull up in front of the castle. They have been labelled by Laura on their booking form as 'poss

183

myst shop' as has everyone else booked in the last two weeks.

No sooner have they got out of the car than Maria is taking photographs. 'It's them, it's them,' Wendy is getting agitated.

'Hang on,' I say, 'half our guests do that. It's a castle and the sun is shining; it's to be expected.'

'Look at the way she's standing,' Wendy counters.

'What?' I go to greet them at the front door.

After the usual pleasantries I give them a tour of downstairs and show them to their room. It's less fluid than usual as Wendy keeps popping out of random doors with stage whispers of advice:

'Remember to point out the step at the bottom of the stairs. Ask them about dinner. Invite them to join us for a drink later… Sign over our savings and give them our children…'

'Wendy, make tea.'

I return to the kitchen and happily explain to Wendy that they aren't the inspectors. They are visiting from Australia where they've lived for four years and have been staying with their son in Kendal.

'Ahh!' Wendy exclaims conspiratorially, 'it's clearly a cover story: They say they've only lived in Australia for four years to cover for the fact they don't have accents, they say they are staying with their son to explain the UK address and that address is in Kendal where the tourist board offices are!' and she rocks back smugly on her heels.

Later at dinner, Maria and Terry are choosing wine and ask some questions about our selection. Wendy comes running into the kitchen. 'They're quizzing us on our wine list.'

'This is getting out of hand Wendy,' I say. 'Just chill out. We do what we do and we'll win or not based on that.'

'But I don't like not winning,' she wails.

'We all know that, remember the Victoria sponge cake debacle at the village show?' I remind her of a less than finest hour she'd rather forget, not for the losing but for her ungraciousness in defeat. 'And then there was the awards a couple of years back when we lost in the sustainable tourism category to a place which was commended for making their own marmalade. You could hardly remain seated.'

'But this is different, we need this, the staff need this,' and she's right. Having been through such financial and political upheaval, we all need something of a pat on the back for still being here.

'Perhaps we should all just get a 'Survival award'. Anyway, what was that earlier with you saying 'look at the way she's standing'? Do inspectors have a certain gait?'

'No, it was just a way she had about her, I don't know.'

While Maria and Terry are enjoying dinner Wendy decides to go up to their room to do a turndown service.

'What the hell?' I say, 'no, absolutely not, I know what you're up to. We don't do turndowns, we never have and you're just going to rifle through their things to find some evidence.'

In the end she doesn't, not because I tell her not to but because she knows in her heart that it's wrong. In any case, we have a party coming up to celebrate fifteen years and any awards aren't going to top that.

♛ ♛ ♛ ♛ ♛

It's been a year since Clarissa Blanchard-Cafferty first unexpectedly turned to Wendy for advice about Martin's apparent breakdown. Since then she has been a regular visitor, offloading across the kitchen table about her marriage; how she knew that Rupert was gay from the day she stumbled into his room when he was fourteen and found him with his penis inserted into his favourite teddy called Maurice; how she didn't quite know how to broach the subject with Martin. There have been revelations about their sex life, other women, trial separations and even mention of an unsavoury episode involving a less than willing ewe.

'Blimey, she really is a living storyline from *The Archers*, isn't she?' I've taken to listening from another room rather than getting involved in the conversations, although I was frustrated when Wendy failed to pursue details of the incident with the ewe.

'She's lonely. You know he is a lot older then she is,' Wendy has grown genuinely fond of Clarissa.

'What's that got to do with anything?' I ask, 'we're friends with lots of couples with big age gaps who are perfectly happy. Martin's just a bigot.'

So it is quite an irony when, a few days later Martin turns up on our doorstep. 'Martin, what a surprise, would you like to come in?' Wendy is already ushering him into the hallway.

'Martin,' I exclaim heartily, 'how lovely to see ewe.' The joke passes him by but it isn't lost on Wendy who is anything but amused, 'pathetic,' she whispers as she passes me on the way to the kitchen.

'What brings you to our door so unexpectedly?' she asks as she sits Martin down in the same spot at the kitchen table from which Clarissa has poured out her heart.

'To be honest, Wend, I am having a rough time of it. Clarissa has asked for a divorce and frankly I don't know what to do.'

He goes on to ask if we knew Rupert was gay and when we tell him we did he seems to retreat into himself. 'You see, everyone seems to have known except me and now everyone thinks I hate him for it and it's just not true. I'd love him no matter what he is. Do you mind if I use the lav?'

'This really is sensational stuff,' I say to Wendy while Martin is out of the room, slipping into my old hack's jacket and relishing the unfolding human interest story.

But Wendy is having none of it, 'stop it Simon, you're not a journalist any more, you're being a complete prick. Here is a man reaching out to us for help and we will be here for him.'

'My God Wendy, have you eaten a self help book from Amazon?' Wendy clicks her tongue against the roof of her mouth as only wives of a certain number of years standing can.

When Martin returns he seems to have brightened. 'The thing is Wend, everyone thinks we're stinking rich, that everything just landed in our laps, that we live some sort of charmed life. But the truth is the recession has pretty much cleaned us out. Rupert and Jenny are OK because we've set them both up but I'm sick of people making assumptions about who we are and what we are.'

'Martin, do you remember when you and Clarissa met us when we first arrived, fresh from London? Do you remember how you spoke to us and the assumptions you made?'

'Bloody hell, Wend, now you mention it...'

'Your problem isn't everyone else because we all make assumptions about each other, your problem is you. Have you spoken to Clarissa? Have you spoken to Rupert? Get Rupert and Hamish down here to the castle for a weekend. Invite Jenny up and bring the family together.'

'Let me tell you this, Martin,' now Wendy's on a roll, 'neither Simon nor I have any parents left. All we have are each other and all the children have are us. Aunty Gloria has stepped into the role of both parent and grandparent to us all and you know what makes that relationship work? Talking. We speak on the phone every week, she talks to the kids, takes an interest, they confide in her. Simon isn't much of a talker but she can get things out of him that nobody else can. Other than Simon's sister and my brother, who are both so far away, we have made a family out of friends because everyone needs support, Martin.'

After he's gone I hug Wendy for a very long time. 'They're just like us, shit scared.'

'More than that though, Simon. They've turned to us for support. Us. We've been accepted. We've arrived. At last.'

We don't win the Small Hotel of the Year award but it doesn't matter because this year we've won something much bigger.

She: 'I could have made a difference to all that.'

I: 'To the family belonging, yes, but not to the local acceptance. I can't blame you for dying. I just wish you'd listened more when you were still here, or perhaps I wish I'd made you listen.'

She: 'Listening is something I can always do, and I like what I'm hearing. You're a good story teller and seeing the funny side of things is a great skill.'

I: 'It's a great mask.'

She: 'So tell me, how is it really?'

I: 'That craving for social acceptance all these years may have had some bearing on the constant ebb and flow of our contentment but it isn't the root of the uneasiness we are feeling now, even as we gear up for our big weekend. With a mountain of unpaid bills, The Gatehouse almost mocking us as it eats through four figures every month and no end in sight to this bloody financial crisis, we are all fighting our own personal battles. It's as if we're just waiting for one of us to lose so we can all surrender.

'My 'life limiting condition' as it has jokingly become known within the family, has empowered me to take a new level of control of and responsibility for my life and physically and emotionally I have not felt as well for years. But this comes with the reality that a lot of what I used to take for granted, when most of us do, I can no longer do, rather I must learn to see the maximum joy in everything I still can. I am likely to have a shortened life span so every day counts just a little bit more. But in quiet moments it is easy to slip into a state of self pity. Why me? Why shouldn't I be able to live life without boundaries like everyone else (although I know that practically everyone has boundaries of one sort or another). And in the ultimate fit of petulance, 'it's just not fair.'

'If, on the whole I am in a good place it is due in large part to Wendy's support.

187

But she is struggling. Usually the family optimist, her one concession to pessimism has always been our annual cash flow crisis when the Christmas bills, VAT and income tax all fall due in January, made survivable by the certainty that it has always been a temporary state. But during this recession those cash flow woes have not been confined to the winter and for the first time she is saying she has had enough. Not since 2001, in the aftermath of Foot & Mouth disease that so ravaged the social and economic landscape of Cumbria has she openly said 'now is the time to sell and get out, I've had enough'. The trouble is, as a business owner, if that's how your business is making you feel, it is likely the worst time to sell up. We both know that which adds to a sense of entrapment. And she still aches for the loss of her father.

'Oliver is doing his best to make the best of what he sees as a bad situation at school. He feels displaced and out of step with the other kids in his year. To compound his frustrations he is head over heels about a lovely girl in the year above, the year where he should be. She also comes from a big, close knit family which hardly helps because he is painfully aware of our family isolation, although they have taken him as one of their own. She doesn't see the year's separation as a barrier but for him it is a constant reminder of how he feels he has been let down by teachers who should have known better. And he wants someone to blame.

'Emily might, on the surface, seem to be the most content of all of us but she is fighting the strongest demons — those that are the residents of every teenager's mind, self doubt, an aching desire for acceptance while being determined not to conform; wanting to befriend everyone while failing to understand why others don't want to be her friend. She is enormously talented and has a desire to share her talent but to many that is nothing more than being a show off. It's something she struggles to process because she doesn't have a jealous bone in her body, she wants only for everyone to be friends with everyone else.'

She: 'In other words, she wants World peace. But she does have lots of friends?'

I: 'Yes, she wants to teach the World to sing...'

She: 'In perfect harmony.'

I: 'She has lots of friends, she has done a good job of creating her own family around herself. Of the two, she's the one you'd have had most in common with although he's the one who misses you because he knew you once.'

She: 'I would have been more involved if I hadn't got sick.'

I: 'Would you, really? You never really came back to us after you'd left. Don't you think the truth is you just didn't have anything left to give, you'd been giving, being taken from, all your life. We've all of us only got so much to give, Mum, I think you just ran out. Nobody's blaming you for that, you definitely didn't leave this life with a deficit. You put an awful lot more in than you took out, for me, for Wendy and even for the kids in the short time you knew them. I'm just glad you're still listening, that's enough for me. What I've learnt is that when someone dies they don't have to be lost. These books have proved that.'

There's a pause. A long pause.

> *She: 'Did you say as much to your father when you wrote 'Undressed For Dinner'?'*
> *I: 'I think so, pretty much.'*
> *She: 'Well it's truer than you think.'*
> *I: 'What do you mean?'*
> *She 'Just that.'*

Chapter Fourteen

We have a party, I find a publisher on our doorstep, a new breed of guest begins to question our abilities and our teenagers eat us out of house and home

As if talk of a party is enough, we feel a renewed optimism which leads us to start to make plans for new marketing and different ways to sell the castle's unique offering. If we have any chance of getting a return from The Gatehouse, we've got to get some money in to do it up. We also decide it's time to be more aggressive with our wedding marketing. There's a new kid on the block offering weddings on a similar scale to us and we can't afford to let them clean up. Advertising spending is often one of the first things to fall away when finances are tight but it's invariably a false economy. There is no doubt that our wedding bookings, although due mainly to a general downturn in weddings booked in the latter half of the recession, have suffered because lack of cash has led to our taking our eyes off the ball of maintaining our profile.

The results are almost instant. Within weeks of a new advertisement appearing in one of the glossy bridal magazines, we have three new enquiries. It's hardly a flood but it's a start.

After fifteen years of hosting and running weddings it would be easy to think that we are unquestioned experts in our field. Some, however, have different ideas and it is true that fashions and crazes run quicker through the wedding market than through pretty much any other, from dresses (vintage is great, but last year's is definitely not), to cakes, fairy cakes last year, cheese cakes this and forget tiers supported on pillars, so last century.

Wendy is showing a prospective couple around the castle and dispensing her well rehearsed patter which, being a sales pitch, is all about the things we can do well and glossing over anything which might present a challenge.

'I like a challenge,' Wendy once said, 'but on my terms.'

'That's not really a challenge then, is it?' but I know what she means. There's no point taking unnecessary risks with someone's big day.

The couple are up from London and have obviously looked at a great number of wedding venues judging from their slightly zoned out demeanour. Wendy gets a second sense of these meetings pretty early on and as I pass her in the hall she shakes her head. It's an odd thing that while we are at the delivery end of the wedding merry-go-round we were never on the receiving end. We didn't go searching for a venue because we lived in the only venue we ever considered; not the castle but an idyllic thatched village cottage in Northamptonshire. There was room in the garden for a marquee holding just 60 – the ideal maximum for any wedding in my opinion – and the church was walking distance away at the other end of the village with the pub as a pit stop exactly half way. Because of this we do still find ourselves floored by certain questions.

'Will the cat be kept out of the photographs?'

'Can we have cats at the wedding?'

'What will your children be doing while we are getting married?'

'I know you say your maximum seated capacity is 46, but can we squeeze in 60?'

'Can we bring our own wine, cake, steak, fish, chef, priest?'

'Can we pay £5 a week until the balance is paid in 2025?'

It's all been asked and we have acquiesced where we can and politely declined where we needed to, our over-riding philosophy being to say yes unless we really can't.

Wendy's current prospects think they are playing their cards very close to their chests, unaware that Wendy has already sussed them. Once the tour is complete they sit down and Wendy runs through the sort of menus we can deliver, at pains to point out that final choices are theirs to make, not ours, numbers and likely timetables, based on our experience of what works and usually focussing on not leaving guests at a loose end to get too pissed before they've eaten anything.

The groom-to-be fixes her a gaze. 'We're thinking about 46 to sit down which you say is your maximum but do you think you can really cope with that sort of number?'

Shortly after they are being shown the door. Politely.

♛　♛　♛　♛　♛

Oliver and Emily too sense that things are picking up. I am in our family kitchen one Sunday cooking a roast. There's a CD on – something from the 1980s, I'm singing away and Wendy comes in with a couple of glasses of wine and a peck on the cheek.

Emily takes one look at the scene and with that inviolable belief, which is the preserve of young people, that her own fate is in no way bound to ours, asks, 'what's all this? Have you both got your shit together at last? I'm so glad that you've finally turned a corner.'

If you can garner the approval of your own teenaged children something has to be going right.

Oliver notices too, 'does this mean we can have some decent food in the fridge at last?'

While things have been tough at times we have always managed to feed the children.

When we lived in the main wing of the castle and shared the castle fridges what we ate as a family didn't really register as a significant factor in anyone's calculations other than the accountant who would ask us annually to estimate the value of 'goods for own consumption'. The children were, of course, very young and their appetites matched their stomachs which were clearly the size of walnuts.

Now we are in our own, entirely separate house, the two small walnut sized stomachs have grown to bottomless pits and an entire supermarket trolley full of food, carefully chosen to feed us for seven days, can be unloaded into the fridge and disappear within 48 hours. Although disappear isn't quite the truth as what actually happens is that the food or the drink is consumed as if by locusts but invariably the packaging remains in the fridge. This defies any logic as, particularly with milk or juice, the carton has to be removed from the fridge, drained and then put back.

Alternatively, the food or drink might be removed from the fridge, be partly consumed in bed and the remainder only discovered when its festering remains, often found underneath a pile of dirty laundry, are the cause of an undeniable stink.

My solution to this is to buy a bigger fridge. Wendy takes this idea on board (with an enthusiasm rarely displayed for most of my ideas for enhancing domestic harmony as they usually involve expense) which strongly suggests that she'd already had the same idea. That three days later a huge American style refrigerator is delivered confirms my suspicions as she doesn't make those sort of purchases without a good deal of internet research.

'What a marvellous idea this was,' I say as we admire the new fridge which is, in fact, practically a new room.

'Yes, wasn't it?' she replies smugly.

Come and see the new fridge we call out excitedly to the children when they get home from school. 'There's nothing in it,' complains Oliver.

'Where's the ice dispenser?' asks Emily, 'these fridges always have ice dispensers.'

'No, it would have to be plumbed in for that,' Wendy explains, 'I did look at it.'

'Yes, your mother's done her research.'

'Ridiculous without ice,' Emily says, although she concedes that it is an impressive addition to the kitchen.

'It does have a turbo can cooler at the back,' I point out, hoping she doesn't ask for further detail.

'Why do you think Americans have to have such big fridges?' I ask Wendy.

'Maybe they eat more, or don't go to the shops as often or maybe they're just determined to keep their place at the top of the international carbon emissions league table.'

'They're the fattest nation on the planet,' Oliver is keen to show he does listen at school.

My logic for having a bigger refrigerator is simple: More space means it's easier to see what's empty and remove it and easier to put back what needs continued refrigeration but within a few days of the new fridge's arrival I can see that my logic is fatally flawed and that a new piece of kitchen hardware does not change the hard wiring inside teenagers' heads. Instead, the new fridge cries out for more to fill it but rather than twice as much food lasting the family twice as long it just means it gets consumed in double the quantity.

As if to compound the growing sense of recovery all around us, weeks before our party I find a publisher for *Undressed For Dinner*. I have known Dawn for many years and she lives in even more isolation than we do, several miles up the hill towards the Yorkshire Dales from where she runs a small publishing house called Hayloft. In all my attempts to find a publisher I had never considered Dawn, always imagining her to be a specialist in serious non-fiction with a particular bent on mountaineering and local history. Though the story which *Undressed For Dinner* recounts might well be a metaphorical mountain climb and will undoubtedly go down in local history somewhere, I consider it a little beneath her and it is only in passing that I mention I have written a book.

I am thrilled when she asks to read the manuscript but hold out little hope of a desire on her part to publish, expecting instead some critical feedback. After all, I doubt she's ever published so many fucks in her life.

'I love it and I'd be delighted to publish it,' Dawn tells me over the telephone a few weeks later.

'This could be our fortune made,' Wendy fantasises, having in her mind already sold the film rights and cast Colin Firth as me with Wendy playing under him at every opportunity.

'If I'd known, I'd have written in some sex scenes for you.'

'Oh I'm sure a screen play adaptation can take care of that,' she chuckles.

'Yes, but we do want to keep it real.'

'Since when did real sell anything? We've been selling a fantasy for years, we'd better keep it going.' She's right of course.

There is to be much to-ing and fro-ing of manuscripts over the summer but a publication date of 1 December is finally settled and there's a real sense of anticipation and excitement about the castle.

'Things are changing,' Wendy says, 'and not before time.'

The weekend of the party is finally upon us and the Saturday dawns cloudless and hot with a similar forecast for Sunday. 'Thank fuck for that,' I congratulate myself, 'you've pulled it off.'

Guests begin to arrive soon after lunch and by teatime we're all tucking into cake. We've tried to remember everyone who has had anything positive to do with the castle. Our closest friends and family are here for the whole weekend and local friends and supporters have been invited for the garden party on the Sunday.

Aunty Gloria is here and Buzz, Wendy's stepmother has flown over from Nairobi. Other friends have travelled from all over the UK and even further afield. Mark, my best man and his wife Sandra have flown in from Munich, happy to have left their two young daughters with their grandparents. It is an emotional event and brings home to us just how many lives the castle has touched. Martin and Clarissa Blanchard-Cafferty join us with Rupert and Hamish. Oliver and Emily look every bit the mature teenagers into which they are growing and both Wendy and I look fabulous, having lost weight and taken every opportunity over the last month to sit in the sun. We're brimming with a renewed confidence and while we aren't promising anyone we'll be here for another fifteen years, there is, at least a realisation that it could be possible.

I take great delight in introducing Dawn to everyone as 'my publisher' and it seems fitting that we should all be enjoying such a perfect weekend, making new memories with a book soon to be published that will set all our old memories in stone.

Ironically, 2013 turns out to be one of the worst financial years since we bought the castle. While wedding bookings are recovering, they are for 2014 and beyond but that is all we need – confidence in the future. That, it seems, is all the whole economy ever needed.

In September we are included in *The Sunday Times* 100 Ultimate Hotels list and we truly feel we have arrived somewhere. Rather like the Blanchard-Caffertys, the press and the hospitality industry are now taking us seriously and giving credence to the slightly bonkers way in which we run our very individual hotel.

She: 'So you pulled through, you survived.'
I: 'Well, we're surviving.'
She: 'Life's just about survival, love, it's how you approach it that makes the difference.'
I: 'I still think it's a shame we didn't have more family to share it with though.'
She: 'Well maybe you do, you just don't realise it.'
I: 'You mean our friends?'
She: 'I may be able to show you if you're open minded enough, which I think you have become.'

What she tells me is nothing short of bonkers – just like the castle itself and that seems a good enough reason to agree.

CHAPTER FIFTEEN

Various brushes with the BBC, some very old guests get more than they bargained
for and some guests from heaven arrive underneath the Christmas tree

With a mention in *The Sunday Times* alongside some of the hotels we
have always held in great esteem we are beginning to feel back at the
top of our game. The Gatehouse is still undeveloped but at the end of
September we finally get word from the bank that it can advance us the
funds we requested at Christmas.

'It's a bit bloody late,' Wendy wails.

'Leave it to me.' It's a while since I've had reason to take anyone to
task and I relish the thought of a fight.

There's an easy air about the castle that none of us can recall having
experienced for a long time. The staff, mostly a happy bunch, are more
content and, as if picking up on this new mood, guests are a lot easier
to please. I have a spring to my step and have begun to take life just a
little less seriously.

So it is that I sit down to write a letter to the bank, because there's
nothing to lose and I'm done with being frightened of upsetting people
in authority, but not before having first telephoned the new manager
to tell her what I am about to do because I reckon if you're going to
shit on someone's head, warn them first as they'll hate you just a little
less when it comes even though they've still got to clear it up. I am also
at pains to tell her that my complaint is not about her personally because it was she who eventually expedited the loan.

My letter is directed at head office and details the length and nature
of the delay in processing our application, the apparent reasons, or excuses, for that delay, the financial implication of the delay by not en-
abling us to have The Gatehouse occupied over the summer and what
I expect as reasonable recompense (the reimbursement of all our

security, legal and arrangement fees).

I don't hold out much hope of a positive response but I'm bloody pleased with the letter and it has made me feel ten feet tall.

Once it's posted there's no time to lose. The Gatehouse needs sorting out, not just because we need it ready by the spring but because it will finally expunge the last ghost of old Augill.

♛　♛　♛　♛　♛

With our enhanced national profile comes some unexpected attention. Siobhan works for the BBC. She needs our help researching 'fresh programming collateral' for the corporation.

'It's all about exploring rural opportunities and how best to enhance them to secure optimal outcomes,' she had explained on the telephone when she first made contact.

We've piqued her interest sufficiently to get her out of the office for a visit and now that she is here her explanations make no more sense. 'Urban deprivation is the easy buzz but the difficult fly in the political embrocation is what goes on behind the barn door in those oh so green fields of England. You are such role models of, you know, finding talent and turning it into potential.'

By a process of elimination Wendy and I work out between us that Siobhan is referring to our work devising and coordinating a young chef competition for fifteen-year-olds. It's the working in collaboration with schools that seems initially to have got Siobhan so excited, 'the symbiosis of the educational establishment and commerce is energising and a real waypoint on the journey to a more integrated way of empowering our youth.'

Wendy spots I am glazing over as Siobhan continues to speak. It is hardly surprising but we have the advantage that Wendy did once work at the BBC during which time she internalised some of the corporation speak and so has a better grasp than me of what is being said.

'Surely everyone doesn't go on like this?' I ask.

'Yep, this is how it is. Nobody actually says anything. That way nobody says anything wrong and can't take the blame when anything goes wrong. But, they are all lined up to take the credit for any success that comes their way.'

'But how do they actually manage to produce anything?' I ask again.

'It just happens – you know, lay down enough manure and the flowers bloom.' We laugh. Wendy obviously got out just in time.

I decide to take a direct line with Siobhan. 'So what exactly do you want from us?' She looks momentarily stunned as she processes all the possible answers to such a direct question.

'I guess what I'm saying is that we want to examine the juxtaposition of success and failure in an outwardly gentle but still brutal environment and show how that stacks up against the equally oxymoronic contrasts familiar to the urbancentric policymakers.'

Suddenly, a light comes on. 'So you want to show that life can be just as shit for some people in the country as it is in London and that it takes others to share their success to help change that.'

'Oh God, yeah, it's as if you're inside my head.'

I don't think so.

Eventually we think we understand each other (although none of us are quite sure). What is clear is that Siobhan wants to make a documentary about how opportunities for young people in rural communities are often less readily available but that when they are taken full advantage of they can have transformational consequences, not only for individuals but for the community itself.

'It's bound to be a BBC2 thing,' I say to Wendy.

'That's pushing it,' Wendy replies, none too happy about the potential stress of hair, diet, chins and what to wear that goes with being featured on TV, 'I'd rather it was on the radio.'

When we tell the children that we have been approached to be in a TV programme Oliver immediately imagines the worst. 'Not *Four in a Bed!* You promised you wouldn't,' and there's real panic in his eyes.

'Emily is a little more saguine. 'No it'll be *The Hotel Inspector.* Dad's got a crush on Alex Polizzi.'

'No I bloody haven't,' I reply testily.

'Ooh the Lady doth protest too much methinks,' Oliver replies.

'Shut it, smarty, just because you've studied a bit of Shakespeare at school.' A little GCSE knowledge is making him frankly insufferable, although I must confess I wouldn't turn down the chance to give Ms Polizzi the chance of a closer look at my mattress protectors.

'It's neither of those, it's…' but I lose the will to continue explaining. Both have already tuned out anyway, satisfied that we aren't going to make tits of ourselves on reality TV.

A few weeks later Siobhan is back in touch. She plans to bring her production team, Gavin, Tamara and Chantal up to see us. Wendy tells me that she is pretty sure that, on joining the BBC most people undergo some sort of personality transformation, of which a name change is an integral part of the process, as she hardly ever encountered anyone with a run of the mill name while she worked there.

'I just about got away with Wendy because nobody knew another one otherwise you might be married to Hermione now. Although strangely, Helen seemed to be quite popular…'

'We can probably just come up for the day,' Siobhan explains, 'since we are now based in,' there's a slight pause and a sharp intake of breath, possibly even an involuntary gag, 'Manchester,' she practically has to spit out the name of Britain's second best city. The move of large parts of the BBC from London to a new northern outpost hasn't gone down well with everyone, especially the 'creative assets'. I resist reminding her that, in actual fact, the BBC is in Salford, Manchester's underprivileged sibling. Besides, where did the BBC move from? Shepherd's Bush. Hardly a shining jewel in London's crown.

Gavin is a much more down to earth sort and he sets out a clear vision of the documentary. We are to stage various elements of our young chef competition and then teachers, students and parents will be interviewed about their attitudes to learning and whether traditional exam based education really works in 21st century middle England where everything isn't always as rosy as the roses around the door might suggest.

It might be the break we've been looking for to get our little competition on the map. Last year we managed to get Sara Medio Danesin, a Masterchef finalist to help mentor our young chefs and judge the final. The year before our MP, Rory Stewart was a judge. This year I am blogging for Jamie Oliver and hoping to get his attention. The BBC as well would be a real coup.

That said, I'm not holding my breath. We've had negotiations with the BBC before which have started promisingly and faltered.

On one occasion we were approached by researchers for *Antiques Roadshow*. They loved the castle but in the end decided there was 'insufficent built infrastructure and historical collateral and that throughput might be compromised by our rurality.'

That's BBC speak for too small, not old enough, too far from Manchester (which is already too far from London). The staff get very excited while the possibility exists until I remind them of the logistical nightmare of serving sandwiches, cakes and tea to herds of antique buffs. In the end the show decides on Lowther Castle, our much bigger, albeit ruined, cousin near Penrith. Wendy and I visit, armed with some tatty old watercolours which turn out to be worth a decent sum and having seen the hash they make of their catering arrangements we are glad to have been passed over.

That's not to say we don't have our day, of sorts. At Lowther Castle we are guilty of repeatedly photobombing the presenters and when the show is aired nine months later there's an unhealthy dose of Wendy and I in many of the shots. I tell friends I really wasn't trying to upstage anyone and that I didn't even notice the cameras but nobody is fooled.

With the economic clouds lifting daily, a half-term school holiday is once again upon us and it's shaping into one of our busiest ever.

Already there's a vile smell at the bottom of the stairs.

'What is that?' Wendy asks me in an uncharitably accusatory tone?

'It's nothing to do with me.'

'Well it's disgusting. It's certainly got all your hallmarks.'

Investigation reveals a festering nappy which has been tossed into the wastepaper basket by the under-stairs door.

Elsewhere there are curtains hanging off poles, sticky ring marks on the polished tables, coke on the Persian rugs and popcorn lurking in the darkened folds of the sofas.

These are the hallmarks of half-term those concentrated week long school breaks in spring, early summer and autumn when families forget that children actually need a rest, parents don't have to feel guilty and so cram too much into too little time all in a futile attempt to prove to themselves and everyone else they are not dysfunctional. We know, we've been there.

In ten days we will have served 370 breakfasts, 150 of them to children under nine. Not bad from fourteen bedrooms. But it started rather inauspiciously with a phone call from Prunella and Michael and yet another example of bad manners.

'Hello, I'd like to book a room for one night. Four poster, nice room, nothing tatty.'

'You're in luck, all our tat is already booked, ' Wendy's not having a good day.

'It's our golden wedding anniversary, we want to stay somewhere special.'

'Augill is certainly special but I do need to point out that the date you've requested is in the middle of half-term and there will be a lot of children in the castle,' Wendy is at pains to make this point to everyone without children who tries to book during the school holidays.

Another couple who booked a night for their honeymoon this half-term were equally averse to children but they loved it regardless, enjoying afternoon tea with several darlings running around them. 'Well, they're not ours, that's all that matters,' they said. She turned out to be a former foster carer. Understandable really.

'Oh neither of us are children people, will they be well behaved?' Prunella persists.

'That I can't say, we do try to keep control but they're not our responsibility.'

'Oh, you ought to make it clear on your website that you welcome children if that's the case.'

'I think we mention it on every page and it's explained in detail...'

'I don't read websites, they're never accurate. We'll book.'

'Are you sure, perhaps another week...'

'No, it's our anniversary, we'll just have to make the best of it.' How inconsiderate of the education authorities not to consider Michael and Prunella's anniversary when planning half-term. Wendy takes the couple's details with a deepening sense of misgiving.

'Now dinner, are you serving dinner?'

'Yes, dinner is served together around one big table...'

'Oh we detest communal dining.'

'Well we can recommend some lovely local pubs and restaurants.'

'No, it's our anniversary. We've been married 50 years. We want to eat in the castle.'

'Well as long as you understand that everyone eats together...'

'We'll just have to make the best of it. Will there be any children eating at the table?'

Wendy resists the temptation to say that children are safely mana-
cled to the dungeon walls at meal times, 'Usually children eat earlier.'

'Will they all be in bed?'

'That I cannot say.'

'Well I suppose we'll make the best of it.'

'OK, can I ask where you heard about us?' Wendy is more than ready
to wrap up the conversation.

'You come highly recommended by friends.' Unbelievable.

We have already been at full half-term capacity for five days when
Michael and Prunella arrive. They are just about to push open the front
door when it is swung back for them by Lottie, six and Sasha, four who
have been staying since the weekend.

'We are princesses and this is our castle. Are you coming to stay?'

'Yes, we're here to check in,' Prunella smiles through already gritted
teeth.

'You're very old,' observes Sasha, 'do you like my princess dress? I
found it in the dressing-up box, would you like to see the dressing-up
box? I think there are some old people's clothes in there too.'

'There might even be a wicked witch outfit,' Lottie adds.

Not a moment too soon Wendy appears in the hall to greet the new
arrivals.

'Oh this is Wendy,' the girls chime, 'she's the Queen of the castle
and she's jolly good at cooking too.' Then, turning to Wendy, Lottie
says in a very loud stage whisper, 'They're massively old, what if they
die in the night? Would there be a funeral?'

Quickly assessing the situation as only Wendy can, she says, 'You
must be Prunella and Michael, how lovely. Congratulations on your anniversary,' and then, a little lamely, she adds, 'half-term, what can you
do?'

Wendy hopes that Prunella and Michael's mood might soften on the
way to their room. But she has forgotten the lingering odour at the
bottom of the stairs.

'What the hell is that?' Prunella asks, almost wretching.

Sensing that another child-related incident might be the last straw,
Wendy sacrifices my dignity on the altar of self-preservation. 'It's my
husband, I'm afraid, he has terrible bowels.

It's a risky strategy but it pays off. Michael, who has so far uttered not a word, beams, 'Oh I know, I'm a slave to mine too.'

'I beg your pardon?' Wendy is taken aback.

'Oh yes, 50 years of it I've had,' says Prunella in a matter of fact sort of way.

Upstairs Wendy feels the ice breaking.

'Lovely room. Pillows, what are they?' asks Michael.

Something I'm surprised you haven't smothered each other with after 50 years, Wendy wants to say.

'You know, pillows, feather or not?'

'Oh feather and goosedown,' Wendy says proudly.

'Allergic. Can't sleep with feathers. Duvet?'

'It's all feather, but we can change it all for you, not a problem.'

Just as Wendy is turning to leave, Prunella barks, 'children!'

Oh Christ. Wendy had thought she'd got away with the children thing. Now Prunella's looking like the bloody child catcher from *Chitty Chitty Bang Bang* in drag.

'What time will they be asleep?' Prunella barks.

'I really can't say but they haven't been up late so far,' Wendy replies.

'Well we'll just have to make the best of it I suppose.'

'Pretty good at that, we've been doing it for 50 years,' Michael says, smiling broadly.

Later on the couple appear for dinner and Prunella is scanning every corner for lurking children. Michael couldn't care less, he's intent on pouring a large whisky.

At dinner conversation flows and it isn't a disaster. All the children are impeccably behaved which has absolutely nothing to do with my threats of locking them in the cinema with *The Smurfs* playing on a loop. Everyone at the dinner table is also impeccably behaved; Prunella has struck fear into the hearts of the entire guest list.

Next morning Prunella says Michael has had the best sleep for years. 'Very gassy all night though,' she confides, 'not sure that spiced parsnip soup was a great choice.' Wendy makes a mental note: Avoid subject of Simon's digestion when trying to break ice, and Prunella and Michael book to return.

'In March, before the schools break up. Weather might not be so good, of course, but I suppose we'll just have to make the best of it,' is Prunella's parting shot.

I turn to Wendy, 'You see, the secret to a long and happy marriage – just having to make the best of it.'

'I already am,' Wendy replies, a little more wearily than I might like, 'I already am,' she looks me up and down, 'has that smell gone yet?'

♛ ♛ ♛ ♛ ♛

The renovation budget for The Gatehouse is customarily tight. We hadn't wanted to borrow any more money but, having had no choice we plan to spend the minimum to make the maximum impact. It has a lot going for it, west facing, nice private garden and a fourteen foot high gothic arched window, one of the castle's most impressive.

'We can keep it all really simple and make the most of the window as the main feature,' I tell our affable builder. He takes a good hard look at what we have – a run down one up, one down lived in by an old man who had done nothing to it for more than twenty years. 'I've got a very clear vision of what it'll look like,' I reassure him, reading a degree of angst on his face.

'I'm glad you have.'

Having given him the budget, I set to calculating the true cost, a figure I plan keeping to myself for as long as possible. With a decade and a half of accumulated crap around the castle it isn't going to be difficult to find furniture so I figure our major expenses will be dry-lining and replastering, rewiring, plumbing, a bathroom and a really imposing bed.

'That sounds pretty much like a whole house build bar the outside walls.' Wendy has good reason to be sceptical of my project budgeting skills.

Our very dear friend, Elaine, a conservation architect, manages to un-endear herself by further pouring water on the flames of my enthusiasm. 'Have you had drawings done? That beam really doesn't look big enough to hold up the whole first floor now you've taken out the walls below it.'

I recount this potentially major hitch to the builder who says he will consult the joiner, who installed the beam, who says he will consult the plumber because the major load it will carry is a bath full of water. The plumber goes back to the joiner who reports back to the builder who tells me they have all consulted a structural engineer who says it's fine.

That's good enough for me.

'I can't allow such things to give me sleepless nights,' I tell Wendy, 'after all we put bathrooms all through the castle without giving the structure of the building a second thought.'

Wendy cuts through my smugness. 'Yes, and look what happened, the hall ceiling came crashing down.'

'Ah, but that's different. The cast iron bath didn't come crashing through the ceiling did it?' I'm determined to hold onto my smugness.

The project will begin after Christmas, giving us what I imagine will be plenty of time to have the suite open for Easter.

'We'll start taking bookings from June then,' Wendy suggests. She's becoming just a little long in the tooth.

My budget gets an unexpected boost with the arrival of a letter from the bank. I'd half forgotten posting my complaint but it has seemingly been passed to the upper echelons of the organisation. The bank agrees to refund all of our fees and, as a gesture of good will, pay us a thousand pounds in compensation.

'It hardly covers the fifteen grand we'll have lost by having the place empty for the best part of a year,' Wendy moans.

'Did you expect anything at all?' I ask, and without waiting for a reply, 'No, I thought as much so stop being so ungrateful. It is a small victory but a significant one.' The builder will know nothing of this extra cash.

Before we know it Christmas is just around the corner. Having categorically promised the children that, having opened for two Christmases in a row we would keep this one for ourselves, we are persuaded by a lovely family to host their private gathering. There are to be just sixteen of them and the deal is sealed when Barbara, an American living in Switzerland, says, 'we will fit in with your family plans, just tell us where to be and when. And really, we want no fuss and nothing fancy.'

'We can hardly refuse, can we?' Wendy pleads with the children.

They know we can't but it doesn't stop them being teenagers about it. 'Im sure there'll be bigger presents in it for us as compensation,' Oliver says to Emily and both shoot us a conspiratorial glance.

While we're starting to prepare for Christmas, there's also the matter of the launch of *Undressed For Dinner* to organise. It has taken nearly twice as long to edit, typeset and print as the original manuscript did to write. We settle on 1 December as the official launch date and we host a get together the previous weekend. It's really just an excuse for another jolly but everyone who comes is good enough to buy a book. I make a speech and read some extracts and for the first time I do feel like a real author. My publisher Dawn promises that she will take care of the sales side of things but we order a supply of books which we intend to flog to guests.

To say it is a dream is to understate one of the defining moments of our time at Augill as we say goodbye to our 2013 Christmas guests but a dream Barbara and her family have been to look after. They have allowed us to have time as a family ourselves, telling us that that is as much part of their enjoyment as their own celebration. They also give us a glimpse into a very different world from the one we inhabit and we realise, perhaps not for the first time, that behind all the trappings of wealth and the privilege that comes with it, we are all pretty much the same, with the same fears, the same desires and the same need to feel loved and appreciated.

'If only we could have Christmas groups like that every year,' Wendy says.

'I wish,' but we do agree that in future, with the memories of the Liverpudlians from the previous year still fresh, Christmas should be one group or nobody.

'Really?' says Laura who has seen and heard it all before and then managed our multiple changes of mind.

'Yes, really. It's time to start taking ourselves into consideration occasionally.'

CHAPTER SIXTEEN

A lesson in not dabbling in social media, an out of control wedding photographer and a beauty parade of bank managers

'This is going to be our year,' Wendy tells me one dark and windy January night as we are curled up together in front of the TV consuming our annual ration of back-to-back dramas while the castle is locked up and empty.

It might be the most desperate time of year for business but there in an undoubtedly special feeling about cosying up in front of a roaring fire surrounded by a castle all of our own, devoid of anyone else to think about. The wind can blow as hard as it likes, the rain can lash the windows but there's nobody to look after, nobody to complain, we're needed by nobody except each other and our children.

'What makes you say that?' I ask, not really needing to as I share the thought.

'It's just a feeling,' Wendy says as she flicks through the advertisements to the next section of an episode of *Grey's Anatomy*. It's all we need, that feeling. Our entire business model is built on gut feeling and, although there have been a few shaky moments, almost always due to our own lack of confidence, it has proved a sound business strategy. After all, this is a people business and the only way to effectively deal with people, given that every one of us is different, is to resort to gut feeling. The difference between businesses that have a similar culture and empower their staff to think the same is always clear from those who try to enshrine customer service as a book or policy.

Our feeling is having a positive effect on home life and all four of us feel very contented, other than Oliver's constant self-professed waking nightmare of feeling he is living in a boarding school because he detests his room and hates sleeping downstairs in an upside down house which we've told him he's just got to get over. We have promised to re-model our house when funds permit but we can put no date on it so it remains an uncertain possibility at best.

The house is filled with music. Emily has found her voice and sings and plays the piano beautifully. When she isn't performing she's listening to music. I can never, and wouldn't, tell her to keep her own singing down but I can be more of an old fart when it comes to her listening to recorded music. I delight in the occasional 'what's this crap?' or 'Emily, I can hardly hear myself think,' after all, I had to put up with it from my father and there is some justice in the repetition of certain aspects of history.

'But dad, music is my life,' she says plaintively.

'Silence is mine,' I reply but there are no prizes for guessing who invariably wins these battles.

But fathers are not without their strategies and I plan my revenge.

The daily journey to school has evolved into an almost ritualistic series of events. It begins with some demonic shouting as the clock registers 8:20. If, by 8:23 this shouting has not elicited a response from one of the darkened pits we know as the children's bedrooms, cursing follows. If Wendy tries to silence this sacrifice on the altar of our guest's comfort and sleep quality, the volume increases.

Once inside the car, there is any one or more of a series of scripted exchanges which involves admonishment about makeup on the seats, warnings about not getting any of that milk on the upholstery or crunchy nut cornflakes down the side of the seats. After the customary rolling of teenaged eyes there are questions about lunch money, home-work and sports kit, although at 8:27 it is too late to fix the absence of any of these. Next is the usual criticism of the radio station, 'oh why are we listening to this crap?' and then usually a tussle to change channels. Here I have gained a distinct advantage by having additional controls on the steering wheel.

Having established that hell will freeze over before we will listen to Radio One and that if they can't listen to Radio Two with good grace I shall simply switch to Radio Four (from which they might actually learn something about the world around them – guaranteed to go down well), there is a brief moment of calm during which Oliver disembarks at the bus stop and Emily completes her makeup in readiness for the remaining eight minutes' driving time to her school. That it is imperative that her makeup is finished by this time might seem odd until you appreciate that the rest of the journey is taken up with selfies.

It is no over-estimation that Emily takes dozens of selfies on her phone every day. I imagine the idea is to keep her various social media profiles fresh but to me the poses are always exactly the same. Slightly at an angle, pouting lips, sultry eyes.

'Why can't you try another pose?' I once make the mistake of asking.

'What's wrong with this? It's my best look,' Emily's reply full of indignation.

'Try showing your teeth or smiling,' I feel like a drowning man so early in the day, 'you have a lovely smile.'

'Oh God, dad, nobody smiles on Facebook.'

'Oh don't be so...'

'Ridiculous, yes, exactly,' and the rest of the journey passes in the uninterrupted company of the Chris Evans Breakfast Show.

Later I decide to have some selfie fun of my own. Somebody, in fact it was Emily, told me that nobody over the age of twenty, 'and that's pushing it', should ever take a selfie and worse still publish it. But this is revenge for all those school run selfies that look exactly the same, not just to each other but to everyone else's too. After all, the internet is supposed to be a place of diversity, a broad church of content and experience.

The next morning, just as I am emerging from my slumber there's a horrified wail from Emily's room. It's difficult to know whether there's any humour in her voice or whether it's pure indignation.

'What's going on?' Wendy asks blearily.

'Well, you know how Em is always taking those pouty selfies?' I'm still feeling quite pleased with my little wheeze.

'Yes, go on?' Wendy's tone suggests she isn't sure she's going to like what's coming.

'I sneaked down to Em's room after she was asleep and took a selfie on her phone.'

'Oh Christ, Simon, why do you insist on making life harder than it needs to be?'

Emily comes clattering into our bedroom with a face of thunder,

'What the hell is this?'

I continue to explain, 'She'd left her Facebook account open on the phone so I posted my picture as her new profile picture.'

Wendy looks at me, then at Emily and then disappears beneath the duvet. I look at Emily and realise I may have made a grave error of judgement.

There's a long silence during which there is much thumbing of the phone in Emily's hand.

'What are you doing?' I ask, nervously.

'I am fixing the enormous damage you have probably caused. This is the most ridiculous thing you could have ever have done.' I'm still not quite sure whether she's truly angry or perhaps that's just hopeless wishful thinking on my part.

Finally she's finished tapping and with one early morning, unmade-up, tousled just-out-of-bed-hair selfie, she shows me her Facebook page. Her dignity has been restored and mine has been annihilated. She has shared my selfie, taken after two large glasses of red wine at the end of her bed in the semi-dark, with all her friends with the caption, 'my dad – loser.'

'And,' Emily throws over her shoulder as she leaves our bedroom, 'I've Snapchatted it too.'

'I think you asked for that,' comes a muffled voice from under the duvet to where I think it is best to retreat for the rest of the day. What a Twit - ter.

☙ ☙ ☙ ☙ ☙

February half-term comes and passes in another frenzy of re-hung curtains, knee-deep popcorn and nappy bags and work is well under way on The Gatehouse. One of the pitfalls of having any sort of building or renovation work done is that there is a period at the beginning of the project when work begins frantically without bills being presented. This can last anything from a month to six weeks. The danger, as I have always found in the past, is that it is all too easy, during the grace period, to wade in with additional ideas and alterations to the scheme which are agreed upon but then never costed, the implications of those rash decisions only presenting themselves in an invoice a month or two later.

So, I steer clear of the construction site, only inspecting progress after the builders have left for the night. As a discipline goes it isn't easy but there's only a very small pot of money in the bank and that pot is even smaller as far as the builder is concerned.

As the wedding season begins we are reminded of some of the aspects of nuptial celebrations that make them so unique. It would be easy to imagine that everyone at a wedding is of the singular mind that the bride, and to a lesser extent the groom, is the centre of attention. Try telling that to some photographers and most bands.

Over the years we have built a comprehensive list of suppliers of all things wedding from cake makers to hairdressers, florists to harpists. Included are photographers and bands who make the grade, not just on technical merit or artistic flair but on empathy too.

One photographer who isn't on our list of recommendations takes the bride and groom into the garden for photographs after the ceremony and they are gone for two hours. They end up at the ruins of Brough Castle, a mile and a half away. Quite how they get there, nobody knows but by the time they return, the bride is in tears, so hungry and thirsty is she, and the party is in full swing without her. Wendy has saved the couple champagne and canapés and we are told later by the bride she had pleaded with the photographer to stop but he just kept going, muttering about light levels and skin tones.

A band that arrives to set up for another wedding is similarly dismissive of their reason for being there. We have cleared the music room for dancing with chairs around the edge of the room. It's a pretty standard arrangement.

When the band leader sees the set up he declares, 'We can't play in here, there's not enough space.'

'This is all the space there is,' I tell him.

'We're going to have to take up all of this area then,' he gestures towards the entire dance floor with a sweep of his arm.

'No, that would mean nobody having anywhere to dance.'

'Well that's not my problem, pal.'

Seeing how much equipment he is bringing in I take him aside. 'Look… pal. You've got enough amplification here for Wembley sodding stadium. This room is 60 feet by 30 and there are 40 guests. Get half this equipment back on your van and your head out of your arse so you can do what you've been paid to do – play music so people can dance.'

Later on, the groom stands up to make his speech in the dining room next door. Just as he begins the band starts a sound check. By the volume it sounds as if, counter to my diplomatic suggestion, he has brought in more speakers and is trying to entertain Glastonbury from Cumbria.

'Can you cut it, the groom is doing his speech,' I ask, drawing a hand across my neck to show that if he doesn't cut it I'll be responsible for something worse.

'Well, pal, we won't be ready to play at eight if we can't do our checks.'

'Do you know what... pal... mate... dickhead... they've come to hear what he's got to say first, you're just the support act, get it?'

♛   ♛   ♛   ♛   ♛

Spring is the time for awards. Wendy thinks we should have another stab at Small Hotel of the Year.

'The trophies in the hall are looking very dated,' she says.

The trophies, all made of solid glass, have, on more than one occasion, looked likely weapons with which to bludgeon somebody in the last few years but whether that means we need a new one, I am unsure.

Among the prime candidates for bludgeoning have been a succession of bankers. We realised that cash was running out about half way through the recession, once the effects of our national award in 2009 had worn off.

It was then that our accountant told us that the banks' doors were not as shut to new business as the media might have us believe, with banks being given state-aided assistance to stimulate lending, and that a refinancing of our borrowing might be key to releasing some working capital.

And so, throughout the recession, we met a string of bankers, all keen to tell us that their banks were the best banks for small business in difficult times. It all started off very promisingly but things were very soon not quite as they seemed.

What started as a bankers' beauty parade becomes a walk of shame. First through the door is Andy. He is regional director for one of the big high street banks so reliant on the government bail-outs to keep functioning back in 2008.

He tells us he has looked at our business, had sight of our accounts and, having been given the show-round usually reserved for wedding prospects, declares we are just the sort of business his bank wishes to support. Will we send him a business plan and any other up to date management accounting figures we can pull together?

Preparing a business plan is no small task but I put in several nights' hard graft to create an inspirational and bullish plan for Augill's future.

And then we hear nothing. I follow up with emails, telephone messages, as does the accountant. Six months later I am told Andy had a personal crisis. But I'm sorry, were we asking Andy to lend us his own cash? Was there nobody to take over his portfolio? Is this really the way to run a bank already answerable to the taxpayer for its very survival?

Next, we enjoy the company of two representatives, 'quite high up,' we are told, from another bank.

'We have avoided the worst of the banking crisis by being clever,' one of the bankers tells us rather too smugly and in a way that seems to suggest that we should be grateful they are meeting us at all. We have given up a busy morning in August to host them, so keen were they to 'secure heads of agreement at the earliest opportunity.' Again, we and our accountant (and his time is far from free) spend considerable resources putting together all the information the bank requires. Six weeks later we have still heard nothing and despite badgering by both us and our accountant a decision either way about their willingness to finance us never materialises.

'Is there something wrong with us?' Wendy asks and I am powerless to answer. It proves to be one of the major causes of our angst throughout the recession, without which we might have had more energy reserved for the people that matter, our guests, our staff, our children and friends. Anyone, in fact, other than flakey bankers and their empty promises.

It dawns on me that we're playing a game and that maybe we're playing to the wrong rules.

'What we're doing is going to banks that don't know us. Let's ask the banks who do,' I tell Wendy. It might seem obvious but then, who really wants to go to their existing bank and say, 'you know, we have a problem'?

So, rather sheepishly, we approach our personal bank, another to be almost wholly owned by the taxpayer, with whom we have both had a relationship since we were teenagers and who did support us when we first bought the castle. The manager knows us well, is personally a fan of what we do and, on being approached, is excited about the prospect of being able to help. Once again we furnish her with all the information she requires and once again we receive no response. After weeks of silence I telephone her for an explanation.

'It's all rather more complicated than I anticipated,' she begins.

'The hell it is, what about some communi-fucking-cation?' and another banking relationship bites the dust.

Our final port of call is our current business bank. We are put in touch with a regional manager who 'has the authority to sanction the sort of lending figures we're talking about'. In order to secure a deal he takes over responsibility for our account.

He is, it has to be said, an objectionable character; very bullish and aggressive. He knows it too. 'I'm not in the business of making friends, I'm all about results.' Perhaps he has forgotten he is talking to owners of a people focussed business. Then, for all of his bravado and following interminable email conversations his line goes dead. It's nothing more than we have come to expect.

In the end we stick with what we know bringing us to where we now are; our mortgage lender stumps up the loan for The Gatehouse, our business bank, with our account now back in the hands of our local relationship manager, eventually comes up with a modest sum to renovate it and with that we realise that, if we are to make a go of things from here it will be on our own, using our own wits and guile and we reflect on how things really haven't changed much since 1997.

She: 'And you find yourselves back where you started?'

I: 'Yes, but a whole lot richer, if not in the bank, then in ourselves.'

She: 'Would things have been any different if I'd still been around, your father, Wendy's Mum and Dad?'

I: 'I think I've already had this out with Dad. The truth is, it wouldn't have been any easier, we'd have had more people, special people to tell us we were getting it right, that they were proud of us.'

She: 'But you must see now that you do, perhaps not in the way you'd have

215

planned in an ideal world but your staff, your friends, the family you've still got...

I: 'But none of them are our parents and everywhere I look our contemporaries, whether they want to admit it or not, crave the approval of their parents. It's about acceptance which I've always assumed is a given between parents and their children. An acceptance which we've had to work so hard to find elsewhere.'

She: 'So is that a benefit or a curse?'

I: 'Ah, well, there you have a point.'

She: 'What you have is the benefit of hindsight. You do have the opportunity of parental approval but on your own terms, from the parents you'd like to have had rather than the ones you did have. In life parents don't have to accept their children, at least not willingly, but in death...'

I: 'Is this leading somewhere?'

She: 'I think you know very well where this is leading... Are you ready?'

I: 'As I'll ever be.'

CHAPTER SEVENTEEN

Awards lost and won, a clueless mystery shopper and Emily hits the big time

Another mystery shopper and another turgid awards night later (turgid, it must be said, only because of the outcome) we still have no new hand blown glass bludgeon for the hall table. The mystery shopper report we receive leaves us incredulous with phrases such as 'the set daily changing menu,' that we have been offering since the day we opened, 'offers little choice,' and 'if a regular maintenance programme on a building of this age is not kept up to date it will begin to deteriorate.'

'You don't say! Do we look like a couple of fuckwits?' I scream at Wendy.

'Obviously,' she replies, 'I can't imagine how we've limped on so long with such an ill-conceived business model. Why don't we go and stay in their hotel? Oh wait, they haven't got one because they wouldn't have the first clue where to start.'

We discuss the report's invaluable findings with the staff and the unanimous verdict is this: We have spent far too long creating a product which breaks the mould, pushes the boundaries and resolutely stays out of the box. Awards only seek to categorise us, compare us and pigeon hole us. We'll have no more of them.

'Is it sour grapes?' I ask Wendy later.

'It was always for the PR,' she says, 'and you know, we do a pretty good job of our PR without the hassle of awards.'

All that said, the following month an award does come our way from a very unexpected direction.

My first book, *Undressed For Dinner* has been well received by those who have read it. My publisher, Dawn entered it for the Lakeland Book of the Year award in the spring and I held out little hope of success, past winners being worthy tomes about such subjects as Wordsworth, the majestic fells of the Lakes and Lakeland poets through the ages. Nevertheless the book is shortlisted and that gets us a free lunch in a marquee on the shore of Ullswater and what's not to like about that?

The tent is full of worthies and it must surely be the year's greatest concentration of Lake District OBEs in one place. We are sitting at a table right in front of the judges' top table but I have long since given up on second guessing such portents. After a tasty lunch the presentations begin. The first category goes to another chap on our table. 'That's it then,' Wendy says, they won't have put two winners on the same table.'

'Shall we just sneak out the back of the toilets then?' I think I whisper, 'I saw some kayaks down by the lake – we could have a lot of fun in them for the rest of the afternoon.'

'Perhaps not just yet,' one of the judges and a colleague of mine at Cumbria Tourism, broadcaster Eric Robson, says into the microphone.

'I've told you about your so-called whispering before,' Wendy giggles.

Eric is clutching my book and before I know what has happened I am accepting a prize for my book in the category about Business and People.

No sooner have I regained some composure than the overall winner, the Lakeland Book of the Year is being announced. Serial author, broadcaster and journalist Hunter Davies, who does, indeed have an OBE, begins talking about my book.

'What to say about this book? On page sixteen,' he begins, always keen to hold the attention of an audience, 'the word fuck appears no less than twelve times.' There is a collective gasp and I am sure, a distinct rustling of crinoline. In my defence, page sixteen does recount the birth of our own son in a broken down ambulance in a pub car park outside Kendal at 3am.

So when he announces that *Undressed For Dinner* has won the top prize, what else can I do but to begin my acceptance speech with 'fuck me'?

When in June The Gatehouse finally opens, only slightly over budget – a vast improvement on previous projects, we think if any mystery shopper were to sleep there they'd be falling over themselves to give us an award. The suite is stunning and it is a fitting fifteenth and final addition to our bedroom stock. Wendy and I are the first to sleep there and I fill the bath to the brim before going downstairs to the sitting room to check that the ceiling is bearing up. The furniture that we have rescued from around the castle all seems to fit together and there is a king sized contemporary four poster bed which dominates the upstairs bedroom.

Friends who have known us throughout our Augill journey tell us that we are not complete without a project on our hands and ask what's next.

There's our own home, The Coach House which Oliver likens to a school boarding house. It's a harsh assessment, particularly given his previous brushes with boarding school but I can see his point. We want open plan living and what we have is a warren of little rooms.

'Surely it's just a case of taking this wall, this wall, this wall and this wall out,' is Wendy's simple assessment.

'I think if we did that the house would fall down,' I offer as my expert opinion.

'Obviously we'd have to put steel beams in. But, all in all, how expensive can it be?'

'Plastering, flooring, re-wiring, plumbing, heating…' I remind her.

'Pff,' which reminds me why Wendy is never to be trusted with renovation budgets.

We're looking at ways of better heating the castle. Solar panels have been ruled out due to a lack of sun and funding a biomass boiler which runs on wood seems ridiculously expensive, no doubt because there are ridiculously extravagant government incentives to install them. I'm minded to wait until the incentives dry up and see the cost of the equipment and installation come tumbling down, much as happened with solar panels.

These are both projects for the future and for now we are content to concentrate on making the best of what we have put together over seventeen years and that includes sharing it with as many people as possible.

For a number of years we have worked with Warcop Primary School, giving every child in the school a chance to cook in a real commercial kitchen. This year we are tasked with doing something a bit different: afternoon tea prepared by the children over two days and served to parents, family and friends. Wendy happily agrees.

'Are you sure?' I ask, 'have you any idea how many people could turn up, there are more than 80 children in the school.'

When it comes to it the whole event runs over two days. Quite coincidentally I have arranged to be away at the other end of the country but it goes like a dream and the sun shines.

In September a German film crew joins us for four days to film Emily's life in an English castle as part of a children's documentary series called 'Look into my World.' Initially excited about the project, as the first day of filming approaches Emily becomes anxious.

'What if they want me to be something I'm not?' she asks as she is doing her nails and applying another set of false eye lashes.

'They just want you to be an ordinary thirteen year old,' I try to reassure.

'Exactly,' she says, 'I am anything but ordinary, surely that's why they are coming.'

Over four days the film crew has Emily doing everything from shopping and feeding the goats to singing and baking a cake.

Some of what she is asked to do is quite out of character and, being German, the film crew are quite matter of fact, 'do it again, please,' being a regular phrase.

'I don't want to do it any more,' Emily complains after day two, 'they're really rather rude.'

'They're not rude, darling, they're German,' I say.

'But they're asking me to do loads of stuff I don't normally do, I thought this was supposed to be reality TV.'

'Darling,' I try to remain patient, 'it's a half hour show and half an hour of you sitting in bed in a darkened room Snapchatting doesn't make good TV.' She knows better than I that there's very little reality in reality TV.

The culmination of the weekend and therefore the highlight of the filming is another legendary Augill party to celebrate Wendy's forty-fifth and Oliver's sixteenth birthday and Emily is to sing.

Originally I had agreed with the producer that the TV crew would follow Emily throughout the course of the weekend getting ready for a family birthday party at which she would sing a surprise for her mum. Between us we had the idea of an informal family get together of about twelve.

Once Wendy got hold of the idea the guest list swelled to 80, Oliver decided he wanted a black tie casino night and Emily's surprise song became a whole set.

'I do hope viewers in Germany don't think this is every day real life in an English castle,' I say. When the show is aired in Germany that seems to be exactly what viewers are led to believe, confirmed by a phone call from my friend who simply asks, 'What on earth did you tell these people about English country life?'

The castle is all about sharing. We share it with guests, we share it for weddings and we open it to schools, for concerts, charities and our own young chef competition. It might sound a little trite, but we believe we are only custodians of this extraordinary place and sharing it with as many as we can, both commercially and otherwise, will be our legacy.

But we don't do any of it without constantly listening to our guests. After sixteen years of serving set menus for everyone to eat together around one big table 2014 is the year we concede, perhaps just a couple of years later than we should have, that that is no longer what most people want. So we introduce a new house menu serving the same great, simple food anywhere in the castle at any time. It's an instant hit with nine out of ten guests staying in to eat rather than, previously, three out of ten. And again, it's all about sharing.

In keeping with the menu's informal style, the food descriptions are pared back – a nod to the offerings of some contemporary new London hotel openings because we're nothing if not *a la mode*.

Mac and cheese is a particular favourite throughout the summer. A superior macaroni cheese, it comes with or without the twist of pancetta. A guest from the Netherlands orders it for lunch but when it arrives she is non-plussed, 'I ordered the mac and cheese,' she says, 'what is this?'

'Mac and cheese, macaroni cheese,' Tiffany explains.

'Oh I thought it was a Mac, I was expecting a burger.'

Tiffany returns to the kitchen and says, as only Tiffany can, 'The lady in the drawing room would like a Big Mac, do we have any?'

'Perhaps she was wondering why there weren't any golden arches above the door.' I say later.

'Who, Tiffany or the guest?' Wendy asks, half exasperated, half resigned.

All in all, we're in a good place now. It isn't the south of France, the sun doesn't shine all the time but it's ours, we have reclaimed the castle and we continue to share it with open hearts and open minds. We are part of the local landscape now and we feel accepted by the people amongst whom we live which is the closest we'll come to parental acceptence. Good friends and the best staff give us that support network we've missed for so long. It's a far cry from where we started in 1997 but is it so far from where anyone thought we might logically end up? Probably not. We're beginning to feel settled, accepted and back on our feet after a gruelling five years.

But good things, it seems, don't last.

CHAPTER EIGHTEEN

The tax man sticks the knife in and death brings a reconciliation

In sixteen years of business we have never given business rates a second thought. They are another tax to be payed and we have just accepted whatever demand falls on to the mat without question, considering them to be none too onerous.

Mrs Shambles, on the other hand, has different ideas. She is a local inspector for the Valuation Office, the government department which decides what businesses should pay in rates. She has written to say that she needs to inspect the castle to assess our rateable value.

I ring an acquaintance who knows more about such things than me and ask his advice. It turns out he knows Mrs Shambles and says he will give her a call to find out what she's up to.

A couple of days later, I am told that Mrs Shambles is inspecting us because another local business has looked up our rateable value online and thinking we're not paying enough, has reported us to the Valuation Office.

'You're fucking joking,' is my involuntary response. I am completely unaware that it's possible to snoop on other people's rates online but I am assured, in a way which suggests I should probably already have known this, it has been possible for some time.

I feel suddenly foolish and naive.

A few days later Mrs Shambles arrives at the castle. She certainly lives up to her name as, for a business meeting, she is pretty bizarrely dressed – a fleece, waterproof trousers and a pair of walking boots. She's a public servant and this is just a downright lack of respect. Of course, in these parts it's nothing less than I've come to expect but it does nothing to improve my mood.

I have been advised to provide only information asked for and nothing more so I sit stoney faced across the table and await her first question.

'So, what exactly do you do here?' Not quite what I am expecting having imagined she would have done her homework so I automatically assume she's trying to catch me out. When she later admits to having looked at our website those suspicions are confirmed so it's probably just as well I don't tell her we're a brothel Monday to Friday with an S&M sex club in full swing in the cellar at the weekends.

For an hour and a half I am subjected to continuous and repetitive questions which I answer truthfully but with no elaboration. She leaves, seemingly content and presumably heading for the hills.

A few days later Mrs Shambles is on the telephone asking me several of the same questions. I try very hard not to sound irritated but know I have failed when Wendy asks me who it was on the phone that so pissed me off.

Four months later a letter arrives informing us that our rates are to be increased by 162% and that the increase is back-dated for a year. Just when we feel we are getting ahead financially for the first time since 2007 – it's a severe blow that risks wiping out our entire profit for the year.

I am, quite simply, numb but Wendy is inconsolable. Between sobs that I have heard too many times during this bloody recession, she wails, 'we could lose it all, Simon. Why, when all we've tried to do is run an honest business, treat our staff well and give something back to the community?'

She's right. It feels like the final straw. We've used every penny of our savings to keep going this far and there's nowhere else to turn. We feel helpless as if we have been kicked in the stomach and then the teeth.

'Oh if only Dad was here,' Wendy says, 'he'd know what to do.'

'Yeah, my Dad too,' I reply.

In truth neither would probably have a better clue than us but from their pedestals, occupied since death, they are the answer we want and because we know we can't have it, it might as well be the answer we need.

We are two children, lost; orphaned and it feels as if nobody has our backs.

'It's time, isn't it?' I ask that evening.

'Yes, it's time. Tomorrow we'll call the agent and get it on the market.'

This might not have been the way we'd have liked to sign off but with my health only set to deteriorate and Wendy suffering from premature arthritis in both knees, we know our days of running a hotel – an intensely physical occupation – are numbered anyway.

'It just feels like we've failed,' Wendy confides.

'If we can walk away with more than we put in, we haven't failed and even if we take a hit, look at what we did, look at the upbringing we gave our children. How many people will they meet who will say they lived in a castle?'

The truth is, the business turns a good profit but we have borrowed too heavily and servicing that debt eats up all the cash we make. This insidious property tax takes no account of our ability to pay, assessed by somebody with little grasp of the reality of running a small business.

'Dad always said cash is king,' Wendy chuckles, pauses and continues, 'I hope he'd have been proud, that's really all that matters in the end but we'll never know, will we?'

'Oh I don't know…'

Events and our own physical failings have made us intensely aware of our own frailty. But, in our mid-forties, we are too young for our own mortality to be a matter of question. True, Wendy's Mum died at 47 and Dad was just 53, both cut down by cancer but they were different times when cancer was a more formidable adversary. Wendy's Dad was just 63 when he was killed in a car crash but accidents are different – not that they don't count but they don't cast the shadow of familial legacy. And all their deaths are separated from our own reality by a generation.

So when I get a call from my younger brother's partner I am ill-prepared for what I hear.

As brothers our relationship is one of contradictions. We aren't close, being two very different personalities, but we have never really fallen out. As adults our lives have just drifted apart and then back together again as if some invisible force is in charge of when we should be in touch and when we shouldn't.

And although we aren't close, we have a knack of knowing what each other is thinking, meaning that we often exchange few words. To a casual observer it might seem a superficial relationship but the truth is that the depth lies in the unspoken, our bond is unseen because even if we share little of the moment we have shared a whole growing up.

He has cancer. It's inoperable and I am told there is nothing but palliative care to be given.

'What do I do?' I ask Wendy. I had hoped never to see the inside of another cancer ward.

'You should go and go soon. Make peace, re-establish a connection. You'll regret it forever if you don't. Go now.'

Jonathan doesn't know I am visiting and when I walk into the room he doesn't look up. I, in turn don't recognise him – he is emaciated beyond recognition and it's only when his eyes slowly lift and meet mine accidentally that I realise it is him. He cannot control his emotions and as I take his hand he grasps it, the bed frame with the other as if these are the last things he has to hold on to now that his life is slipping away. There is no physical strength left in his hands but there is something else. Something I cannot determine.

He gestures at his throat and I realise with utter horror that he cannot speak. He has had a tracheotomy. My horror is not because of what has happened but because this is exactly the same cancer that killed our father.

'You came. I didn't know you would,' he mouths to me and in an instant I am once again standing at the bar with Dad, conversing without words in the easy manner we never shared when he could speak.

'Of course I came, how long have you been in here?'

'Three weeks,' and again there are tears rolling down his face, out of sunken sockets and over bones where cheeks should be.

'Why didn't you let me know before?' With the help of an iPad and a pen and paper he tells me how scared he has been, how he'd been to his GP six months ago and had been sent away with antibiotics for a throat infection. The cancer was aggressive and when his throat haemorrhaged and he was rushed to hospital tests revealed it had spread to his lymph glands. There was nothing to be done. He hadn't wanted anyone to know until he had the facts, he said.

'But I'm your brother, I would have come and supported you,' how dare he exclude me from this drama, keeping it to himself, so selfish. I am ashamed of the anger that starts to well up in my chest but I can't stop it. I have a right to be involved, it's his duty to include me, his crime that he's the last. After him there's nobody – we're all that's left of each other's growing up.

My younger brother, the only person left who shared my childhood, who shared the ups and downs of life in our childhood home, the only person who still truly understands those silly jokes about our parent's foibles and peccadilloes, the only person with the same blood, made of the same DNA as me is going to die.

His father's son. He lived like him and now he will die like him too. Why shouldn't I be angry? Most of his life has annoyed me since he has never been an easy person to know. But he has always had a smile for everyone and every situation. Infuriating sometimes when, in the midst of an argument or a weighty discussion, a grin begins to spread across his face.

Hopeless at keeping in touch and yet always surrounded by people and never on his own. He has a winning way with women and everyone who knows him will tell you of his cheeky grin, his special chuckle or that certain glint in his eye. Just like his father.

When I returned to England to settle down after several years of travelling it was Jonathan who persuaded me to accompany him to a party of old school friends, telling me I needed to get back into the swing of things. It was there I met my wife Wendy and Jonathan was always proud of his part in bringing us together, reminding me at every opportunity.

Jonathan had two wives, several engagements and more girlfriends than Peter Stringfellow. In fact, I can't remember a time when he wasn't with someone. Unsurprising as, like Dad, he was hopeless on his own. Both had been utterly spoilt by their mums.

Those who know him will say Jonathan has always been happy, always joking, charming, sociable and up for a laugh. All traits inherited from Dad, but all that masks a man who struggles with life.

In the end life has got the better of him. I am grateful his illness, its similarities with Dad's inescapable, promises to be mercifully short. Grateful as much for myself as for him.

'I know what you're thinking,' he writes. No you bloody don't, and then as I catch his eye I see him looking into my thoughts, reading my resentment, recognising the conflict between my need to be needed and my desire not to be part of it at all. I understand why he didn't call for three weeks.

We have four months together after I first see him in hospital during which I do all the talking – of course – and during which there are several afternoons of silence. But it's a silence full of significance because it's a sharing. Not of the present because we both know there is nothing of now left, but of a mutual past. It is a reaffirmation of our history, that he may die with a sense of belonging and I might find some meaning to a grief I would otherwise have resented.

On one of these afternoons I tell him of our plans to sell the castle. I don't expect he really cares, it has never been part of his life and I always imagine it as a source of some resentment. I explain how we soldiered on through the recession only to be dealt a blow of such finality by the Valuation Office.

I talk, as I always do on these afternoons, into the middle of the room, filling the empty space with words because seeking interaction from someone who cannot speak seems selfish but also, because I am selfish, as a way to avoid looking at his face – once so beautiful now grotesque with cancer.

When I do glance at him I see he is crying. There is no need to ask why; I squeeze his arm gently as he writes.

'I'm sorry. I was always so proud of what you achieved up at the castle but I never told you. You deserve to be proud of it too. Don't ever let the buggers get you down. Whatever you decide to do you can walk away with your heads held high. I am just sorry we didn't make more effort to be closer as I'd have loved to be more involved. It has been an epic journey. You're both very brave.'

In mid-April, obliging my request that he should avoid Easter, Jonathan dies and I am with him. There is no dramatic last gasp, no sudden regaining of consciousness for a final farewell, spasm or throe of death but there is something – an almost imperceptible departure. It would be fanciful to say there is a light breeze which for a fleeting moment stirs the curtains as something, someone departs. There is no breeze but it is as good a way as any to describe the moment. And while it is an experience which I would be in no hurry to repeat it is a privilege to have another person cradled in your own arms at the point their life ends.

Why? Perhaps because they have put their trust in you to be there? Perhaps because there is nobody else to be there and you are? In our case because we were given the chance to build bridges, mend walls and plant seeds of reconciliation before he died. I had the privilege of being able to do that with both my father and my mother and for that I must always be grateful. But it also reminds me that Wendy had that with neither of her parents. She was kept at arms length from her mother's extended illness and her father was snatched suddenly by a car accident. For her closure, that most ghastly of Americanisms has been elusive. For me it has been a treasured gift.

> She: 'He's here now.'
> I: 'I know, I think he was always destined to be happier there than here.'
> She: 'He loved you. He just didn't know how to tell you.'
> I: 'I know that. I could say the same. Sometimes our brotherly rivalry got in the way. Too often really. I wish…'
> She: 'No, stop. None of that now. We have a final chapter to write.'

THE FINAL CHAPTER

We find what we've been searching for

'You know…' I turn to Wendy who's yet again checking her status on Facebook.

'What?' she asks absent-mindedly.

'Why have you become so obsessed with that? You're always on it these days.'

'So are you.'

'Not as much, I'm not picking a fight, I'm just interested to know what fascinates you about it, most of it's trivia and nonsense.'

'Well, it fills a hole doesn't it?' She is speaking into the room as she puts down her 'phone.

'What sort of hole?' I ask.

'I imagine that most people who have proper families talk mostly about nothing in particular. It's all just noise in the background but when it's all put together, that's the stuff that makes individual people into a family of people. That's what I miss. We have a pretty amazing life and I don't regret any of it, even the shitty bits. We are really so very lucky. But wouldn't it have been all so much more worthwhile if we'd had a family to buzz it all around and who could have made that noise about it?'

'You mean parents?'

'I mean parents, yes.'

'Anyway, what were you going to say?'

The slightest of shivers caresses the hairs on the back of my neck and I tense very slightly before correcting myself.

A little too self-consciously I roll over and rest on one arm, failing miserably to appear nonchalant as I nearly miss the edge of the bed, 'nothing, I mean, are we busy this Saturday? I have some people I'd like you to meet, all of us to meet.'

'Who?

'Visitors, they're only going to be here for one night but they're very keen to meet us all as a family.'

'Who the hell has taken a one night booking on a Saturday night? Honestly, I really do…' Wendy is winding up for a rant.

'They're not our usual sort of guests,' I'm trying to adopt my most soothing tone.

'I hate it when you get all cryptic. Who are they, are they going to make us an offer for the castle?'

'I doubt that but they may well give us a different perspective on all of it. Saturday, put it in the calendar.'

The next day I wake the children for school to be greeted by the usual salutations, 'piss off', 'turn the bloody light off' and 'why don't you just butt out of my life?'

Ever so calmly – because that's the tone that annoys them most – I say, 'I just want you both to know that we have some guests coming on Saturday and I need you both to be here for them. If you'd like a friend here too, that's fine.'

'Oh God,' Oliver moans, 'what d'ya have to spring that on us now for?'

'Just please make sure you don't go out.'

I'm as nervous as anyone when Saturday morning arrives. In fact nothing can really prepare us for what's about to happen. When it was first suggested I thought my mind was playing tricks. Maybe I still do. All I know is that the four of us are to be together and to avoid being disturbed. At least I've kept quiet about who is actually coming so Emily won't tell me I'm ridiculous if they don't appear and anyway, if I had told the others who's coming they'd have said I was mad.

At eleven o'clock, Oliver, Emily and Wendy are gathered in our sitting room. I have made tea and as I put the tray down in the middle of the room I'm struck by the similarity to a scene way back when we first arrived here of my mother bringing tea to ease the brewing awkwardness of a moment. I pull myself up to my full height but I'm shaking. This is, without doubt, the weirdest thing I am ever going to have to say and I can feel my collar moistening.

'You all know that I have been writing a second book and that all throughout the time I've written both books I have been asking you all questions about parents and grandparents, right?'

'Yes…' they're either feeling very edgy or very frustrated.

'You should know that I wrote neither book entirely by myself.'

I am so nervous now, I take a deep breath so I can deliver my line in one go, otherwise I know I'll choke on the emotion. 'I don't really know why, or how – I imagine it's very rare and I think Nanny Mary helped and if you ever tell anyone else this has happened they'll never believe you.'

They're looking at me very oddly now and I can see they are agitated, not knowing what is going on.

'Daddy,' I'm pulled up short, Emily hasn't called me that for a good couple of years, 'are you having one of your breakdowns?'

'Don't be stupid, Emily,' Oliver retorts, 'they only happen after much drinking and never in the mornings.'

That little exchange has brought me back to the here and now and I'm grateful for it as I am still unsure of what is going to happen, knowing only that it promises to be something most people only dare to dream.

Emily and Oliver, please say hello to your grandparents, Wendy say hello to both our mums and dads. There should be an awkward silence but this is no ordinary social call and instantly an easy calm falls upon the suddenly extended family gathering as the room fills with the last people anyone was expecting.

Emily is first to speak, her eyes wide as a toddler's, her demeanour that of the thirteen-year-old she is and the six-year-old she never wanted to leave behind, rather than the eighteen-year-old she is always trying to be. 'Hello, Nanny,' she beams at my mum and all at once this is the most natural of encounters, 'come and have a look at the art room, it's got lots of your old brushes and stuff and you'll adore some of the things I've been doing.'

'I will do, but first…' she moves over to Oliver and cups his face gently between her bony but silky soft hands, 'hello lovey, I've missed you so much but I haven't been far away, promise.'

Oliver sobs quietly and throws his arms around his Nanny. 'Just like our Saturday mornings together used to be when you were little,' she whispers, 'do you remember how we'd sit on the front step together with hot chocolate and biscuits?' and he gently nods his head further into her breast, his thumb involuntarily finding his mouth.

While Mum and Oliver are getting reacquainted, Emily stands up and gives her other Nanny, Val, a hug. 'I think I must have inherited some singing talent from you,' she tells her, 'because I certainly didn't get it from Nanny Mary.' Perhaps because she shared little living history with any of her grandparents Emily seems to be taking this most unorthodox of scenarios in her stride. Val smiles with her eyes and her whole face lights up, her prominent cheek bones catching the light, 'you have a beautiful voice, much lovelier than mine but I smoked, please promise me you'll never do anything that stupid, not with a voice like yours my darling.'

'What lovely skin you've got,' Emily says, staring at Val's almost translucent features.

Dad just smiles at me, we're old pals now, after all, we've written a book together, but he's dead keen to meet Wendy, 'you've made a fine man of my boy, I think we would have got on, I hope we would because I couldn't have asked for a better wife for him or mother for my grandchildren. I've tried to help him avoid making the same mistakes I made, you know, where I've been able to, shall we say, influence things, but really I think that's mostly down to you.'

As Mum is led into the art room by a chattering Emily, Oliver is left gazing in awe at Mike and John, his two granddads whom he has never met. They each gaze down on him with gentle, benevolent smiles, Mike's slightly lopsided grin, his head and shoulders bent a little to one side; John's framed with his salt and pepper, slightly ginger moustache with his pipe still hanging from one corner of his mouth. 'Dad says you always had trouble keeping that alight,' Oliver says to his Granddad John.

There's a hearty, throaty laugh, 'no need now, it's just for show and he passes it to Oliver to handle. I hear you're a rugby man, cricket was my game.'

'Oh I like cricket too,' Oliver jumps in, eager to please, 'but Dad's not very good at it, so we didn't really keep it up.'

'Maybe we'll have a game, you and I?' Dad says to Oliver. The boy looks confused and the old man just winks, 'we're not as far away as you think if you open your mind.'

Wendy's dad, Mike has been chuckling all the way through the conversation and now Oliver turns to him, 'you have come a very long way from Africa today.'

'It's no distance at all any more, as your Grandad John says, keep an open mind. Next time you visit, if you'll let me, and with your mum's help I can take you on safari to the places we all used to go.'

I've less catching up to do with my mum and dad, and I'm keen that the children shouldn't miss out on all the overdue attention. 'Oliver, why don't you take Grandad John downstairs and show him the Xbox.'

'The Xbox?' Oliver can hardly believe what he's hearing.

'Oh yes, Grandad was a sucker for every gadget going, he'll be blown away by that.'

'Whatto, that sounds wizard, come on Oliver.'

As he moves past me I am struck by a new sensation. The sweet, nutty, slightly acrid smell of pipe tobacco smoke. I haven't noticed it before, haven't smelt it since he died but there's no mistaking it now. It's what I remember most about him while I was growing up. Our house never smelled of tobacco smoke despite my father and mother both being heavy smokers but he always smelled of tobacco smoke. Not the cloying stench of stale cigarettes, that bitter sharp smell that tastes yellow, but a wholesome, rounded aroma. Imagine the smell of fish at a fishing port. It lingers on well after the fish have been landed – everything, everywhere, everyone smells of it, the smell is imbued into everything it touches, can never be washed away. The place would be wrong without it. It would be called a stench anywhere else but when it fits its purpose it becomes an aroma and aromas are the stuff of lasting memories. It's like that now. It fits him. He would be incomplete without it. Now I can see him, hear him, smell him. He is whole.

I turn back into the room where just three people are standing now. Wendy hasn't said a word, I doubt she's able. There are tears streaming down her face and she's fighting to regain some sort of composure. Her mum and dad are standing side-by-side smiling. They're in no hurry. He is dressed in his safari shorts, long white safari socks and a fishing jacket all topped off with a floppy cotton hat. She is made up and panto-ready, dressed as Robin Hood.

'Hello Mum, hello Pops,' and she falls into their arms. 'I'm so sorry,' she mumbles into her dad's chest, 'for all the trouble I caused you when

I was younger. But I've done this for you, all of it is to thank you for everything you did, everything you had to put up with.'

'My darling girl,' Val gently moves Wendy away so she can see her face. Their eyes meet, 'you have nothing to be sorry about. What you've had to go through, losing me when you were just fourteen, your dad in that awful crash, is more than anyone twice your age could expect from life.

'Don't do any of this for us, do it for you, for your beautiful family, my darling, darling girl.'

'Remember,' her dad continues, 'there's no hurt left in us now. The cancer died with your mum and Simon's dad. There's no disappointment, just love. That's the only thing that survives death because it's the only thing that really matters. We're here now as we were at our happiest in life.'

It takes Wendy a few moments longer than she'd like to pull herself together, they may be precious moments wasted, 'Mum, this is Simon, he's been taking care of me.'

'You've been taking care of each other.'

Emily comes back into the room. 'Look what Nanny has just shown me how to do,' and she holds up a perfect watercolour sky. She then looks around the room, 'why are you all wearing the same things as in the photos we've got of you all on display?'

'Because this is how you best remember us,' they're all talking at once. 'What you need to do is open your hearts to us and we can be whatever or whoever you want now. That's why we're here darling, in fact, we've always been her, you just didn't know us.'

Emily swings round and there they are, on top of her piano, all looking just as they do now.

'You've been here all the time,' she giggles before her voice breaks and she is no longer able to hold back her sobbing. Not a sad sob for the departed but happy sobbing for the reunited.

'And if you want, we can be part of anything.'

Mum turns to me, noticing I have been the quietest in the room. 'Are you OK lovey? You're very quiet.'

'I guess I've less catching up to do than everyone else,' I smile weakly.

'Something's up though and I think I can guess what it is.'

After a lengthy pause which hangs unencumbered only because it is in the company of people who have all the time they need, I whisper, 'Jonathan?'

She takes my face in both hands as she did earlier with Oliver and as she did so often when I was little, 'He doesn't feel the need my darling. He's at peace and he doesn't believe you have any more that needs to be said.' It's all I need to hear.

'Remember,' she says softly, 'we are never far away – you just have to ask, just open your heart.'

Epilogue

The Magic of Augill that so beguiled us when we first encountered it will live on, whether in our hands or those of others who will make it their dream.

That magic was itself inspired by the magic of Les Mimosas, a chambre d'hôte in south west France that was, for so long the embodiment of our dream. Perhaps that dream is not to be, perhaps it is still to be fulfilled – certainly the house remains, beckoning us south towards the sun. What I do know with some certainty is that we are already living a different dream. At times it is an awakening one, a dream of shadowy horizons and uncertain futures, but mostly it is a dream of fulfilment. In what other life could we be such an important part of so many people's lives, make other people's dreams come true? How many people dream of owning a castle?

We touch and are touched by so many. It is a privilege to live in such a place as Augill Castle, our time here has been and continues to be a journey during which we have learnt to know and accept that as long as we do what we do with open hearts and minds, we will never be alone.

The most important thing we can exchange with another person is love and once there it cannot be taken away. It may fade or be eclipsed by other emotions – anger, disappointment, resentment, jealousy – but it won't die as those weaker emotions wither and perish and so neither will the people who loved us and who we have loved.

Augill Castle is for all of them.

Death is nothing at all. It does not count. I have only slipped away into the next room.

Nothing has happened. Everything remains exactly as it was.

I am I, and you are you, and the old life that we lived so fondly together is untouched, unchanged.

Whatever we were to each other, that we are still. Call me by the old familiar name. Speak of me in the easy way which you always used.

Put not difference into your tone. Wear no forced air of solemnity or sorrow. Laugh as we always laughed at the little jokes that we enjoyed together. Play, smile, think of me, pray for me.

Let my name be ever the household word that it always was. Let it be spoken without an effort, without the ghost of a shadow upon it.

Life means all that it ever meant. It is the same as it ever was. There is absolute and unbroken continuity. What is death but a negligible accident?

Why should I be out of mind because I am out of sight? I am but waiting for you, for an interval, somewhere very near, just round the corner. All is well.

Henry Scott Holland, 1847-1918
Regis Professor of Divinity, University of Oxford

...because we are all searching for something or someone and because who or what we seek is often much closer that we ever realise.

It is not the critic who counts; not the man who points out how the strong man stumbles, or where the doer of deeds could have done them better. The credit belongs to the man who is actually in the arena, whose face is marred by dust and sweat and blood; who strives valiantly; who errs, who comes short again and again, because there is no effort without error and shortcoming; but who does actually strive to do the deeds; who knows great enthusiasms, the great devotions; who spends himself in a worthy cause; who at the best knows in the end the triumph of high achievement, and who at the worst, if he fails, at least fails while daring greatly, so that his place shall never be with those cold and timid souls who neither know victory nor defeat.

Theodore Roosevelt, 1858-1919

...because no matter what the empty personalities of the civil service or the faceless critics on the internet throw at us, we toiled, we made this place. It is our triumph to say we lived in a castle, to have been able to give others the chance to sleep in a castle and... to stop for breakfast.

ABOUT THE AUTHOR

It was at the age of eleven Simon learnt the power of words having written a piece at school which made his English teacher cry.

Words have been his companion ever since.

He was born in London and his family relocated to the West Country three years later – it was all, he says, his fault, a story for another time – but he has always considered himself a Londoner at heart.

He went to a very fine public school and then chose a university based on the quality of the nearby beach.

An exciting spell in international hotel management took him around the world from Jersey to Jakarta via Sydney, Perth, Singapore and eventually back to London.

After completing a post-graduate diploma in journalism he spent several carefree years reporting on everything from dog shows to murder trials on a series of evening newspapers and then, quite inexplicable, bought a share of a West End restaurant with his new wife, Wendy. Eighteen months later, even more inexplicably, they bought an empty, near derelict castle at the foot of the Pennine fells in Northern England; a decision yet more puzzling for the fact that their dream was to move to southern France.

The rest is history and the inspiration of his first novel *Undressed For Dinner*, Lakeland Book of the Year in 2014.

Today, alongside running the castle, he maintains a writing career which has morphed from print journalism in the 1990s to blogging and content writing in the 21st century. He contributes regularly to travel sites including The Good Hotel Guide, Sawday's Special Places and Best Loved Hotels.

He works as a small business advisor, a hotel reviewer and often entertains as an after dinner speaker. He has been a school governor for fifteen years, most of those in the chair that nobody else seemed keen to claim and for four years was a director of Cumbria Tourism, one of the UK's leading destination marketing organisations.

In January 2016, after a second trip to the Middle East as part of a diplomatic mission, he set up a non-profit organisation, Bridges Not Barriers to empower young people to become international ambassadors for peace.

Simon continues to live and work at Augill Castle with Wendy, their two children Oliver, 17 and Emily, 15, the ashes of his brother, mother and grandmother with which he confesses he doesn't know what to do, and a shrinking menagerie which at press consists of a dog, a cat and one hen called Cindy.

You can find out more about Simon's writing at:
www.SimonTemple-Bennett.com

and his work with international young people at:
www.BridgesNotBarriers.com.

Also by Simon Temple-Bennett, the award-winning
Undressed for Dinner
Lake District Book of the Year 2014.